More Praise for *Big Questions, Worthy Dreams*

"Making meaning is a challenge at all stages of life, but perhaps most of all during the emerging adult years, when most young people leave their family home and then have to find a new place in the world. In this book, Sharon Daloz Parks explores with insight and empathy the many ways that today's emerging adults struggle to answer their big questions and reach their dreams —and how, as mentors, we can help them get there. This book will be a valuable resource for parents, professors, administrators, employers, and all others who care about emerging adults and want to see them thrive."

—Jeffrey Jensen Arnett, Clark University; author of *Emerging Adulthood: The Winding Road from the Late Teens Through the Twenties*

"*Big Questions, Worthy Dreams* is welcome relief from recent portrayals of university students as character-flawed consumers. Parks's skillful presentation of developing 'consciousness, conscience, and competence' in emerging adults challenges university colleagues to reclaim their shared project of higher education with enlarged imaginations and renewed purpose."

—Patricia O'Connell Killen, academic vice president, Gonzaga University

"In this book, Sharon Daloz Parks has given us a rare and precious gem that shines a deeply sensitive and profoundly sweet light into the core meaning of higher education. With an intellectual edge honed by experience, she writes with her characteristic compassion and brilliant reflections on the big questions of our time. Her search and explorations reignite the spirit, purpose, and calling of our common work as mentors and educators seeking to understand how to help form more responsible global citizens. Give this book to yourself and as a gift to a friend."

—Manuel N. Gomez, vice chancellor, emeritus, University of California, Irvine

"I read *Big Questions, Worthy Dreams* when I first became a rabbi on campus. The copy is well worn and overflowing with underlined passages. Sharon Daloz Parks's wisdom and insight continue to enlighten and inspire all who work with emerging adults across lines of profession, discipline, and faith."

—Rabbi Josh Feigelson, educational director, AskBigQuestions, an initiative of Hillel: The Foundation for Jewish Campus Life

"From today's vantage point, the things at stake in this tenth anniversary edition are even more profound and urgent than they were the first time around. This is not a little story about young people. It is a big story about humanity and the persistent quest for meaning and purpose. Parks begs us to get young people on the mat and wrestling with life's big questions, and to help them build authentic lives that do right by those questions. The moment is now, the responsibility is ours, the key is mentorship, and the payoff should be big—for all of us."

—Richard A. Settersten Jr., author, *Not Quite Adults: Why 20-Somethings Are Choosing a Slower Path to Adulthood, and Why It's Good for Everyone*

"This is the classic work on emerging adulthood, now updated to reckon with the bewildering and very big questions the past decade has delivered up: think 9/11, Facebook, global recession, climate change. Scholarly, wise, elegant, and deeply insightful, the book is an indispensable resource for all who work with people in the awe- and angst-filled years between 18 and 32, all who interact with them, and all who care about their safe passage into mature and compassionate adults. And, as Sharon Parks helps us see, all of us should care, because the stakes are high. Mentoring from "hospitable" adults can make all the difference in how high they set their sights and now, more than ever, upcoming generations have fateful choices to make about their lives and our common future that we need them to take up faithfully and fully awake. Parks, a master teacher, lights the way—theirs and ours."

—Diana Chapman Walsh, president emerita, Wellesley College; board chair, The Broad Institute of MIT and Harvard

"No one who cares deeply about people in their twenties should be without this book. In Sharon Daloz Parks's lyrical company we learn so much more about their biggest possibilities—and our own."

—Robert Kegan, author, *In Over Our Heads*; professor, Harvard Graduate School of Education

"Parks's clear voice in *Big Questions, Worthy Dreams* is simultaneously that of a scholar, clinician, ethicist, and priest—that of a rare and capable generalist who can nurture both teachers and students . . . [and] reveal the architecture of the process by which we merge the questions of ultimate reality with the immediate needs and duties of our generation. Stunningly transparent. Essential insight."

—Janet Cooper Nelson, chaplain of the university, Brown University

Big Questions, Worthy Dreams

Mentoring Emerging Adults in Their Search for Meaning, Purpose, and Faith

Revised Edition

Sharon Daloz Parks

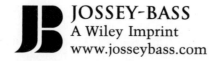

JOSSEY-BASS
A Wiley Imprint
www.josseybass.com

Published by Jossey-Bass
A Wiley Imprint
989 Market Street, San Francisco, CA 94103-1741—www.josseybass.com

Credits appear on p. 320

Jossey-Bass books and products are available through most bookstores. To contact Jossey-Bass
directly call our Customer Care Department within the U.S. at 800-956-7739, outside the
U.S. at 317-572-3986, or fax 317-572-4002.

Wiley also publishes its books in a variety of electronic formats and by print-on-demand. Not
all content that is available in standard print versions of this book may appear or be packaged
in all book formats. If you have purchased a version of this book that did not include media
that is referenced by or accompanies a standard print version, you may request this media by
visiting http://booksupport.wiley.com. For more information about Wiley products, visit us
www.wiley.com.

Library of Congress Cataloging-in-Publication Data
Parks, Sharon Daloz, date
    Big questions, worthy dreams : mentoring emerging adults in their search for meaning,
purpose, and faith / Sharon Daloz Parks.—2nd ed.
        p. cm.
    Includes index.
    ISBN 978-0-470-90379-7 (hardback); 978-1-118-11384-4 (ebk); 978-1-118-11385-1
(ebk); 978-1-118-11386-8 (ebk);
    I. Title.
    BL42.P37 2011
    207'.50842-dc23

Printed in the United States of America
REVISED EDITION
HB Printing   10 9 8 7 6 5 4 3 2 1

The Jossey-Bass
Higher and Adult Education Series

Dedication

James W. Fowler III

intellectual pioneer,

faithful professor,

masterful teacher,

friend

Contents

Preface

In recent decades, there has been mounting public awareness of something particularly powerful and poignant—and sometimes confounding—about the "twenty-something" years, harboring, as they do, both potential and vulnerability. No longer adolescents, young, emerging adults have achieved critical strengths, yet in a complex and demanding culture, they remain appropriately dependent in distinctive ways on recognition, support, challenge, and inspiration as they make their way into full adulthood. Not only the quality of their individual lives but also our future as a culture depends in no small measure on our capacity to recognize emerging adults, to initiate them into the big questions of their lives and our times, and to give them access to worthy dreams.

This book is intended to inform and inspire renewed commitment to the practice of mentoring and to invite reconsideration of some of the institutional and cultural patterns that affect emerging adults. Its purpose is to serve as a bridge across the divides between generations and to encourage a more adequate recognition of what is at stake in the response of all who interact with emerging, young adult lives.

In 1986, I published *The Critical Years: Young Adults and the Search for Meaning, Faith, and Commitment*. Anchored in constructive-developmental research and theory, it revealed a new stage or era emerging in the human life span and a vital set of tasks in the development of adult meaning-making. After it went out of print yet was still being used, I was invited by Jossey-Bass to rewrite the work—creating a new book. *Big Questions, Worthy Dreams: Mentoring Young Adults in Their Search for Meaning, Purpose, and Faith* retained the essence of the earlier work while expanding the focus from the traditional undergraduate period to a broader recognition of the power of the twenty-something years as a whole. It also reflected an expanded awareness not only of the importance of mentors, but also of the vital significance of "mentoring environments."

That was a decade ago—a decade in which *Big Questions, Worthy Dreams* has been widely used, and now I am privileged to have been invited to offer a tenth anniversary revised edition. Because the book describes core processes of human becoming that do not change dramatically, much of the book is the same. But there are also changes because I continue to live, learn, and grapple with new questions; because other scholars and theorists have provided additional traction in our understanding of this "new" era in the human life span; and because the cultural landscape is shifting at whiplash speed, affecting the aspirations and anxieties of young, emerging adults and all the rest of us.

Notably, our economic and political life has become yet more brittle, volatile, and global—both enlarging and constraining young adult aspirations. Today's emerging adults are "digital natives"—connected and distracted in unprecedented forms. Emerging adults now move in not only a religiously variegated world in which religion and faith have become problematized and polarized, but also a world in which hybrid and atheistic claims have gained currency along with various forms of fundamentalism. In this context, it has become all the more essential to recognize, as this book does, that the word *faith* in its broadest, most inclusive form is an activity that all human beings share. Whether expressed in religious or secular terms, *faith is the activity of making-meaning in the most comprehensive dimensions of our awareness*. This understanding of the word *faith* is increasingly crucial not only for making one's way in a multireligious world, but also for recognizing, in any case, that the ways in which we do or do not make sense of the *whole* of life profoundly affects our personal and collective life.

The primary concern that initially fueled my research and writing was that although young people rightly discover a critical perspective that calls into question their inherited, conventional faith, and although they may then be able to increase their respect for the faith of others, they often are left adrift in a sea of unqualified ethical relativism, unable to compose a worthy faith of their own. This concern remains. But my more recent concerns are two. First, too many emerging adults are not being encouraged to ask the big questions that awaken critical thought in the first place. Swept up in religious assumptions that remain unexamined (and economic and political assumptions that function religiously), they may easily become vulnerable to conventional assumptions and miss being invited to their own authentic and worthy dreams. This was a significant influence in shaping the first edition of *Big Questions, Worthy Dreams*. My second concern affecting this revision is this question: for those who do achieve a capacity for critical thought, why is critical thought apparently so difficult to sustain beyond the borders of a narrow expertise—that is, why is it inadequately applied to the broader challenges now facing our society and world? Too often the collective work of all citizens is dodged through denial, misdefinition, or an inappropriate deference to authority. Moreover, during the past decade, I published a book, *Leadership Can Be Taught: A Bold Approach for a Complex World*, focused on the need for adaptive leadership in a society where there has been a growing sense of a "crisis of leadership" across sectors. Emerging adulthood is a distinctively vital time for the formation of the kind of critically aware faith that undergirds the trust, agency, sense of belonging, respect, compassion, intelligence, and confidence required for citizenship and leadership in today's societies. And yet if emerging adults and their potential mentors simply operate on the current default settings, the formation of self and society that is needed may not occur.

In some quarters, emerging adults are being more effectively recognized in both their potential and vulnerability. This revised edition is offered as a companion to that good work and is intended to inspire the imagination of yet others. It is written particularly for those who meet young adults in the context of higher education and spans the unfortunate chasm that often exists between the academic concerns of the faculty and "student services." But it is intended also for supervisors and other potential mentors in the professions; business, corporate, and nonprofit workplaces; and the broad range of communities and agencies in which young adults live, work, and seek recognition, support, challenge, and inspiration.

This book draws on forty years of teaching, counseling, research, and study with young adults in college, university, and professional school contexts, as well as in workplace and other settings both formal and informal. Unless otherwise cited, quotations from young adults themselves are drawn from my research at Whitworth University (in collaboration with Gonzaga University), Harvard Divinity School, Harvard Business School (in collaboration with the Tuck School of Business and the Darden School of Business), the Harvard Kennedy School of Government, from the study reported in my book with colleagues *Common Fire: Leading Lives of Commitment in a Complex World,* and from more informal conversations—most recently at Seattle University, the Whidbey Institute, and other places where I have served as speaker and consultant. In most instances names and identifying elements have been changed because anonymity was a condition of the research interviews; thus, any similarity to actual people or organizations is accidental. To each of the interviewees who so graciously and continually confounded and informed my understanding, I want to express my ongoing and deep gratitude.

There are, however, some who in their emerging adult years (past or present) have made essential contributions that can be acknowledged here: Peter Bloomquist, Peter Dykstra, Danielle

Hendrix, Hannah Lee Jones, Hannah Merriman, Julie Neraas, Elana Polichuk, Wendy Evans Sewall, Scott Shaw, Cindy Smith, Greg Spenser, Susan Hunt Stevens, Kendra Terry, Drew Tupper, Sarah Waring, and Tyler Whitmire.

From the beginning and for always I am grateful to David Erb, Duncan Ferguson, James Fowler, Beverly Harrison, Fritz Hull, Vivienne Hull, James Paisley, Robert Rankin, William R. Rogers, William G. Perry Jr., and George Rupp—apart from whom my study of young adult faith might never have been launched or, once launched, might never have found a voice and a home. I am also deeply indebted to many colleagues from a wide range of institutions—particularly faculty, administrators, and campus chaplains—who have generously shared their insight, competence, skepticism, and the inspiration of their commitment to the next generation. These include Keith Anderson, Chris Cobel, Jeff Dalseid, Jon Dalton, Tony Deifell, Craig Dykstra, Dave Evans, Josh Feigelson, Lucy Forester-Smith, Marianne Frase, Ron Frase, Diana Gale, Steve Garber, Cheryl Getz, Keith Howard, Jim Hunt, Linda Hunt, Chris Johnson, Heather Johnson, Julie Johnson, Robert Kegan, Patricia Killen, Sharon Lobel, Steve Moore, Ian Oliver, Mark Nepo, Parker Palmer, Suzanne Renna, Mary Romer, Michelle Sarna, Rick Spaulding, Terry Stokesbury, Ed Taylor, Michael Waggoner, Cathy Whitmire, and Arthur Zajonc.

This revised edition would never have come to be without the invitation and colleagueship of Sheryl Fullerton, senior editor at Jossey-Bass, and the competence of her colleagues, especially Joanne Clapp Fullagar, Susan Geraghty, Alison Knowles, and Jeff Puda, and I remain grateful for the earlier and considerable editorial gifts of Sarah Polster, Karen Thorkilsen, and Kate Daloz.

Finally, I am grateful beyond measure to my husband, Larry Daloz, for his steadfast presence, encouragement, and assistance as in our life together we have navigated the throes of yet one more book—sharing the faith that working on behalf of the next generation to provide leadership and mentorship within a new global commons is worthy of our best and ongoing efforts. And I am grateful in another and very special way to my stepdaughter, Kate Daloz, and my stepson, Todd Daloz. They were among the young adults to whom the original *Big Questions, Worthy Dreams* was dedicated—both then recently graduated from college. Now, married to Edward Herzman and Susannah Walsh, who entered their and our lives when they were all still emerging adults, I have had the privilege of watching the four of them complete their twenty-something years and become full adults, including becoming parents and moving into their own professional competence and commitments. They deeply inform my best imagination of the courage, costs, and gifts of the twenty-something years lived with an artful faithfulness—willing to ask big questions and to pursue worthy dreams.

Summer 2011   Sharon Daloz Parks

Chapter One

Emerging Adulthood in a Changing World

Potential and Vulnerability

A talented young man, recently graduated from an outstanding college, still trying to heal from his parents' divorce, and somewhat at a loss for next steps in his search for a meaningful place in the world of adult work, is asked by his dad and stepmom, "When you think from your deepest self, what do you most desire?" To their surprise he quietly responds, "To laugh without cynicism."

Having been admitted to a top-tier law school, but uncertain about that path, a bright young woman deferred admission for a year "to give myself some breathing room" and took a job to try something new as a community organizer in a nonprofit working to improve the quality of K–12 education. Three years later, she says, "It was hard. I learned that recruiting and training volunteers was time-consuming and emotionally draining. But it was amazing to see people you recruited lobby their elected officials, speak eloquently at a school board meeting, and show up five thousand strong to rally at the capitol. I'm increasingly interested in education policy, and though I'm uncertain about my next steps, I'll never regret not going to law school three years ago."

A young man from Guyana, twenty-six years old, is the proud owner of a small flooring company and a part-time student at a community college. One of his teachers observes that though last term he only occasionally slouched into class, he seems to have made some kind of decision and now attends regularly, alert and ready. "His papers have improved by about 200 percent, and he contributes to the friendly, thoughtful tone of the class. He is obviously working very hard both for class and in his business. He has dyslexia, and writing is very labored for him, but he has shown a tremendous amount of thought, effort, creativity, and truly beautiful insight—especially in a paper he wrote about being a young father. He is someone I really, really respect and am generally rooting for."

A college student remarks with candid self-awareness that she and her peers are in a "self-centered" time in life, busy with identity and vocation questions, and aren't yet thinking in terms of larger questions about justice or meaning. She is neither apologetic nor precluding that her perspective will change.

A class of undergraduate business majors is invited to divide into small groups and share their values. One student after a bit concludes, "I don't have any." He's asked, "Well, why are you here?" He responds, "To make money—like everyone else." Another student in the group comments quietly, "But there has to be some meaning, too."

A freshman in her spring term at a state university remarks that she wishes she could find a "church home," longing for what she had in her hometown three hundred miles away. She says she is coping in the meantime by attending an off-campus evangelical college youth group, where there is a lot of warmth, singing, and community. She also participates in a small, challenging study series offered by the campus ministry. What's missing is a kind of wholeness or integration she can't quite grasp.

In the bowels of the university physics lab, a sophomore, raised in Middle America and steeped in a mainline conventional faith, has discovered that the lab is a good place to learn how people from the Middle East and Asia make sense of today's world. It is his perception that the faculty is not aware of this conversation.

A young woman graduating from college offered to work for free for a start-up tech company to show what she could do as a Web designer. Three years later, with a full-time job at the heart of the organization grown large, she says, "I got here because I've worked hard, I'm a leader, and it was inside me. On the other hand, it is bizarre to be in a position of enormous responsibility. But like others my age, I know the whole scene better, I'm quick, I'm on it, I grew up with it. I fell into it. As my astrologer says, I can move on if I want with a certain amount of material whatever—but not necessarily have it define me for the rest of my life."

A young woman, twenty-seven years old, confessed, "I'm told I have lots of potential and can go anywhere. I don't know what choice to make next. I'm paralyzed by opportunity."

A recent college grad, twenty-six years old, intelligent, and well traveled, declares that her life is "a daily struggle" between "Am I becoming what was given—inherited—or really creating my own life?"

A twenty-something comments, "You have to remember that I have lived in a different environment every year for six years. So have most people I know. Nothing is stable and we switch between worlds all the time. We go from having money to being broke . . . from being surrounded by friends, to being lonely, to having friends again. . . . Those kinds of major transitions would make anyone refigure the way they think about the world, especially if they are already grappling with issues of identity, career, and life-goals."

A guest blogger writes, "Admittedly, some of us are resistant to settling into the 'traditional cycle' of adulthood, but is this because we are sloughing off responsibilities or because we are waking up to a new set of responsibilities?"[1]

For each of these young, emerging adults—and for all of us— there is much at stake in how they are heard, understood, and met by the adult world in which they are seeking participation, meaning, purpose, and a faith to live by. This book is dedicated to a reappraisal of the meaning of emerging adulthood and the crucial transformation it harbors for all of us.

In varying roles (including professor and researcher), I have taught, counseled, studied, and learned with young adults in

college, university, and other professional and workplace settings. In the late 1960s and early 1970s, I witnessed the power
of young adult energy to sway a society. I wondered at the apparent disappearance of that energy once the Vietnam War ended
and the television cameras had departed from campus.

Over subsequent decades, however, I saw that same energy
reconfigure and weave itself into the fiber of our cultural life. In
the eighties and nineties, I watched emerging adults—particularly
in professional schools—seeking a place in a new global commons
that ambivalently welcomed, encouraged, exploited, and discouraged their participation.

Now, in the early part of the twenty-first century, I continue
to watch young adults—both in North America and abroad—
reach for a place of belonging, integrity, and contribution that
can anchor meaningful hope in themselves and our shared
future—while the tides of globalization, cynicism, polarization,
and consumerism, coupled with an uncertain economy and a
shifting social-political milieu, play big roles in charting their
course. I have observed among some of the most talented many
who simply have been lured into elite careers before anyone has
invited them to consider the deeper questions of meaning and
purpose. Others are fiercely determined to find a distinctive path
and to make a difference in a complex maze of competing claims
and wide-ranging opportunities. Still others are simply adrift and
yet others feel themselves essentially locked out of viable, meaningful choices.

A New Era in Human Development

Across forty years, my scholarship has been primarily in the fields
of developmental psychology and education, leadership and
ethics, theology and religion. Insights drawn from these domains
have served as useful interpreters of emerging adults, as I know
them. At the same time, young adults themselves have continually prompted me to notice that even some of the "disciplined"

interpretations of emerging adulthood are misleading. By young, emerging adults, I mean people typically between eighteen and thirty-two years of age—the *twenty-somethings*.

When I began my initial studies, there was some recognition of theoretical awkwardness in the transition from adolescence to adulthood, but this period was typically described as "prolonged adolescence," a merely "transitional time," a "moratorium," or "regression." Cultural assumptions allowed that some might go through a period of idealism soon to be outgrown yet generally implied that adulthood begins, or should begin, with the completion of formal schooling, entering the world of full-time work, and establishing a family—around the traditional age of perhaps twenty-two or so (if not earlier). Later, such popular descriptions of young adults as Generation X, Generation Y, and more recently Slackers, Millennials, and Boomerang Kids extended the timeframe. But these attempts to describe and normatively define twenty-somethings in media-manageable terms have primarily served to cast them as a market while finding them resistant to categorization.

Since 2000 or so, particularly through the work of Jeffrey Jensen Arnett and his colleagues but notably others as well, this postadolescent-not-yet-full-adult era that early on Kenneth Keniston described as *youth* (1960) and I described as *young adulthood* (1986) has become more visible to scholars and the general public.[2] Currently the designation *emerging adulthood* has gained considerable traction, but other terms also such as *the odyssey years, failure to launch, preadulthood, quarter-life crises,* and *waithood* signal the growing consciousness of this "new" era in the human life span that challenges both scholars and popular culture.

Keniston named this postadolescent period *youth*, which is problematic in obvious ways.[3] I have previously used the term *young adult*, which is both appropriate and problematic in other ways. As the term *emerging adult* is useful within the growing scholarship exploring this developmental era (though more problematic when speaking directly with twenty-somethings), I am choosing here to use both terms but to privilege the term *emerging adult*. *Adult* connotes a sense of responsibility for one's self and others—*emerging* connotes the exploratory, ambivalent, wary, tentative, and appropriately dependent quality that is characteristic of early adulthood.

Bewildering Ambiguity

When does one cross the threshold into adulthood? The response of North American culture is, indeed, ambiguous. Chronological age does not serve as a consistent indicator and the rites of passage that might mark that threshold are various: obtaining a driver's license, social security card, or credit card; sexual experimentation; reaching the legal drinking age; graduation from high school, college, or professional school; marrying or partnering; full-time employment; establishing one's own residence; parenting a child; becoming eligible to vote; becoming subject to military registration; becoming subject to being tried as an adult for criminal behavior; financial independence; capacity to be responsible for one's own beliefs and actions; and to make responsible life decisions and enter binding legal contracts. Each of these serves to some degree as a cultural indicator of adulthood, yet the legally established age for these passages ranges from sixteen to twenty-one (and beyond in relationship to some financial contracts and health care) and is not uniform from one jurisdiction to another.

In this maze of contradictory cultural signals, it is difficult to have a clear sense of what to expect of either oneself or others. Establishing an occupation, finding a mate, and starting a family all endure as indicators of adulthood. But as the human life span has been extended and as a postindustrial, technological culture has made it both easier and more difficult to make one's way into the world of adult work and other commitments, the twenty-something years take on new significance.[4]

Thus even an indicator such as "becoming established on one's own" no longer seems useful when some eighteen-year-olds are "on their own" because they have left dysfunctional families in search of healthier ways of life; when others who would have been expected to "leave the nest" by the age of at least twenty-five have moved back home, even though they have graduated and may be working full time; when professional education may extend into one's early thirties; when it is common to change jobs or careers several times in one's twenties—and across a lifetime; and when what is important to learn and incorporate into one's adult identity becomes increasingly complex and controversial.

In this changing milieu, many parents find themselves surprised, if not dismayed, and ponder whether and for how long it is appropriate to provide financial support. Corporate planners are challenged by the fluidity and short-term horizons of young adult ambitions. Financial magazines feature young entrepreneurs earning "adult" salaries who are appearing to bypass higher education altogether. Many emerging adults themselves, even those who have achieved some of the traditional markers of adulthood, wonder when and if they really are "grown up." Young mothers with partners who do not yet seem ready to be fathers have few guidelines for determining what they may ask, claim, or demand—and at the same time young women are experiencing more professional opportunity and personal latitude than previous generations were allowed. Young men are discovering that their traditional roles—procreate, provide, and protect—are being significantly recast in new gender role assumptions, an overpopulated planet, a globalized economy (in which increasingly "brains" trump "brawn"), and the changing conditions of warfare.[5] Governments and other authorities may be irritated when emerging adults mount a protest against a perceived injustice. Correspondingly, however, established adult culture feels at least mild uneasiness if its young seem passive, dependent, "not pulling their weight," oriented to absolute security, and bereft of idealism. All are bewildered if the sort of self-confidence, aspiration, and commitment that are associated with movement into adulthood are not as evident as they expected.

Three Central Questions

Thus, embedded in this question of when one becomes an adult are three central questions: What is the key marker that defines the threshold and shapes the tasks of emerging adulthood? What are these tasks and the timeframe these tasks imply? What kind of environment best serves the tasks of young, emerging adulthood?

Twenty-somethings do many things. They seek work, find jobs, change jobs. They party and play. They earn undergraduate, master's, doctoral, and professional degrees. They have a yen for travel—from one country to another and from one company to another. They create art, claim adventure, explore and establish long-term relationships, form households, volunteer in their communities, become parents, initiate important projects, and serve internships. Sometimes they protest and make demands. They try to become financially independent. Some go to prison. Some deal with major health and other physical and emotional stresses. And some emerging adults die too young.

It is my conviction that the central work of young, emerging adulthood in the cycle of human life is not located in any of these tasks or circumstances per se. Rather, the promise and vulnerability of emerging adulthood lie in the experience of the birth of critical awareness and consequently in the dissolution and recomposition of the meaning of self, other, world, and "God." In the process of human becoming, this task of achieving critical thought and discerning its consequences for one's sense of meaning and purpose has enormous implications for the years of adulthood to follow. Emerging adulthood is rightfully a time of asking big questions and crafting worthy dreams.

What is the timeframe this task requires? It takes a while.

I was in conversation with a young woman who halfway though her sophomore year of college reflected, "I have been thinking lately a lot about thresholds. When does one become an adult? When we graduate from high school? Or college? Can a piece of paper signify that we are adult? It seems at times that it is easier to meet new adults who recognize me as I am now than to be with adults who see me as I used to be." Later, when I expressed appreciation for her comments, she added, "It seems to me that one becomes an adult when *you know that you have a life*. Do you know what I mean?"

When we shift from just "being a life" to "knowing we *have* a *life*," we achieve an undeniably different form of consciousness. New possibilities and responsibilities appear for both self and world. Whether or not this transformation occurs and how a young adult is (or isn't) met and invited to test this new consciousness will make a great difference in the adulthood that lies ahead. We are helped to grasp the potential significance and scope of this shift in consciousness—and why it takes a while— by an understanding of the development of human meaning-making in its most comprehensive dimensions, the development of "faith."

The Search for Meaning, Purpose, and Faith

We human beings are unable to survive, and certainly cannot thrive, unless we can make meaning.[6] If life is perceived as utterly random, fragmented, and chaotic—meaningless—we suffer confusion, distress, stagnation, and finally despair. The meaning we make orients our posture in the world and determines our sense of self and purpose. We need to be able to make some sort of sense out of things; we seek pattern, order, coherence, and relation in the dynamic and disparate elements of our experience.

As we will see in Chapter Two, this capacity and demand for meaning and purpose is what I invite the reader to associate with the word *faith*. For most of us, this represents a shift from the usual connotations. Faith is often linked exclusively to belief, particularly religious belief. But faith goes far beyond religious belief, narrowly understood. Faith is more adequately recognized as *the activity of seeking and discovering meaning in the most comprehensive dimensions of our experience*—that is, *faith* is as much a verb as a noun. Faith is a broad, generic human phenomenon. To be human is to dwell in an ongoing process of meaning-making, to dwell in the sense one makes out of the whole of life—what is perceived as ultimately true and trustworthy about self, world, and cosmos (whether that meaning is strong or fragile, expressed in religious, multireligious, humanist, naturalist, or secular terms). This understanding of meaning-making and faith provides a comprehensive lens through which we may perceive and interpret the multifaceted and often tangled features of emerging adult lives. The twenty-something years are especially ripe for vital transformations in meaning-making and the re-formation of faith.

To become an emerging adult in faith is to discover in a critically aware, self-conscious manner the limits of inherited or otherwise socially received assumptions about how life works and what counts—and to compose more adequate forms of meaning and faith on the other side of that discovery. But we don't do it alone. The quality of this recomposition and its adequacy to ground a sense of purpose and a worthy adulthood depends in significant measure on the hospitality, aspirations, and commitment of adult culture as mediated through both individuals and institutions. Understanding the potential significance of the re-formation of meaning, purpose, and faith in the twenty-something years may deepen our appreciation of the courage and costs of the journey toward a mature, adult faith, and encourage us to reexamine our assumptions about the formation of adulthood, our participation in the lives of emerging adults, and our own capacity to live meaningful adult lives. Indeed, because the future of our planet may depend on us all becoming more conscious, critically aware, mature adults, we may see that a resilient and vibrant society finds its orientation, in part, in its commitment to the formation and flourishing of emerging adults.

A Disciplined Inquiry—A Developmental Perspective

Within this broad, comprehensive frame of meaning-making, insights from constructive-developmental and social psychologies assist in revealing and interpreting key features of the work of emerging adulthood. Increasingly, as the human life span has been extended, human development is understood as a complex process that includes changes in biological, cognitive, emotional, social, spiritual, and moral dimensions. As we shall see in Chapters Three through Six, when we trace the process of the development of critical thought and the reorientation to authority and community it requires, we can discern an era or stage in human becoming that has its own work, its own strengths and limitations, and its own integrity.

The perspective described here has taken form in dialogue with several psychosocial theorists (Piaget, Erikson, Perry, Levinson, Keniston, Kegan, Gilligan, Belenky and her colleagues, and more recently Arnett and his colleagues, along with others). This work also stands within and critically elaborates the interdisciplinary study of faith development pioneered by James Fowler.

But the primary dialogue that shapes my thinking has been necessarily with young adults themselves. They have continually challenged my assumptions about human development, the formation of faith, and educational-professional practice. Listening carefully to emerging adults grappling with the particular stresses of making meaning in these complex times continues to prod me to amend those theories (including my own) by which young, emerging adults are interpreted.

Developmental theories have primarily described the movement to mature adulthood as a three-step process whereby conventional (or adolescent) meaning-making develops into a critical-systemic faith (or order of consciousness), which then evolves into a mature adult form of meaning-making that can hold both conviction and paradox. Encouraged initially by the seminal work of Kenneth Keniston and informed by my own observation and research first published in 1986 as *The Critical Years*, it is my view that this developmental journey is more adequately grasped as a four-step process. That is, I believe there is a distinctive emerging adult way of making meaning in the often murky and overlooked territory between conventional faith (adolescence) and critical-systemic faith (adulthood). In the years from roughly eighteen to thirty-two a distinctive mode of meaning-making can emerge, one that has certain adult strengths but understandably lacks others. This mode of making meaning includes (1) becoming critically aware of one's own composing of reality, (2) self-consciously participating in an ongoing dialogue toward truth, and (3) cultivating a capacity to respond—to act—in committed and satisfying ways.

Role of Imagination in Human Intelligence

Further, in Chapter Seven, I will draw attention to the relationship between how we know and what we know, that is, to the difference between the cognitive form or structure (for example, critical thinking) and the *content* those structures hold. Though constructive-developmental theorists have concentrated primarily on describing the formal structures of each stage or "order of mind," careful consideration must also be given to the formative power of the content: the images and concepts that our structures of mind hold and to the role of imagination in human intelligence. Moreover, as these are the stuff of the young adult "Dream"[7]—an imagination of one's best future—they inevitably play a vital role in both informing and inspiring the formation of adulthood.

From this perspective, we can see this under-recognized territory as the birthplace of adult vision and can recognize how every feature of cultural life potentially shapes or misshapes the narrative offered to the imagination of emerging adults. And this brings us to our third central question: What kind of environment, social milieu, and culture best serves the tasks of those in the twenty-something decade?

Mentors and Mentoring Environments

Emerging adults embody a postadolescent quality of new strength yet are at the same time appropriately dependent on others, particularly the presence and quality of mentors and mentoring environments—educational, economic, political, religious, and familial. They are ripe for initiation into big questions and ready for access to worthy dreams. Emerging adults are, therefore, especially vulnerable to whether or not such questions are posed and how their dreams are seeded, assessed, and nurtured. They are vulnerable to if and how they are recognized, supported, challenged, and inspired. They are vulnerable to promises—made, broken, and kept.

As we will see in Chapters Eight and Nine and in the Coda, within a distracted, indifferent, or exploiting culture, emerging adulthood may be squandered on dreams too small to match the potential of the emerging adult life. In the good company of thoughtful mentors and mentoring communities, however, emerging adults can navigate the complex tasks at hand and galvanize the power of ongoing cultural renewal.

For many reasons, the practice and wisdom of mentoring has been weakened in our society. We compensate for this loss with a professionalism that is too often delivered without the "life-giving, caring field once provided by elders."[8] This has contributed to fragmentation and loss of transcendent meaning for which no amount of professional expertise can compensate and has spawned assumptions that tragically widen the gap between generations. Restoring mentoring as a vital social art and a cultural force could significantly revitalize our institutions and provide the intergenerational glue to address some of our deepest and most pervasive concerns. Thus this book is for all adults who directly and indirectly are investing themselves in the promise of young adult lives, and it is for those who yet may be persuaded to do so.

Becoming Adult in a Changing World

We live in "cusp time"—one of those great "hinge" times in history. The young adult task of composing and recomposing meaning and faith now takes place in a culture making its way through a similar task, as now we are all negotiating a turning point in the flow of history. This threshold time is shaped by new technologies that have spawned accelerated, permanent change and unprecedented conditions prompting reconsideration of every feature of life. In the intensification of our experience of an interdependent global reality, we increasingly recognize that we must birth a new cultural imagination on a planetary scale. This larger, dynamic context is a primary catalyst in the growing recognition of emerging adulthood as a discrete era in human becoming. The tasks of emerging adults are a microcosm of the transition we are now making as a culture, as we move into the reality of a new global commons.

The New Commons

The commons is a powerful image buried deep in the core of human experience. In ancient societies, it was and remains the crossroads at the center of the village. It has also taken the form of the great plazas and squares in cities around the world. In New England, it was the classic patch of green where everyone could pasture a cow. That commons was framed by an ecology of institutions—the general store, town meeting hall, school, church, bank, post office, the doctor's house, newspaper office, an inn or pub, the sheriff's office with the jail, and a flock of households with the farmlands beyond. People gathered on the commons for commerce and communication, play and protest, memorial and celebration, and worked out how they would live together over time.

The commons is not a pristine, idyllic, romantic image. Whether in the form of Main Street or the wharf; the church, synagogue, or mosque; the bodega or the stoops of the brownstones; the marketplace or the ball field—the practice of the commons always embraced a mix of the best and the worst of human life. But the notion of the commons always presses toward inclusion, and the experience of a commons anchors a sense of a shared life within a manageable frame.[9]

Today our shared commons is global in scope and personal in impact. Travel, communication, and nuclear and biological technologies along with a growing environmental consciousness have spawned a global market, a collision of cultures, and we are all cast into a new global commons, increasingly more keenly aware that we are a part of a vast tissue of life—a shared life within an *un*manageable frame. In this new commons, society has become yet more complex, diverse, and morally ambiguous. As addressed in *Common Fire: Leading Lives of Commitment in a Complex World*, there is an enormous need for an understanding and practice of human development that prepares people to become citizen-leaders in this new commons, able to engage the great questions of our time and to participate in discovering and creating responses to challenges both new and ancient. Democratic societies are dependent on a complex moral conscience—a citizenry who can recognize and assess the claims of multiple perspectives and are steeped in critical, connective, and compassionate habits of mind.[10] Recognition of the importance of emerging adulthood and a reappraisal of the relationship between generations and the work we need to do together throughout our culture are essential elements of this challenge. Emerging adults require an initiation into viable forms of meaning, purpose, and faith that can orient and undergird their response to our new reality. Our capacity as a culture to provide this initiation is a critical feature of our vocation as a species on the edge of a new cultural landscape (Chapter Ten).

The Distinctive Role of Higher Education

In its best practice, higher education is a vital expression of that vocation, playing a primary role in the formation of critical thought and consequently in the formation of viable, adult meaning-making and faith. Higher and professional education is not the only context where critical awareness can be cultivated and informed, but it is distinctively vested with the responsibility of teaching critical and connective-systemic thought and initiating young lives into a responsible apprehension, first of the realities and questions of a vast and mysterious universe, and second of our fitting participation within it. Higher and professional education is intended to serve as a primary site of inquiry, reflection, and cultivation of knowledge on behalf of the wider culture—and a privileged place of formation in the process of human development.

Invariably, issues pertaining to the development of character and conscience—cognitive competence, integrity, freedom, responsibility, skillfulness, empathy, generosity, professional courage, wisdom, and fidelity—will be threaded through society's expectations of the purpose and life of the academy. All are qualities associated with exemplary citizenship, leadership, and the best of the intellectual life. The fate of these qualities is embedded in our assumptions about the formation and claims of adulthood. How these qualities are formed and re-formed in the lives of emerging adults appropriately shapes educational goals, cultural aspirations, and the conditions of accountability for students, faculty, administrators, supervisors, and all who interact with twenty-somethings. Though this is contested territory, there is renewed awareness that these concerns belong at the center of the life of the academy.[11] As such, institutions of higher education hold a special place in the story of human becoming, particularly in the process of becoming an emerging adult in the imagination of "faith." Creating and stewarding mentoring environments—formal and informal—are primary means by which faculty, administrators, and the many others who are directly and indirectly related to emerging adults inevitably, by intention or default, play a formative role in their lives. Seen from this perspective, every subject, discourse, and methodology in the curriculum of higher and professional education and every class, program, lab, dorm, and athletic team (as well as their analogues in the related contexts of adult work and the wider society) potentially contributes to the formation and transformation of emerging adult meaning-making.

It is enormously difficult to make meaning, to compose a faith, within the intensified complexity of today's commons, but it is particularly appropriate to do so in the institution charged with teaching the value and practice of critical reflection. It is especially difficult, however, if the practice of critical reflection stalls out in mere unqualified relativism, without engaging in the ongoing hard work of discerning the terms and conditions within which fateful choices—both personal and collective—must be made within an increasingly complex, diverse, morally ambiguous world. Some would argue that meaning-making and its moral, ethical consequences are not the business of higher education, that its proper task is to discover and teach empirical truth, and that issues of meaning, purpose, and one's take on ultimate reality are more appropriately dealt with elsewhere in society. Yet society itself has not always made this assumption.

At the beginning of the story of American higher education (the founding of Harvard College), we find this statement of purpose: "After God had carried us safe to New England and wee had our houses, provided necessaries for our livelihood, rear'd convenient places for God's worship and settled the government: One of the next things we longed for, and looked after was to advance Learning and perpetuate it to Posterity: dreading to leave an illiterate Ministry to the Churches, when our present Ministers shall lie in the Dust."[12]

For these forebears, learning and faith were integral to each other. Moreover, both were at stake in the establishment of higher education. The little college, which was at once a divinity school and the seed of one of the world's finest universities, was charged with preparing people who could responsibly nurture human faith—that is, viable meaning-making relative to the whole of life—on behalf of future generations.

Today, as our social reality has become dramatically more complex, higher education has become a multi-institutional reality composed of colleges, programs, institutes, centers, laboratories, and graduate and professional schools—all invested in related professional sectors. Further, every college and university is linked to a vast network of trustees, alums, parents, funding agencies, and other members of the wider commons who have a stake in what we know and how we learn to become citizens in the twenty-first century. Within this dynamic complexity, the questions of the relationship between the extraordinary knowledge development of our time and the questions of purpose, meaning, faith, and ethics have become both more difficult and more urgent.

This book, therefore, is addressed in a particular way to those who directly affect the lives of emerging adults within higher and professional education: faculty, administrators, trustees, counselors, chaplains, coaches, residence hall staff, and others. But higher education no longer dwells in any kind of reality separated from the fabric of our society as a whole, and emerging adults, whether or not they are engaged in higher and professional education, are affected by work supervisors, parents, older adult friends and relatives, and a wide range of professionals, including policy makers, business executives, religious leaders, attorneys, social workers, and all who shape the media—musicians and other artists, directors, producers, publishers, commentators, and webmasters. Thus, while giving particular attention to the experience of emerging adults in the context of higher education, this book recognizes the mentoring role of all who affect the lives of twenty-somethings (see especially the Coda).

A Complex Call

In 1990, Kotre and Hall observed that if a new stage of life is emerging, it is

> confined primarily to the middle class, but that is where childhood and adolescence first took root. Wider recognition . . . will depend on the prosperity and educational demands of society at large. If young adulthood becomes accepted as a season of life in the twenty-first century the way adolescence did in the twentieth, it would be the second stage to fill the widening no-man's-land between the biological and social markers of adulthood. Twenty-five extra years of life . . . have stretched the lifeline. . . . Much of the resulting tension is being felt between childhood and adulthood.[13]

Now two decades later, there is growing evidence that society is beginning to create a larger cultural space for twenty-somethings. How this cultural space will be used remains the critical question.

This book offers a complex call—across all sectors of the new commons—to those who would mentor the next generation. It is offered also to relatively older emerging adults themselves who, having traveled some of the terrain described here, may find confirmation of their own struggling and aspiring integrity and affirmation of their finest and boldest dreams. As today's generations must make meaning in the midst of an intensifying personal and global complexity and an expanding universe, and as both younger and older adults stand on a new frontier in the history of human meaning-making, it is an invitation to all of us to recognize with new strength how emerging adults and their mentors serve to fuel the power and promise of cultural resilience and renewal, seeding an imagination of a worthy adulthood and the promise of our common future.

Chapter Two

The Deep Motion of Life

Composing Meaning, Purpose, and Faith

When I was invited to work with the faculty of a prestigious business school as they began to readdress ethics in the MBA curriculum, a longtime colleague from another field said, with a cynical glint in his eye, "Oh, you get to ask those students what their ethics are!" I responded, "Well, yes, but what I really want to understand is how they make meaning."

Most of us recognize that we human beings may or may not act in a manner that corresponds with what we say our ethics are. But human beings do act in ways that are congruent with what we ultimately trust as real and dependable—what makes sense at the end of the day, what we think we can really count on. We humans act in ways that are congruent with how we make meaning.

In our meaning-making, we search for a sense of coherence, connection, pattern, order, and significance. In our ongoing interaction with all of life, we puzzle about the fitting, truthful relationships among things. We search for ways of understanding our experience that make sense of both the expected and the unexpected in everyday life.

Over time, we can grow in our capacity to make meaning in ways that are trustworthy and dependable, aligning with the deep currents of life itself. A child may make meaning of his parents' divorce by telling himself, and us, that his parents are divorced because they caught it (like a disease) from another family in the neighborhood who suffered divorce just a few months earlier. We find this bit of heroic meaning-making poignantly charming, fitting for his age—and perhaps not without truth—but we know that in time he will tell the story differently.

But how does this change happen? How do our ways of making meaning become more adequate, dependable, and satisfying? How do we learn to make meaning in ways that orient and sustain a worthy adult life?

These are questions that invite us to reflect on how adult faith is formed. Most people, however, do not immediately recognize that meaning-making is a central feature of the experience of faith and the ground of our ethics. When I told my cynical colleague that I was interested in the meaning-making of MBA students as a way of understanding their ethics, he was intrigued. If I had said I was interested in their faith, he might have found it odd or inappropriate in a culturally plural, professional setting, or he might have simply concluded that ethics and faith or religion go together—all important, but somewhat marginal in the "real world."

Points of Departure: What Faith Is and Isn't

Faith is a multifaceted phenomenon and we perceive it best when we consider it from several angles of vision.

Faith and Religion

Indeed, for many, faith is simply equated with religion. Thus the word *faith* has become problematic in a changing and religiously plural world. This is particularly true within any setting—governmental, educational, or commercial—where the multiple perspectives characteristic of our new global commons are especially evident. Among some people, personal and cultural ambivalence about matters of religion make *faith* a charged, negative word, best avoided in any case. For others, it is a strong and positive word with a venerable history that dwells at the core of human life. For yet others, faith has simply become a matter of indifference. If recognized as a part of human life—even an important part—it is nevertheless seen as only a part and considered separable from other important elements of life, such as career, relationships, political commitments, economic life, and so on. Those who view faith this way assume it is something one may choose or choose not to incorporate into one's particular lifestyle. From this perspective, faith becomes merely a single and optional element in the complex calculus that is required to negotiate contemporary adult life. Thus many in today's society assume faith to be at most a personal matter, preferably confined to the private sphere—and a disturbing point of contention in public life.

In contrast, there are those (particularly some who have a strongly defined and intensely held set of religious beliefs) who assert that a particular form of faith (theirs) fully interprets and may be arbitrarily imposed on all experience (theirs and others')—and may thus be used to justify both personal and political-public commitments, sometimes in violent and even terrorist terms. And common to many understandings of the word *faith* is the assumption that it is something essentially static. You have it or you don't. When faith is linked with religious dogma, the word is not generally used to connote something dynamic that undergoes change, transformation, and development over time.

Faith and Spirituality

There is, however, some shift toward a more spacious connotation when faith is associated with spirituality. Growing numbers of people in professional and other walks of life are apt to say, "I'm not religious, but I am spiritual." Though religion may be perceived as problematic, there remains an awareness that everyone asks religious questions—questions about matters of ultimate concern, especially questions that take us into the Mystery of life that we all share. Some people are more attuned to such questions than others. But if spirituality begins at the crossroads of awe and angst, human beings inevitably step into those moments when we are in awe of the vastness of the universe or confounded by the agony of the innocent. These are not puzzles to be solved but realities that are integral to the experience of being human. Spirituality may be helpfully understood as "one's lived relationship with Mystery."[1] In corporate and educational spheres there is, in some quarters, growing comfort with speaking of spirit, spirituality, and soul. In large measure, these words typically connote a personal rather than a public sensibility, although book titles addressing these dimensions of experience are highly visible in the public square.

This turn to a recognition of spirituality and an acknowledgment of soul is rooted in a longing for ways of speaking of the human experience of depth, meaning, moral purpose, transcendence, wholeness, intuition, vulnerability, tenderness, courage, the capacity to love, and the apprehension of the animating essence at the core of life—*spirit* (English), *pneuma* (Greek), *prajna* (Sanskrit), *ruha* (Hebrew), *spiritus* (Latin). As Parker Palmer has articulated so helpfully, it arises from the hunger for authenticity, for correspondence between our inner and outer lives.[2] In a society grown weary and restless with hardening definitions of who and what counts in determining what matters—what we will invest our lives in and how we will name that investment—there is a desire to break through into a more spacious and nourishing conception of the common life we all share. In this context, the words *faith* and *faithfulness*, connoting trust, relationship, and loyalty, find place and resonance.

Faith: A Human Universal

A reconsideration of the word *faith* assists us in reclaiming an enlarged sense of meaning and purpose and yields ways of understanding the contemporary resistance and attraction to things religious and spiritual. A central feature of the perspective offered here is that faith is integral to all of human life. It is a human universal; it shapes both personal and collective behavior. Faith is manifest in a multitude of personal and cultural forms. Its expressions in language and ritual, ideology and practice are, however, always particular and finite. Faith is a dynamic phenomenon that undergoes transformation across the whole life span, with the potential for a particularly powerful transformation in the emerging adult years.

A careful exploration of the word *faith* is more than an exercise in etymology. If we are to recognize the significance of the dynamics of meaning-making and faith in the experience of emerging adults and their implications for the role of mentors and the institutions that influence the formation of adulthood, faith must be emancipated from its too-easy equation with belief and religion and reconnected with meaning, trust, and truth.

Faith and Belief

In contemporary English usage, *faith* is used primarily as a noun, strongly associated with religion, and frequently used synonymously with belief. This has not always been so. The eminent historian of religion Wilfred Cantwell Smith elegantly traced the relationship between the words *faith* and *belief*. He has shown that because in English *faith* was used only as a noun, to *believe* was chosen as the verb. This was appropriate, for in earlier centuries "the Anglo-Saxon–derived word 'believe' meant pretty much what its exact counterpart in German, *belieben*, still means today: namely, 'to hold dear, to prize.' It signified to love, . . . to give allegiance, to be loyal to; to value highly." The Latin *credo*, meaning literally "I set my heart," was translated as "I believe," and thus was not a mistranslation.[3] "To believe" connoted an essential human activity involving the whole person.

In recent times, however, the word *belief* has shifted. Smith traces three important migrations in the use of *believe* that have altered its meaning: first, from the personal to the impersonal— from a relationship with Being to dogma; second, a shift in the subject of the verb, from "I believe" or "believe me" to "he, she, or they believe"; and third, from conveying the linking of the heart with truth to increasingly connoting a lack of trust and confidence—"Do you really think that is so?" "Well, I believe so."[4]

As a result, belief has come to suggest primarily a cognitive enterprise. Further, it connotes mere opinion—or even the dubious or false—rather than matters of truth, reality, and ulti-mate importance. Thus, when the word *faith* is used synony-mously with *belief,* it takes on these same connotations. Consequently, these impersonal, propositional, and narrowly cognitive connotations separate faith from the personal, affec-tive, visceral, and passional dimensions of being and knowing. In addition, the association of faith with what is dubious links it with "irrational knowledge" and consigns it to the private, emo-tional sphere, divorced from both public life and the life of the mind.

These shifts in the meaning of the words *faith* and *belief* have critical significance in contemporary culture. They are a part of the postmodern reorientation of our relationship to knowledge, affecting our most cherished institutions and assumptions— specifically our assumptions about faith, religion, belief, and what we can trust, imagine, and hope for. Religion itself has had a role in these currents of change. For example, Christianity, in Smith's view, has fallen into the "heresy" of requiring belief as the primary evidence of faith.[5] Faith, a more fundamental dynamic than belief, has been obscured.

Whenever belief has become mere intellectual assent to abstract propositions, and whenever specific religious proposi-tions have become meaningless, impersonal, dangerous, or at least dubious to a large number of postmodern people, then by synonymous usage faith has come to be equally meaningless—particularly to the critically aware mind. If faith is discounted, the human landscape becomes arid, and hope and commitment wither; the human spirit grows parched and not much more than a prickly cynicism can be sustained. Therefore, if we are to recover an adequate understanding of human faith, we must be clear that when we use the word *faith* we are speaking of something quite other than belief understood in these ways. Faith is not simply a set of beliefs that religious people have; it is something that all human beings do.

Faith and Truth

This distinction between faith and belief is particularly important when we are concerned with the relationship of faith to truth. Every person, profession, and sector of society has a stake in the adequacy of truth claims. Commitment to truth requires a questioning curiosity and relentless and rigorous examination of one's most elemental assumptions. In the face of new understanding, one may come to perceive an earlier experience of faith—an earlier way of making meaning—as now outgrown or otherwise irrelevant. Indeed, if faith is understood as static, fixed, and inextricably bound to a particular language or worldview, it must be discarded as obsolete if the integrity of intellect and soul is to be maintained in a dynamic world. A richer perception of faith, however, enables us to recognize that fidelity to truth may indeed require changing a particular set of beliefs—and spur the ongoing task of discerning a more adequate faith.

Faith and Skepticism

Any attempt to recover a generic understanding of the word *faith* in a way that may illuminate essential human capacities and commitments—including the commitment to truth—is bound to encounter skepticism. Yet skepticism itself may be closely related to faith. For faith to become mature, it must be able to doubt itself. Skepticism combines the power to question with an openness to being convinced. Skepticism can be a healthy form of doubt. It may or not reflect the loss of a once-shared trust in a universe of meaning, however that was defined. Cynicism, in contrast, functions as a kind of armor against disappointment and despair. It may also function as a thin veneer of public sophistication, glossing over a private, lonely void that neither the rational mind nor economic success can fill. In our time, we have become at once scientifically informed, philosophically relativistic, disappointed and disillusioned in many quarters, and dubious about our future. Yet ironically faith can come alive in an engagement with radical uncertainty.

Faith—a Matter of Meaning

Though faith has become problematic, the importance of meaning has not. William G. Perry Jr., who has contributed so much to our understanding of meaning-making in young adult-hood, often remarked that the purpose of an organism is to organize, and what human beings organize is meaning. Meaning-making is the activity of composing a sense of the connections among things: a sense of pattern, order, form, and significance. To be human is to seek coherence and correspondence. To be human is to want to be oriented to one's surroundings. To be human is to desire relationship among the disparate elements of existence.

Patterning, testing, and recomposing activity occurs as part of the deep motion of human life and manifests itself in meaning. The mind does not passively receive the world but rather acts on every object and every experience to compose it. This composing activity occurs even at the level of basic perception. For example, when we perceive a tree, we compose it, organizing its various parts into a whole—branches, leaves, trunk, roots, textures, colors, height, breadth, and whatever we may know of the intricate systems by which it is nourished or threatened through the seasons of its existence. Though we may all encounter the same tree, each of us composes a different one. Moreover, in interaction with the tree we compose, we each make different meanings of it. Some of us see the subject of a poem; others see a lucrative number of board feet; and still others see a source of shade, shelter, or a threat in a strong wind.

It is much the same with our experience of a handshake. We compose a sense of warmth, sincerity, strength, aloofness, ambivalence, or mere social custom according to how another grips (or fails to grip) our hand. This perception is composed from our cultural history, our mood in the moment, our knowledge of the person, and a whole host of other elements in our environment. Though we may shake hands with the same person, each of us composes a different perception.

We compose the discrete elements of our every day, such as trees and handshakes, into an overall pattern that orients and grounds us. Even to get out of bed in the morning we depend on some familiar pattern of relationships among coffeepot, shower, and breakfast—whatever constitutes our ritual of initiation into a new day. There is, however, an important distinction to be made. Though there may be times when getting up in the morning is indeed a heroic act, nevertheless, the primary concern here is not with meaning-making at the level of only the discrete and mundane. Rather, when we speak of faith, we direct our attention to the desire of human beings to live at more than a mundane level—to make meaning of the *whole* of life.

We reserve the word *faith* for meaning-making in its most comprehensive dimensions. In other words, whenever we organize our sense of a particular object, a series of activities, or an institution, we are also compelled to compose our sense of its place in the whole of existence. Human beings seek to compose and dwell in some conviction of what is ultimately true, real, and dependable within that vast frame. Either unconsciously or self-consciously, individually or together, and taking more or less into account, we compose a sense of the ultimate character of reality and then we stake our lives on that "reality"—the meaning we have made.

Forms of Faith

It is this activity of composing and being composed by meaning—this "faithing"—that I invite the reader to associate with the word *faith*. As such, faith has many facets and is manifest in our experience in several forms.

Faith as Primal Force of Promise

William F. Lynch, a Jesuit who reflected deeply on the nature of faith and hope, described faith as "the most elemental force in human nature."[6] He invites us to imagine faith as coming into force "as soon as promises begin to be made to it"[7]—that is, at the very dawn of human existence, in the womb. (Although he used this image only as a metaphor, prenatal psychology suggests that it may indeed be more than metaphor.[8]) We cannot remember but we can imagine that we first come to consciousness in a rudimentary sense of trustworthy pattern, wholeness, and relation—a sense of an ultimate environment that intends our good.

Then, in the experience we call birth, we undergo what must seem like utter chaos: sound louder than ever before, light, touch, breathing for the first time. The task of the infant is to recompose that which was promised at the dawn of existence, a felt sense of trustworthy pattern and relation. Erik Erikson described an infant's first task as the establishment of "basic trust."[9] As I am describing the process, however, the first task of human being is to reestablish basic trust.

In most religious traditions, a ritual occasion marks one's entry into a social world of meaning and purpose. In Jewish, Islamic, and Christian traditions, the community gathers around the infant and does an extraordinary thing. The child is affirmed as "child of the covenant"—child of primordial promise. What is most significant about this declaration is that the adult community knows that though the infant may with good care be able to reestablish a trustworthy sense of relation and wholeness, this task is not accomplished alone, nor is it then accomplished once and for all. Over and over again, life will require the encounter with the unexpected. Again and again, we undergo the loss of our most cherished patterns of meaning and anchors of trust as we discover their insufficiency. In the ups and downs of daily life, human beings experience the ongoing motion of a dialogue between fear and trust, certainty and doubt, power and powerlessness, alienation and belonging. Yet mature faith has learned that though the forms of faith are finite, the promise is kept. It is from this struggled knowing that the adult community addresses the new infant as a child of the promise.

Thus, to speak of faith is to point toward the meaning-making that frames, colors, provides tone and texture, and relativizes the activity of the everyday. All human action is conditioned by a felt sense of how life really is (or ought to be) or what has ultimate value.

A Center of Power, Value, and Affection

Fowler has described the activity of faith as "intuiting life as a whole"—a wholeness that is felt as a sense of relatedness among self, other, and "a center of power and value" that some would name "God."[10] Up to this point, we have spoken of faith without speaking of "God" per se. In the dynamic activity of composing meaning, whatever pattern of meaning we ultimately depend on functions as "God" for us. In other words, whatever serves as the centering, unifying linchpin of our pattern of meaning and holds it all together—that center functions as "God." As the theologian H. Richard Niebuhr recognized, "To deny the reality of a supernatural being called God is one thing; to live without confidence in some center of value and without loyalty to a cause is another."[11]

Many and Lesser Gods

In the times in which we live, many people might best be understood as "polytheists," juggling as it were many gods. They find themselves living fragmented lives, piecing together various scraps of discrete meaning, each with its own center of value, power, and affection, each with its own god. Polytheistic faith is composed by those who may have "intuited life as a whole" but have only been able to compose an assortment of "isolated wholes." For example, many people yearn for a sense of deep integration in their lives but experience even the worlds of home and work as quite separate, each sphere oriented to differing values, expectations, and loyalties.[12]

There are those, however, who construe a single pattern of meaning and thus dwell in a faith with a single cause or center, such as the success of their careers or other ambitions. Yet they are unable to relate the center to any larger frame of trustworthy meaning. Niebuhr described this form of faith as "henotheism." Their sense of self, world, and God is cohesive because the boundaries are tightly drawn. The center they rely on to anchor ultimate meaning is, however, inadequate in the face of the variety, complexity, and tragic elements of human experience. Their henotheistic faith is vulnerable to competing centers and to any significant shift in the conditions of personal, professional, or cultural life. This form of faith can also be the "cramping faith of blind and fanatical particularism" or "narrow faith."[13]

Henotheistic faith may take such forms as devotion to a child or commitment to artistic achievement, scientific inquiry, a political dream, or a business venture. The question is not whether these are worthy and valuable forms of engagement with life. The question is, Do self, world, and "God" collapse when the child dies or a permanently injured hand can no longer play a musical instrument or the funding for the laboratory dries up or one is defeated in an election or the business enterprise ends in failure? The challenge that drives the motion toward mature adult faith is grounded in the question, Is there a pattern of meaning, a faith that can survive the defeat of finite centers of power, value, and affection?

One Embracing the Many

H. Richard Niebuhr directs our attention beyond polytheism (which depends for its meaning on many centers and gives its partial loyalties to many interests) and henotheism (which centers in a god who is "one among many possible gods") to "radical monotheism." This is a pattern of meaning, a faith, centered in "One beyond the many"—a centering of power and value adequate to all of the ongoing conditions of the experiences of persons and their communities.[14] This could, however, be expressed as "One embracing the many."

In a Buddhist sensibility, this ultimacy might be described as *Sunyata*, usually translated as "emptiness." This use of the word is intended to convey a consciousness of the very foundation of the universe, the vast "mystery underlying even darkness—from which the earth itself with its mountains, oceans, buildings, animals, people, and clouds is born."[15]

When we speak of faith as the composing of meaning in these most comprehensive dimensions, we mean a sensibility of life that not only transcends (is beyond us) but also permeates and undergirds our very existence (is within, among, and beneath us). To speak of God as a gift of faith is to seek to name an orienting consciousness that is both transcendent and immanent, both ultimate and intimate.

Faith as Truth and Trust

When the activity of meaning-making is recognized in these comprehensive dimensions, we begin to perceive how both truth and trust are at stake in the composing of faith. A worthy faith must bear the test of lived experience in the real world—our discoveries and disappointments, expectations and betrayals, assumptions and surprises. It is in the ongoing dialogue between self and world, between community and lived reality, that meaning—a faith—takes form.

Yet the meanings human beings compose range from "murky shadows to shimmering points of illumination."[16] If a person composes self and world in a manner that constellates an ultimate sense of mistrust, a conviction of a universe of, say, indifferent or malicious randomness, for her such randomness is what is true and trusted. This is her faith. But interestingly, the word *faith* is most typically used to convey the affirmation of a trustworthy ultimacy, having dependable characteristics in a more conventional (though not necessarily a simplistic) sense.

Faith is generally understood as a form of meaning-making that is a quality of human living that at its best grounds capacities for confidence, courage, loyalty, and generosity—and even in the face of catastrophe and confusion enables one to feel at home in the universe (though one's apprehensions of it may be complex, dynamic, shrouded in mystery, and variously described). But the tension remains. If we understand faith as a human universal, two questions necessarily haunt us: If one composes a faith that is trustworthy, is it true? If one composes an ultimacy that is not trustworthy, is it faith?

This way of perceiving faith may trouble those who take for granted that faith always has to do with God as defined by their religious traditions. For them, to speak of faith in generic terms without necessarily referring to God as previously conceived seems confusing, if not beside the point. It is helpful, therefore, to explore further the intimate relationships among faith, trust, and truth.

Faith—to Set One's Heart

The relation of faith to trust and truth is illuminated by Smith's study of the notion of faith across cultures, specifically in his discussion of the Hindu word *sraddha*. The word *sraddha* permeates Hindu literature and is assumed in all religious sensibility. As such it functions as an Indian concept of faith. *Sraddha* "is a compound of two words, *srad* (or *srat*), heart, and *dha*, to put." *Sraddha* "means placing one's heart on." This tradition has said that "the religious life, whatever its form, begins . . . with faith; and faith, in its turn, is one's finding within that life (one's being found by) something to which one gives one's heart."[17]

Sraddha in itself leaves unspecified the object of faith. It can be recognized, however, that one gives one's heart only to that which one "sees" as adequate, trustworthy, and promising. Indeed, Smith notes the Hindu insight that "in fact, the universe and human beings were created in such a way that faith is the intrinsically appropriate human orientation towards what is true and right and real, its absence or opposite (*asraddha*, unfaith, disinterest) being recognized similarly as the proper human attitude to what is false and awry."[18]

"Faithing," then, is putting one's heart on that which one trusts as true. It is a bedrock trust that the pattern one sees is real. Faithing, in other words, is the ongoing composing of the heart's true resting place. Thus, learning to see and to know in increasingly adequate ways is critical to faith.

The Canopy of Faith

We may think of faith, therefore, as the deep ground, the loom on which the rest of the particular threads of life's tapestry find their place. Or the activity of faith might be imagined as the weaving of an overarching "canopy of significance" that embraces, orders, and relativizes all of our knowing and being. Both metaphors convey faith as infinitely transcendent in character and simultaneously profoundly immanent. Faith is an activity that at once reaches infinitely beyond and intimately within the particulars of existence.

The metaphor of the canopy of faith has been made accessible to many cultures through the classic play *Fiddler on the Roof*. When the second daughter chooses to follow her revolutionary lover into Siberia, her father waits with her for the train that will carry her away from her family home. He acknowledges that they do not know when they will see each other again. Then his daughter gives him a gift. She responds, "I promise you I will be married under the canopy." This is a gift to her father, for in a Jewish wedding, the canopy represents not only the home that is formed by that union but also the whole household of Israel. She is promising her father that the fabric of meaning into which he has woven his life will be sustained and will transcend both miles and ideology. Later, we watch his canopy of faith stretched to its limits—and perhaps beyond its limits—when his youngest daughter chooses not to be married under the canopy.

Particularly because many in contemporary life find their meaning in forms that are not articulated in religious terms, we are often unaware that we have nevertheless woven a canopy of significance—a faith that we hold and are held by—until people we value do not choose to affirm that on which we discover our sense of life has ultimately depended. For some, awareness of the patterns that have been deeply woven into our personal and collective life emerges only in the suffering of the unraveling or rending of those weavings that held a personal or public trust.

If our daily living is dependent on a comprehensive fabric of meaning, the questions of faith are at once large and intimate, as all those who grieve or otherwise suffer meaninglessness know. "Why should I get out of bed in the morning?" "What is the purpose of my existence and the existence of others?" "Does anything really matter?" "What can I depend on?" "Are we ultimately alone?" "What and whom can be trusted as real?" "What is the ultimate character of the cosmos in which I dwell?" "What is right and just?" "How, now, shall we live?" Whenever we allow such questions to permeate the fiber of our lives, we discover new depths, and enlarged vistas often catch us by surprise. Our sense of the possible and the impossible is vulnerable to being reordered.

Faith as Purpose and Act

Faith—one's sense of the ultimate character of existence—not only centers the mind and provides a resting place for the heart. It is also the orienting and motivating guide of the hand. Faith orients one's sense of purpose and is manifest in action. In *The Path to Purpose,* William Damon describes purpose as "a stable and generalized intention to accomplish something that is at the same time meaningful to the self and consequential for the world beyond the self." He casts "purpose" in contrast to "goals and motives that come and go" in that "[a] true purpose is an *ultimate concern*. It is the final answer to the question of *Why? Why* am I doing this? *Why* does it matter? . . . A purpose is the reason *behind* the immediate goals and motives that drive most of our daily behavior."[19] When we examine our deepest purposes, we discover that they emerge from the meaning we make in the dimensions of faith. (It must be acknowledged that there are noble and ignoble purposes. But as with the word *faith*, when we speak of "a sense of purpose" we tend to set it in accord with an enduring, positive, moral intent.[20])

In this way, faith is intimately related to doing. We human beings act in accordance with what we really trust and what truly moves us—in contrast to what we may say we value. We act in alignment with what we finally perceive as real, oriented by our most powerful centers of trust (or mistrust). Thus our acts, powered by a deeper faith, often belie what we say (or even think) we believe. Our faith is revealed in our behavior.

Our actions are consistent with our verbal declarations only if these declarations reflect our actual convictions about ultimate meaning and are not superseded by unspoken commitments, loyalties, and fears oriented to other, more compelling centers of power, value, and affection. Faith makes itself public in everyday acts of decision, obedience, and courage. Faith—our sense of ultimate meaning and purpose—is the ground of ethics and the moral life. Faith is intimately linked with a sense of vocation—awareness of living one's life aligned with a larger frame of purpose and significance. It is from this perspective that I might have responded to my cynical colleague regarding the ethics of MBA students by saying, "I want to understand their meaning-making at the level of faith—what they ultimately trust will work and count as they act to sort out the fitting relationships between themselves and others—as they make decisions and deals in their crafting of life."

Through the Valley of the Shadow

Betrayal, loss, fear, and death pose fundamental challenges to faith, yet they may also be integral to the life of faith most profoundly understood.

Faith Betrayed

Faith as a primal, elemental force of promise permeating the whole of life is manifest most inescapably and often treacherously in faith betrayed. Lynch refers us to the mythical Medea for an appreciation of the primal power of faith. Medea has been "terrible" in her fidelity to Jason the Argonaut. She has followed him everywhere and given up everything. When he abandons her for Creusa, the princess of Corinth, Medea says she made a mistake when she "trusted the words of a Greek." She then murders her own children and Creusa, demonstrating the limitless fury that floods the vacuum created by faith's disappearance, thereby revealing the power of this primal force transformed into one of its fierce forms. Lynch continues:

> The furies insert themselves in a terrible way into human affairs precisely where the greatest faith has been violated, where a

mighty word has been given but is now betrayed. In every case the Fury attacks the violator of a word written out in the most primitive and earthly forms of nature, the form of mother, who is word to her child, the form of wife, the form of friend, the form of father. All these forms are words carved out in the deepest realities of nature itself, making promises without opening the lips and demanding belief for very survival's sake. . . . The energy and power of human faith become visible in the size of this fury. We tend to reduce faith to a sweet pious dimension, weak rival and challenger of knowledge. We know it best through its embodiment in fury. And through its incarvement, without words, in the very deepest structures of human life. Aristotle knew this well in *The Poetics* when he chose these violations of kinship and fidelity as the most tragic forms of tragedy. They are.[21]

In most societies, there is a legal distinction between crimes of passion and other crimes. Such tragic moments arise when the very fabric and center of one's meaning—one's sense of wholeness, connection, and belonging—is violated, broken, shattered. The promise is broken. Faith erupts into fury. These are the Furies who rage in witness to the world as it "ought to be."

Faith as a Suffering

Any attempt to rethink the category of faith in relation to contemporary life is insufficient without recognizing faith as a "suffering" as well as a virtue of reasoning and willing.[22] Suffering in its broadest sense means "undergoing" and to be "totally affected"; thus, suffering may include not only physical and emotional pain but also the kind of deep betrayal just described as well as the suffering of doubt, of yearning, of being overwhelmed, of drifting without moorage or goal, of prolonged struggle, and of bleak despair.

Shipwreck, Gladness, and Amazement

During my own graduate studies, it happened that the professor I most frequently heard applauded was Richard R. Niebuhr. The reasons were not immediately obvious because he did not seek to capture the student imagination either with entertaining anecdotes or with a lecture style designed to dazzle by the aesthetic of its systematic outline. Rather, when he lectured it was as though he was generously allowing others to be present to his own contemplation. As he reflected on the material for the day, he would sometimes, for example, pause and look out the window, waiting for the word to come that would fittingly name what he was learning to see and understand. When the word did come, it did seem to be the right, fitting word. And when applause broke out at the end of class, it was perhaps because we were especially grateful for the naming of intuitions that dwell in the deepest currents of human experience.

When Niebuhr reflects on human faith, he does so, in part, with the metaphors of "shipwreck, gladness, and amazement."[23] These metaphors connote the subjective, affective, dynamic, often bewildering, and transformative nature of the experience of faith.

Metaphorical shipwreck may occur with the loss of a relationship, violence to one's property, collapse of a career venture, physical illness or injury, defeat of a cause, a fateful choice that irrevocably reorders one's life, betrayal by a community or government, or the discovery that an intellectual construct is inadequate. Sometimes we simply encounter someone or some new experience or idea that calls into question things as we have perceived them or as they were taught to us or as we had read, heard, or assumed. This kind of experience can suddenly rip into the fabric of life, or it may slowly yet just as surely unravel the meanings that have served as the home of the soul.

To suffer, I have said, means to undergo and be totally affected. If people undergo the break up or unraveling of what has held their world together, inevitably there is some degree of suffering. When we suffer the collapse of our sense of self, world, and "God," we are disoriented—drained of those rich connections that yield significance, delight, and purpose.

When I first began to reflect on the experience of emerging adult faith, a colleague recalled that as a freshman his dream was to become a basketball star. He was not very tall, and he had come to college from a small-town high school. The second week of the season, he was cut from the team. He remembers going to the showers and sobbing for two hours. He suffered the collapse of meaning—his sense of self, world, and "God." To undergo shipwreck is to be threatened in a total and primary way. In shipwreck, what has dependably served as shelter and protection and held and carried one where one wanted to go comes apart. What once promised trustworthiness vanishes.[24]

Early in my experience of college teaching, I was a part of the teaching team for a course for first-year students in the curricular core. I became aware that one of the young men in my section seemed less than satisfied with the course, so I invited him to linger for a moment after class for some conversation. I assumed that in general he was adjusting well to college. He was on the football team; his older brother (also an athlete on campus) had paved the way for him. But as we talked, I began to realize that there was more going on than his dissatisfaction with the course. He wasn't entirely sure that he was comfortable with being "just a football player"—feeling that perhaps this identity was forged more by his high school newspaper than by his own sense of self. Then, after telling me briefly about his parents' divorce, he looked directly at me and quietly said, "Do you know what it is like to have lost everything you ever really loved?"

We didn't get around to discussing the course very much that day. But in that moment, I felt some gladness that I could tell him that I did know something about it. My parents were not divorced, but I had undergone other experiences in my mid-twenties that, in retrospect, I realized had quietly devastated assumptions about my self, how the world worked, and even my sense of God.

On the other side of these experiences, if we do survive shipwreck—if we wash up on a new shore, perceiving more adequately how life really is—there is, eventually, gladness. It is a gladness that pervades one's whole being; there is a new sense of vitality, be it quiet or exuberant. Usually, however, there is more than relief in this gladness. There is transformation. We discover a new reality beyond the loss. Rarely are we able to replace, to completely recompose, what was before. The loss of earlier meaning is irretrievable and must be grieved and mourned. But gladness arises from the discovery that life continues to unfold with meaning, with connections of significance and delight. We rarely experience this as a matter simply of our own making. As the primal, elemental force of promise stirs again within us, we often experience it as a force acting on us, beneath us, carrying us—sometimes in spite of our resistance—into new consciousness, meaning, faith, and purpose.

This gladness is experienced, in part, as a new knowing. Though this knowing sometimes comes at the price of real tragedy (which even the new knowing does not necessarily justify), we typically would not wish to return to the ignorance that preceded coming to the new shore. We do not want to live in a less-adequate truth, a less-viable sense of reality, an insufficient wisdom. There is deeply felt gladness in an enlarged knowing and being and in a new capacity to act.

But here we must resist any temptation toward glib piety. To repeat, when we wash up on a new shore of knowing, there may be diminishment as well as enlargement. Something is always lost. This diminishment may potentially lead, however, to a more adequate understanding of how it is that human beings are continually enlarged and diminished in the course of ongoing experience. Yet surely some tragic outcomes challenge a notion of faith as a dynamic of shipwreck, gladness, and amazement.

My own reflections on this matter in relation to young adulthood continue to be tugged into discipline and mystery by the suicide of a close friend, the husband of one of my college roommates, when we were all twenty-seven years old. When Dan died, another of his friends said of us, "Before Dan died, we were all 'star-spangled.' After he died, we knew that tragedy could strike any of us." In the face of a promising life seemingly unfulfilled, and another (his wife's) forever set on a path quite different from her choosing, we suffered a kind of shared shipwreck. We were initiated into yet larger dimensions of consciousness and deepened questions of meaning, purpose, and significance. Now decades later, life and faith have been recomposed, but there remains a shared ache, a shared knowing, and a sweetness among us that from time to time render us reverent again before the Mystery we all share.

The questions that suffering and death pose to us are questions of faith: Is there any form of meaning, any faith that can without delusion embrace both our small and great sufferings? In today's world, not only our own suffering but also that of millions of others is made known to us through contemporary media. The threats to meaning that confront us on the scale of collective experience surely challenge any cursory affirmation of the dynamic described here as faith. Specifically, the task of making meaning on the scale of vast shared suffering has been almost overwhelmingly confounded by our awareness of genocide in many differing places and times, including our own. Yet it is, for example, Holocaust sufferers themselves who give us some of the most compelling instances of the capacity of the human spirit to reconstitute meaning and faith of the most profound integrity. Victor Frankl, a Holocaust survivor, has written, "But not only creativeness and enjoyment are meaningful. If there is a meaning in life at all, then there must be a meaning in suffering."[25]

Thus the gladness on the other side of shipwreck arises from an embracing, complex kind of knowing that is experienced as a more trustworthy understanding of reality in both its beauty and horror. It is in this sense that Richard Niebuhr describes such gladness as an "intellectual affection."[26]

Such gladness is accompanied by amazement. The power of the experience of shipwreck is located precisely in one's inability to immediately sense the promise of anything beyond the breakup of what has been secure and trustworthy. Until our meaning-making becomes very mature, in the midst of shipwreck there is little or no confidence of meaningful survival. The first time we are self-consciously aware that faith itself has been shattered is, after all, the first time. How could we know that even this might be survived? Even if we accept the dissolution of our self, world, and God with steely and sophisticated courage, we may expect nothing more. Then, when we are met by the surprise of new meaning, we are amazed. Passover is the celebration of amazement. Easter is what happens to us when we look back and say, "I survived that?!"[27] Faith is informed by joy as well as by pain.

The Deep Motion of Life

The metaphors of shipwreck, gladness, and amazement point toward the dynamic, transformative nature of faith. They help us recover faith as a verb, a powerful activity provisionally distinguished from static notions of religion and belief. Faith as a dynamic, multifaceted activity is an active dialogue with promise.[28] The motion of shipwreck, gladness, and amazement describes not only major crises of meaning that punctuate the story of our lives but also the tumbling, rocking, flowing motion of our every day, as we dwell in a continual dialectic between fear and trust, hope and hopelessness, power and powerlessness, doubt and confidence, alienation and belonging.

This ongoing, meaning-making motion of faith is named in many traditions as the activity of spirit and Spirit. Across traditions, the word *spirit* is typically rooted in words such as *air*, *breath*, *wind*—the experience of power moving unseen. Faith is formed and transformed in the unseen but sometimes deeply felt motion of ongoing life. As we are beginning to see, it may be said that it is the strategy of Spirit—or if one prefers, the deep current of life—to "release our tight hold on the foreground of life and turn toward the vast background" over and over again.[29] The ongoing process of shipwreck, gladness, and amazement shakes us loose from our focus on little loves and puts us in touch with the mystery of the wider force field of our lives. Each time, our souls are stretched and reordered, at least in some measure. We find that all we love and wrestle with is recast as something closer to a sense of right proportion. We are perpetually invited to participate more consciously in the deep motion of faith, learning to wonder in a larger frame and awakening to bigger questions and larger dreams.

Faith as Rational and Passional

The power and motion of faith includes, but is more than, cognitive activity and a reordering of mind narrowly understood. Yes, faith is intimately related to knowledge, yet it is also prior to knowledge in any formal sense. The faith of the infant, for example, is composed by a rudimentary cognition that relies on, discovers, and composes meaning through sensory, affective modes of knowing. Trust (or mistrust) is grounded in an affection that informs cognition. So it is with adults. As Fowler and Keen have put it, "In faith the 'rational' and the 'passional' are fused."[30] A trustworthy ultimacy is composed by feelings as well as thoughts, by being touched as well as by intellectual persuasion. This is not to say that faith is irrational. It is to say that faith has affective and cognitive dimensions. As in all being and knowing, affect has an ordering power.

Verb and Noun

To suffer shipwreck, gladness, and amazement on the journey of faith is to relinquish the pattern of ultimacy one has seen, known, felt, and acted on—and to discover a new faith. Therefore, even as we recognize the word *faith* as a verb, it remains also a noun. Faith is a composing and a composition. Faith is not only the act of setting one's heart, but it is also what one sets the heart on. When we say people have a strong faith, we mean first that they confidently engage in the activity of faith in their ongoing meaning-making, testing, trusting, and acting; and second that they have found the pattern of shipwreck, gladness, and amazement to be true and trustworthy. They dwell in a consciousness of an intricate, intimate pattern of life that is continually in motion and yet holds at the level of ultimacy. Their faith is manifest as trust, knowledge, emotion, value, and action, permeating every facet of their existence. Their faith changes—it develops—over time, undergoing transformation and growth toward greater adequacy.

The journey through shipwreck, gladness, and amazement can have particular and transforming power in emerging adult lives. It can be understood as one way of describing the deep process by which we become at home in the universe.

Chapter Three

Becoming at Home in the Universe

A Developmental Process

It has been said that *home* is the most powerful word in the English language. It is where we start from. It is what we aspire to. To be at home is to have a place in the scheme of life—a place where we are comfortable; know that we belong; can be who we are; and can honor, protect, and create what we truly love.

Reflecting on the political cynicism of American society and the ironic detachment that characterizes many in his generation, at the age of twenty-four, Jedediah Purdy wrote, "We doubt the possibility of being at home in the world, yet we desire that home above all else."[1]

To be at home within one's self, place, community, and the cosmos is to feel whole and centered in a way that yields a sense of power and participation. Parker Palmer has described his experience in midlife of contending with the ill-fitting dreams of his future and toxic expectations of self he had carried for many years. This journey took him though the slough of despond. When asked how it felt to emerge from depression with, as he put it, "a firmer and fuller sense of self," he responded, "I felt at home in my own skin, and at home on the face of the earth for the first time."[2] Wilfred Cantwell Smith wrote, "Faith, then, is a quality of human living. At its best, it has taken the form of . . . a quiet confidence and joy which enable one to feel at home in the universe. . . ."[3] To be at home is to be able to make meaning of one's own life and of one's surroundings in a manner that holds, regardless of what may happen at the level of immediate events. To be deeply at home in this world is to dwell in a worthy faith.

Emerging adulthood has much to do with big questions about home: Where do I live? Whom do I live with? Where and with whom do I belong? What can I honor? What is worthy of shelter and protection? Where can I be creative and thrive? If Robert Frost was right that "home is the place where they have to take you in," emerging adults do, indeed, also ask, "Does my society have a place for me? Am I invited in?"

These are questions of meaning, purpose, and faith. They are not just about where to spend the night. In emerging adulthood, as we step beyond the home that has sheltered us and look into the night sky, we can begin in a more conscious way to ask the ancient questions, Who am I under these stars? Does my life have place and purpose? Are we—am I—alone?

In our time, however, I believe that these ancient questions are being slightly recast. We continue to speak of composing a worldview, yet we sense that this world is too small a frame. Consciousness of the circuitry of life—ecological and technological—increasingly expands world into universe. Today's emerging adults grew up within the imagination of *Star Wars* and other interstellar fantasies. For many, such planetary odysseys have held spiritual significance. Simultaneously, a new story of the universe is coming to us from the sciences and creating a new dialogue with religion. Either directly or indirectly, through the shifting forms of culture, we, as individuals, a species, and a planetary community are learning in new ways that we inhabit a vast universe. We are the first generations who have seen the earth from space and have taken account of whole galaxies as features of our geography.

I remember a conversation with an eight-year-old boy one afternoon when I noticed that he was playing with a globe. I assumed that it was a map of Earth, "our world." When I actually focused my attention on it, I was a bit surprised that it was, in fact, the moon, with the craters and valleys mapped and named.

My young friend was quite familiar with them. I learned from his mom that he often flew his toy spaceships around that globe and that he asked her one day if she ever thought about how we could be standing upside down as well as right side up, depending on how we thought about our planet moving through space. Yet when, shortly thereafter, I speculatively asked him if he would like to live in space someday, he responded with a bit of distress on his face, "No." When I asked why, he said that he would miss his mom and dad.

Distant realities of many kinds are increasingly brought into our immediate experience, expanding our sense of place. The search for meaning, purpose, and faith takes place within an enlarging field of awareness. Particularly for emerging adults, up and down (along with top-down) has rapidly become a less meaningful way of speaking. It is thus that the ancient question shifts: "Who am I *under* these stars?" is becoming "Who am I *among* these stars? Can I be at home in the universe; among vast stellar spaces; among my own varied and conflicting yearnings; among diverse cultures; among multiple perspectives, theories, and ideologies; among a wide array of possible futures? And if I make this move rather than that one, who and what will I miss?"

Ironically, the same set of dynamics can conspire to cause people to draw smaller boundaries, to carve out some manageable frame so as not to be obliterated by the vastness. This is the temptation to fortify one's turf, especially acute when global awareness and the accompanying encounter with greater diversity prompt and require a refined definition of self. Awareness of an expanding universe can thus go hand in hand with greater differentiation of the participants within it. There can be a tendency to identify home as only a relatively small, manageable, exclusive unit or network rather than also recognizing one's participation in the whole panoply of life within a larger frame. Thus a move toward greater differentiation can be life-enhancing or it can become shallow, tribalistic, and dangerous. To avoid the latter, it is vital that a capacity for trust, confidence, and humility be developed in ways that make it possible for the soul to wade into the deepening complexity of today's world, resisting distraction and illusion. This is particularly challenging for the growing number of persons—many of whom are emerging adults—for whom the complexity of today's world is experienced *within* as well as outside the self. International travel, immigration, marriage across ethnic and cultural boundaries, and persistent forms of prejudice intensify the challenges of composing a sense of inner coherence, finding place and purpose, and becoming truly at home in the universe.[4]

The Formation of Trust and Power

If it is a responsibility and privilege to participate in the process by which others become at home in the universe, what do we know as to how this may come about? One of the perspectives that informs my respect for another's process of becoming is the discipline of constructive-developmental psychology—careful study of the unfolding of consciousness and competence through time and space. This perspective, like other disciplines, has been composed over time through successive conversations among theorists and the populations we have studied. Although there are a host of voices in this conversation, it is useful to recognize the contributions of key voices in composing the point of view we are using here to understand the potential and vulnerability of emerging adult lives. There are two well-known grandfathers of this discipline.

In his classic *Childhood and Society*, Erikson traced eight ages of human unfolding, linking biological development to a series of life tasks:

1. *Infancy:* trust vs. mistrust
2. *Toddlerhood:* autonomy vs. shame
3. *Early school age:* industry vs. inferiority
4. *Later school age:* initiative vs. guilt

5. *Adolescence:* identity vs. role confusion

6. *Young adulthood:* intimacy vs. isolation

7. *Adulthood:* generativity vs. stagnation

8. *Later adulthood:* ego integrity vs. despair

As each stage with its corresponding task is engaged, if the task is resolved in the positive direction, then the person gains strength and more satisfying participation in his or her emotional and social world.[5]

Erikson believed that there is a particularly ripe time for each life task to be taken up. But he also believed that once a task is taken up and worked initially in its own time, it is continually reworked in relation to the tasks of the following eras. It is interesting that Erikson's first tasks (planted at the core of our unfolding, to be reworked and strengthened throughout life) are trust and power. These basic life tasks, successfully achieved, create the capacity to trust that one is held well and the confidence that one can affect one's world. In whatever measure they are not taken up well, they yield mistrust, shame, guilt, and feelings of inferiority. Although no life can avoid these feelings altogether, resolving these tasks in a positive direction honors the potential of human life. Erikson's later stages can be seen as yet more complex elaborations of the dynamics of trust and power that are foundational to our lives. In our study of people committed to the common good in the face of the complexity, diversity, and moral ambiguity of the new commons, a good enough sense of trust, along with the confidence that one has power to make a difference, were, indeed, key elements in the formation of their lives and commitments.[6]

Erikson's original scheme (and its later refinements with his spouse and colleague, Joan Erikson) has significantly influenced educators and clinicians and has been widely critiqued and elaborated. Its broad application has long since confirmed its intuitive power and fundamentally shaped our maps of change and growth through the human life cycle. In the Eriksons' view, people move through these life stages and their tasks ready or not, as biological changes inevitably unfold across a lifetime.

The radio personality and cultural commentator Garrison Keillor has observed, however, that though we move through life and its tasks ready or not, we do not necessarily become adult. It is said that he has remarked, "You don't have to be very smart to be an adult; some people prove it to you. They get promoted every year at their birthday when they ought to be held back because they still have work to do." Being an adult in terms of chronological age is not necessarily the same as having the capacity to negotiate the rapids of life in ways that can be trusted as competent and mature. If we focus only on the number of birthday candles—or, as we shall see, only on the tasks Erikson describes (vital as they are)—we may find we become adults without growing either knowledgeable or wise. We need additional perspectives to understand more fully the development of consciousness that is now needed. Understanding the gap between just getting promoted every year on our birthday and learning to see, know, and act in the complex ways that can lead to competence and wisdom is the passion that animates the discipline of constructive-developmental psychology.

Evolving Capacities of Mind

Jean Piaget is the second grandfather of constructive-developmental psychology. His understanding of human development was grounded in the intellectual tradition of Immanuel Kant, James Mark Baldwin, George Herbert Mead, and John Dewey. Originally a biologist (and at the age of sixteen a recognized expert on mollusks!), Piaget became a genetic epistemologist as a result of his fascination with the logical consistency of children giving the "wrong" answers in IQ tests. This fascination led to another set of powerful insights into human development.

We can begin to grasp what Piaget was after by reflecting on this now well-known passage from the popular author, Robert Fulghum:

> All of what I really need to know about how to live and what to do and how to be, I learned in kindergarten. Wisdom was not at the top of the graduate-school mountain, but there in the sandpile at Sunday School. These are the things I learned:
>
> Share everything.
> Play fair.
> Don't hit people.
> Put things back where you found them.
> Clean up your own mess.
> Don't take things that aren't yours.
> Say you're sorry when you hurt somebody.
> Wash your hands before you eat.
> Flush.
> Warm cookies and cold milk are good for you.
> Live a balanced life—learn some and think some and draw and paint and sing and dance and play and work every day some.
> Take a nap every afternoon.
> When you go out into the world, watch out for traffic, hold hands, and stick together.
> Be aware of wonder. Remember the little seed in the styrofoam cup? The roots go down and the plant goes up and nobody really knows how or why but we are all like that.[7]

What is delicious about this passage is that we hear it through two differing forms of consciousness. We are at once both our present age and also six years old. We know what Fulghum is writing about because of how we knew these things as children. We also know that the passage conveys more than what we knew as children because of our subsequent experience and the meanings we have made of it. Thus his words take on more meaning. Though they refer to concrete things that are supposedly simple, they simultaneously hold a subtle complexity—if, that is, we have learned to see, hear, and act in ways that are more complex than when we were six years old. Not everyone does.

Piaget deepens our understanding of why some people are able to compose a larger and more adequate sense of truth over time. He has helped us to see that not only do we human beings compose our world but we also develop in our capacity to do so.

Through careful and elegant observation, Piaget discerned that, in interaction with their environment, human beings develop increasingly complex structures (or capacities) to receive, compose, and know their world. He observed, for example, that infants know their world through performing certain sensorimotor operations by means of which they can begin to dependably relate to their environment: grasping, sucking, and the like. But infants cannot hold in the mind the rattle they learn to grasp and hold in their hand. For them, out of sight is literally out of mind. Toddlers, by contrast, can hold an image in mind but cannot coordinate images—cannot, for example, put items in sequence. Nor can they distinguish between dream and waking reality. School-age children, however, can become liberated from a world in which all images float free as they develop the capacity for "concrete operations," the capacity for ordering and categorizing the world of concrete reality. This is the age of beginning to organize things in a more fixed way, recognize cause and effect, and create "collections"—rocks, stamps, or a series of cards.

It is not until later—the cusp of the teenage years—that one can begin to practice abstract, symbolic thought, or what Piaget called "formal operations." This capacity makes it possible to think propositionally, hypothetically, inferentially, and symbolically. Possibility is no longer a subset of concrete reality. Reality becomes a subset of possibility. It becomes possible to "spin out an 'overall plan' of which any concrete event . . . is but an instance. Put most simply . . . 'what is' [becomes] just one instance of 'what might be.'"[8]

Thus Piaget has helped us understand that all knowing is shaped, in part, by an underlying structure of thought as well as its particular content. Even a bright child of nine who uses concrete operations to receive and compose his or her reality simply cannot know, cannot make meaning, in the same way that may be possible for a fifteen-year-old who has developed formal operational structures of thought. Consequently, such life events as achievement or defeat in school or athletics, the death of a parent, or the potential consequences of drug abuse are grasped and known differently in each era of human development. Terror and comfort, understanding and wonder, may take quite different forms for an infant, a child, an adolescent, and an adult.

Moreover, we do not move through this kind of development ready or not. Piaget would have agreed with Erikson that biological maturation plays a significant role in human development, but he saw it as a necessary but insufficient condition for developing some aspects of cognition and affect. The kind and quality of our interactions with our environment are also critical. A fourteen-year-old, for example, may be ready biologically to develop the abstract thought required for basic algebra but will have difficulty developing this capacity if her environment does not encourage the development of abstract and symbolic thought. We develop the capacity—the structures—to think and feel in increasingly complex ways only if the situations we encounter present us with both the challenges and the resources to do so. Thus, this school of psychology is best understood as a social psychology because it pays attention not only to the unfolding of an individual's life but also to the power of the context—the quality of relationships and institutions—within which individuals live and do or do not become at home in the universe.

We are still discovering the implications of Piaget's insight. Though not easy, it is intriguing to consider what it means that how a person perceives reality, makes meaning of it, and consequently acts is dependent in part on his underlying pattern or structure of thought, and that this underlying structure can grow and develop in identifiable ways. (Using a computer metaphor, we might say that a person's grasp of reality is dependent on the capability of the inner software program as well as the nature and quality of the information available.) When we explore the implications of this insight, not just for child development but also for adult growth and development, the implications for learning; teaching; parenting; advertising; management practice; and social, political, and religious life are enormous. Above all, this perspective reminds us yet again that what is said is not necessarily what is heard. What is intended is not necessarily what is received. And each of us plays a part in the becoming of others.

A Powerful Conversation

Theories of human growth and development have become powerful at this time in our cultural life primarily as a consequence of two new conditions in our society: (1) people are living longer and thus undergoing more change across the life span, and (2) our society is becoming more complex and requires people to develop greater competence as workers, spouses, parents, and citizens.

It is not surprising, therefore, that one of the places where this perspective has been seriously explored is in graduate schools of education, where scholars and teachers grapple with the question of what, where, and how people learn. In the 1970s and early 1980s at Harvard's Graduate School of Education, a notably generative conversation convened around the work of Lawrence Kohlberg, who pioneered the implications of Piaget's work for moral development. Among the many who participated in those seminars were Robert Kegan, Carol Gilligan, and James Fowler.[9]

Kegan: Shifting the Focus

Piaget focused his attention on the development of cognition in the individual child. As a consequence, Piagetians and neo-Piagetians were often perceived as concerned only about childhood, cognition, knowing, the individual, stages, and the discontinuities in human development (what is new and changed in the person). As important as these dimensions are, however, they neglect other dimensions that are also integral to becoming at home in the universe: adulthood, emotion, being, the social process, and continuities in development (what in the person persists through time).

Robert Kegan has contended that these "neglects" are actually unitary. He has effectively argued that all of the neglects in the Piagetian story of development are embraced if we return to Piaget's central insight: human becoming takes place in the interaction between the person and his or her environment, between self and other, self and world. These neglects become unitary when they are gathered up in a larger conception: the transforming motion of the self-other relation, which is the daily motion of life itself.

In his primary books, *The Evolving Self* (1981), *In over Our Heads* (1994), and with Lisa Lahey, *Immunity to Change* (2009), Kegan observes that ongoing self-other differentiation and relation is one of the most significant, robust, and universal phenomena to be found in nature. In the relationship of self and other, we are constantly sorting out what is what, who is who, and how we are all distinctive yet related. But, he says, the full significance of the self-other relation is obscured if we fail to recognize the motion that gives rise to it. He calls this motion "meaning-constitutive evolutionary activity," by which he refers to "something that is more than biology, philosophy, psychology, sociology, or theology, but is that which all of these, in their different ways, have studied . . . the restless creative motion of life itself."[10]

Individual persons are not their stages of development but are a motion within which what has been called stages of development are merely moments of dynamic stability—a temporary balance. In his later work, Kegan has shed the language of stages altogether and prefers to speak of "orders of consciousness": distinct patterns of making meaning that, evolving over time, can hold complexity with increasing adequacy.[11] The more adequate our pattern of meaning-making, the more developed, conscious, and (in this sense) mature we may become.

Kegan has pushed Piaget's theory of cognition in childhood to a broader theory of the formation of persons across time and space—a theory of the self in motion. The activity of cognition is but one actor in a larger drama: the composing of meaning. This drama has everything to do with adulthood as well as with childhood.

Kegan is moved by the dignity and the "astonishingly intimate activity" of a person—at any age—laboring, struggling, and delighting in making sense. If we look through a developmental lens, we see that the heart and art of life is not a static structure—a stage or a series of stages. It is a motion in which what one is "subject to" evolves so as to become "object." Growth involves a process of emergence, from embeddedness in the assumed truth of one's perceptions to the dawn of a new consciousness in which those same assumptions become available for more conscious assessment. Thus Kegan suggested that it is useful to recognize that a person is always both an individual and an "embeddual," meaning that we are embedded in our perceptions until we can distinguish between our perceptions of the other and the other itself.

An important step toward mature adulthood, for instance, is the evolution from "I *am* my relationships" to "I *have* my relationships." Whether I cherish, wrestle with, or despair over my relationships, if I *have* them instead of *being* them, I participate in them differently. Though I continue to depend on them in profound ways, I am less fused with them. I can respond as a self to the other from a more self-aware "ordering of consciousness"—a more complex way of making meaning.

This perspective is grounded in the conviction that truth is a relational phenomenon. It modifies the sharp divisions between subject and object that have dominated Western ways of knowing without dismissing the importance of these distinctions. A person remains "in relation to" that which one may also "take as object." Thus, how we compose knowledge and make meaning is shaped by the context in which we love and work, think and feel.

Gilligan: A Different Voice

It is, however, Carol Gilligan, seeking to understand moral decision making in real time and using the lens of gender, who retold the story of human development in a manner that most clearly reveals the power of connection as well as differentiation. Listening to the voices of women as they made moral judgments, she and her associates described an evolving understanding of moral choice in a world in which "all things being equal never are." The journey of development, as she tells it, unfolds in a language—a voice—that seeks to express more adequately the reality of ongoing relation and responsibility. This voice (expressive of both male and female experience but traditionally tending to be more evident in the voices of women) contrasts with the juridical voice of differentiation and rights identified in Kohlberg's account of the development of moral reasoning in males.[12] The voice Gilligan identified focuses not on the differentiation of subject from object but on the *relation* that orients subject to object, self to other, self to truth, self to possibility.

Gilligan has portrayed the distinctions between these two voices with the example of two young children playing together and wanting to play different games. The girl says, "Let's play next-door neighbors." The boy replies, "I want to play pirates." The girl responds, "OK, you can be the pirate that lives next door." The children might have resolved the conflict by the fair solution (Kohlberg). They could have taken turns playing each game for an equal period. This solution would honor the rights of each child and keep the identity and truth of each child intact, while providing opportunity for each child to experience the other's imaginative world. But, observes Gilligan, "the inclusive solution, in contrast, transforms both games: the neighbor game is changed by the presence of a pirate living next door; the pirate game is changed by bringing the pirate into a neighborhood." The inclusive, relational solution creates not just a new game but a new image of self, a new relationship, and a new truth.[13]

The importance of this relational perspective is heightened in a society and world in which growing numbers of neighborhoods feel threatened in some measure by intensified social diversity and the specter of random or organized violence. Because together we must create new, life-bearing realities, the potential contribution of this perspective cannot be overestimated.

Fowler: Development as the Motion of Faith

The developmental perspectives of Erikson, Piaget, Kegan, and Gilligan are deeply resonant with the dynamics of the formation and re-formation of faith, as described in Chapter Two. In them we hear a process of composing meaning, making sense, and ordering the relationships among things in ways that transform being, feeling, knowing, and doing. Indeed, James Fowler, a theologian and ethicist, and already familiar with Erikson's perspective, joined the Kohlberg seminar and became the most significant pioneer in bringing a constructive-developmental perspective to our understanding of the formation of faith. In response to Fowler's work, early on Kegan affirmed that to incorporate a dynamic notion of faith into the constructive-developmental insight is not to add something at the periphery of the developmental perspective but to speak from its heart.[14] When constructive-developmental theory moves beyond focusing on stages to focusing on the deep motion of life that gives rise to consciousness, it moves into the experiences and phenomena that have been a feature of people and their communities of faith for as long as people have given expression to the reality of being alive: "The constructive-developmental perspective has not yet found a way to do justice to what Whitehead called the ultimate reality of the universe—its motion. Much less has it recognized the religious dimension of our relation to this reality, what Buber spoke of both as an inevitable lifelong tension between the I-Thou and the I-It, . . . the sacredness of the everyday."[15]

Incorporating the methodology used by other constructive-developmental theorists, Fowler and his associates mapped the relationship between developmental psychologies and transformations of faith across the life span.[16] Informed by theological and psychological perspectives and by the patterns that began to emerge from analyzing hundreds of interviews, he articulated a framework by which to interpret the development of faith in a series of six stages.

Beginning with his now-classic *Stages of Faith: The Psychology of Human Development and the Quest for Meaning*, across three decades and in a wide range of publications and forums, Fowler has shown how evolving forms of logic, perspective taking, moral judgment, world coherence, the boundaries of social awareness, symbolic function, and the locus of authority all affect the life of faith.[17] Similar to the work of other Piagetians, Fowler's has had a cognitive and stage-structure bias. He has, however, not only forged linkages between psychological development and human faith but also has contributed significantly to the extension of constructive-developmental insights into adulthood.

Fowler's attention to shifts in the locus of authority in the maturing of faith provided a key girder for building a bridge in my own thought between the formation of faith and human development in the young adult years. It was Perry, however, who drew the essential outlines of an architecture that spans the chasm between unexamined trust and a critically aware form of making meaning in the emerging adult years.

Perry: The Art of Listening to Young Adult Meaning-Making

William G. Perry Jr., or just "Bill" as we knew him, was a master educator, therapist, and theoretician who, with his colleagues, forged a groundbreaking and widely applied study of human development in the context of higher education. Founder of Harvard's Bureau of Study Counsel, Perry and his colleagues accompanied scores of students as they made their way through the rapids of young adult life. As described in his *Forms of Ethical and Intellectual Development in the College Years: A Scheme*, Perry identified nine sequential modes in which students composed truth as they pitched and bucked from assumed ways of knowing to taking responsibility for their concepts and commitments. His work is characterized by an extraordinary quality of careful and compassionate listening and by a sensitivity of interpretation that serves as a model for researchers who are willing to value the integrity of human experience more than theoretical tidiness. One of his favorite axioms was, "The person is always larger than the theory."

Perry embodied practiced reverence for the courage and costs of growth. He paid deep respect to how difficult it is to compose and recompose reality and truth on the other side of discovering the finitude of every form of "Authority." He described with careful nuance the journey of intellect and soul that requires holding on while letting go—making one's way through the valley of the shadow of doubt, struggling to retain something enduring while a new way of seeing and trusting is being configured. He understood how it feels from the inside when certainty must be relinquished for integrity. He believed that to be present to the growth of another is "to worship before great mysteries." The insights into the development of emerging adult faith elaborated in the chapters that follow are substantially informed by Perry's capacity to listen with rigorous respect to the underlying patterns of emerging adult meaning-making or, as he put it, to the "music beneath the words."[18]

A New Place in the Life Span

In American society prior to the Civil War, the human journey was typically described as a movement from infancy and

childhood to adulthood. Major transformations in society after
the Civil War effected such real change that adolescence emerged
as a "new" stage in human development. In the 1960s, Kenneth
Keniston observed how the same magnitude of change was creating yet another recognizable era in the human life span.
Employing philosophical, sociological, and psychological perspectives, he held a rich appreciation of the dynamic, shifting
interaction between culture and person:

> Psychological development results from a complex interplay of
> constitutional givens (including the rates and phases of
> biological maturation) and the changing familial, social,
> educational, economic, and political conditions that constitute
> the matrix in which [people] develop. Human development can
> be obstructed by the absence of the necessary matrix, just as it
> can be stimulated by other kinds of environments. Some social
> and historical conditions . . . slow, retard or block development,
> while others stimulate, speed and encourage it. A prolongation
> and extension of development, then, including the emergence
> of "new" stages of life, can result from altered social, economic
> and historical conditions.[19]

Among such changes, he cited particularly a shift in the
percentage of students who finish high school and begin college
within accelerated social change: "a rate of social change so rapid
that it threatens to make obsolete all institutions, values, methodologies and technologies within the lifetime of each generation; a technology that has created not only prosperity and
longevity, but power to destroy the planet, whether through
warfare or violation of nature's balance; a world of extraordinarily
complex social organization, instantaneous communication and
constant revolution."[20]

In this social milieu, Keniston argued that we would do well
to notice that many young people are not adequately described
as either adolescent or adult. This is because "the twenty-four-
year-old seeker, political activist, or graduate student often turns

out to have been through a period of adolescent rebellion ten years before, to be all too formed in his or her views, to have a stable sense of self, and to be much further along in psychological development than his or her fourteen-year-old high school brother or sister."[21]

Keniston's description of the characteristics of this new era in human development was an early signal, drawing attention to distinctive, identifiable forms of postadolescent meaning-making. Keniston provided compelling confirmation of my own perception and research that within, for example, Kegan's and Fowler's fourth stage (or order of consciousness) there are actually two separate, identifiable stages. Between the assumed knowing of stage three and the critical, systemic knowing of stage four's "full adulthood," we can see the outlines of a critically aware but yet young adulthood. As acknowledged in Chapter One, Arnett— also informed by Keniston—has subsequently galvanized further recognition of this new era spawned by social change, naming it *emerging adulthood*. The five hallmarks of emerging adulthood as he describes them are identity explorations, instability, self-focused, feeling in-between, and age of possibilities.[22] Whether or not what he describes is a new developmental "stage," in contrast to a new societal pattern or phase, remains to be adjudicated, as does the question regarding to what degree these descriptors are culture specific—especially the description, "self-focused." This book participates in that conversation.

Discovering Another Neglect

After reflecting on my own experience with young adults and allowing my perceptions and thinking to steep in the strength of developmental perspectives, I published an initial critique and elaboration of theory.[23] Though the insights that had emerged among those of us who were working to elaborate constructive-developmental theory were proving strong and useful, I noticed that I was vaguely but persistently uneasy. From the beginning, there was a healthy recognition within the field that every theoretical perspective has its limits. I knew, nevertheless, that there was some sense of a significant deficit in these powerful, useful perspectives, and it subtly haunted me.

I was aware that though the metaphor of development itself was a rich one, with an imposing pedigree, it was also problematic. Development connotes incremental but qualitative growth and enhanced adequacy. As some critical social theorists have well argued, however, the language of development is aligned also with certain imperial economic and political impulses (requiring "them" to be like "us").[24] I was keenly attuned to how the force of this critique alerted us to conditions of exploitation in the service of development and had to be taken into account.

But it was not until I was reading the draft of a manuscript that would subsequently receive two national awards, written by a then-distant colleague, Larry Daloz,[25] that I discovered the still deeper source of my uneasiness. A chapter in which Daloz described the relationship between a mentoring professor and three older adult students (a man and two women) disturbed me. All three students had been affected by their encounter with higher education, and each underwent a significant challenge to assumptions about self, world, and "God." In the author's analysis, however, only one of the students, the male, had "grown" or "developed." The two women seemed not to have "moved" because they were choosing to "stay" in their context, maintaining commitments to family and community in settings that appeared to place constraints on their opportunities for enhanced thought and being. Yet it was fully apparent to me that both of these women, having recomposed their ways of seeing, knowing, and being, were undoubtedly acting in new ways, though remaining within their same context.

I urged him to think some more about his analysis, and after some discussion sorting out the distinctions between movement and growth, he recast that portion of the manuscript. Meanwhile,

I discovered a key to another feature of the story of human development: its prevailing metaphors.

Journey

As typically told, the story of human development is framed by the primary metaphor of journey. Developmental psychologies are attractive, in part, because they are so resonant with the many secular and religious myths that feature the journey motif. The journey metaphor is powerful; it grasps essential elements of our experience of moving through life.[26] It has special power in relationship to spirituality and the life of faith. Our desire to soar is readily fused with a conviction of aliveness, a confidence of spirit. Journey language is a language of transcendence, crossing over, reaching, and moving beyond. When we feel we are not yet *what* we ought to be, we are prone to feeling we are not *where* we ought to be. The journey metaphor can also convey a sense of movement down into, through, and beyond the swamps of confusion or despair. As such, journeys toward greater enlighten- ment or sanctity are dominant motifs across many cultures, often anchored in practices of pilgrimage.

The metaphor of journey also evokes adventure, courage, and daring. In Western culture, it is linked strongly with the meta- phor of battle, the slaying of dragons, and the triumph of con- quest. Going out to conquer is a primary element in all of the heroic myths. "The hero ventures forth from the world of common day into a region of supernatural wonder: fabulous forces are there encountered and a decisive victory is won: the hero comes back from his mysterious adventure with the power to bestow boons on his fellowman."[27]

The metaphor of journey is pervasive in American culture. Increasingly, however, journey has signified going forth without necessarily leading to a return. On discovering the New World, explorers went out and often did not go back, and in a culture of emigrants, the dominant experience is departure and journey without return. Since the Enlightenment, we have become profoundly aware of the relativized nature and partiality of our knowledge, particularly our knowledge of "Truth, God, and Ultimate Reality." We feel, as it were, bound to an ongoing, uncompleted search, an infinite quest for more adequate approximations of reality.

Yet if we build on the work of Robert Kegan, Carol Gilligan, and Nancy Chodorow (a social psychologist), a larger imagination comes into view. The map of the psyche that portrays a journey is perhaps particularly salient in male experience, yet only half of a larger human reality. Chodorow has suggested that the emphasis on heroic separation may be shaped significantly by the fact that for most children the primary caregiver is female. For males, therefore, a central task in becoming a self is separation or differentiation, going forth and heading out. By contrast, for females the task of becoming a self requires identification with, attachment, and connection.[28] Men, therefore, tend to tell their stories primarily in terms that celebrate moments of separation and differentiation. Women tend to tell their stories in terms of moments of attachment and relation.

Thus the dance of self and other in the story of human becoming might best be understood as reflecting "two great yearnings": one for differentiation, autonomy, and agency, and the other for relation, belonging, and communion.[29] There may well be a polar preference between the genders, but each gender has the capacity and the need to fulfill both yearnings. Thus if we listen to both voices, we hear additional metaphors.[30] I began to realize that it was insufficient to work exclusively with the metaphors of journey, traveling, and adventuring. The story of human growth and development is more richly comprehended if we cast it also in the metaphors of home, homesteading, dwelling, and staying.[31]

Indeed, men and women alike know that a good life is composed of both venturing and abiding.[32] The ventures that matter most are the ones that enable us to become truly at home in the universe. If we embrace this larger conception of the story of human development, we recognize the power of home places as well as the power of travel. The image of journey in the story of optimal human development is transformed into pilgrimage. That is, the word *journey* is rooted in the French *jour*, meaning simply a day's travel. A journey can be a profound and life-changing experience, or it can be endless and without purpose. The practice of pilgrimage is a going forth and a returning home that enlarges the meaning of both self and home.

Home

From this perspective, we should be concerned that some of our most powerful contemporary myths presuppose the destruction of home or even the home planet, as in the *Star Wars* epic. Simultaneously, a primary suffering of our time is homelessness, both domestically and in the growing number of refugees worldwide. Moreover, a fundamental question of our time is, "Can we all dwell together on the small planet home we share?" Martin Heidegger observed, "To be a human being means to be on the earth as a mortal. It means to dwell."[33] Yet with the Industrial Revolution, the household was separated from the means of production, bifurcating the relationship between the genders and shearing the home away from the workplace and the public place. As a consequence, the arts of dwelling became associated with one gender alone. They became a subjugated knowledge, removed from public discourse, and we are all the poorer for it.

Thus at this pivotal, dangerous, and promising moment in history, the development of human life and adequate forms of meaning, purpose, and faith may be dependent in part on the liberation, reappropriation, and renewed companionship of the metaphors of detachment and connection, pilgrims and home-makers, journeying and homesteading, pilgrimage and home.

Psychotherapist and Zen trainer John Tarrant has reflected on the legend of Shakyamuni, the historical Buddha, observing that in setting off to bend his life toward prayer and meditation, Shakyamuni abandoned his family:

> It is said that on the night he left, he paused in the doorway in silent farewell to the woman and child sleeping there, and didn't dare to wake them. If we imagine their confusion when they woke the next morning, we see that if the man has found a sure path, he has asked his family to bear the desolation and loss that is the underside of his certainty. . . . By leaving the child and the woman, Shakyamuni conformed to the familiar pattern that for the sake of developing the spirit, we must turn away from the world and our ties. The same gesture appears in Jesus' rejection of his mother. But this means to turn away also from the trees and the fate of the planet and the soul, which loves these things. If we are to have a marriage of soul and spirit, we will have to find a way to walk back eventually through the charged doorway and find the wisdom of the sages in that small, quiet room where the woman and her child are sleeping still.[34]

It has become increasingly clear that there is value and healing in incorporating into our understanding of human development an imagination of becoming at home. A part of becoming adult is finding our place in the new global commons in which we now find ourselves. We are beginning to recognize that this becoming is not so much a matter of leaving home as it is undergoing a series of transformations in the meaning of home. We grow and become both by letting go and holding on, leaving and staying, journeying and abiding—whether we are speaking geographically, socially, intellectually, emotionally, or spiritually. A good life and the cultivation of wisdom require a balance of home and pilgrimage.

In this way of seeing, though we may move from one geographical location to another, the growth of the self and the development of faith may be understood as transformation of the boundaries that have defined home. These boundaries may be continually revised outward to embrace the neighborhood, the community, the society, the world, and even the inexhaustible universe in which we dwell. While we make this journey of transformation in which our sense of inclusiveness and ultimacy is continually expanded, we experience home as a familiar center surrounded by a permeable membrane that makes it possible to sustain and enlarge our sense of self and other, self and world. From this perspective, an ethical orientation for our time can be formulated in terms of hospitality to the stranger.[35] Our imagination of development becomes not only a ladder but also a series of concentric circles or perhaps a spiral that honors both. Thus we can imagine human becoming both as a process of moving on and as a process of recentering.

As we explore critical features of the development of emerging adults, it is vital that we learn to do so with an eye to both venturing and dwelling. If we understand human development not simply as departures and arrivals but also as transformations in the meaning of home, then the emerging adults with whom we have the privilege of making meaning may become more viably at home in the universe. If we accompany them well and provide good home places along the way, they may grace us all by becoming citizen-leaders, adults who can both belong and distinguish themselves, connect and separate, venture and dwell. To be good company, we need to understand the transformations in thinking, feeling, and belonging that are embedded in the promise of emerging adult lives.

Chapter Four

It Matters How We Think

Who or what has authority in my life? Whom can I trust? To what can I give my heart? These are among life's biggest questions, and they dwell at the core of meaning, purpose, and faith. They are asked again and again across a lifetime. How we respond is in part a matter of how we think, which may undergo significant transformations over time. Noticing whether and how we place our trust in authority is one way of observing these changes.

In a society riddled with strong allegiances to the values of self-sufficiency, freedom, and infinite choice, questions of authority (intimately linked with trust) are often hidden from view. Yet every day we are not simply making choices. We are also swayed, moved, enticed, compelled, persuaded, and more or less swept along—in varying measures obedient to powers that are acting authoritatively on us, influencing our perceptions and judgments.

There are many such powers in our lives. We sometimes trust the opinion of a friend without actually checking the facts. We assume a published report in a reputable journal is accurate. We look to the boss or CEO for orientation and direction. We may respect traditional scriptures. We want to trust our physician. The opinion of a valued colleague carries weight with us. We may be cynically sophisticated about advertising, yet we know we are affected by it. We pass on to the next generation admonitions given to us in our youth. We entrust people we love to the care of professional people whom we do not know. When we are stressed and fearful we look to some source of authority for reassurance. We may pray—at least under certain circumstances. Placing our trust and vesting authority are an integral part of weaving the fabric of life.

Over time we may learn the appropriate limits of our trust. Recently, I heard a young child explaining a scrape on his face: "I hurt my nose, but not very badly because God is always with me and taking care of me." He is being taught by authoritative voices in his world that he lives in a caring and dependable universe. By the time he is a young adult, however, it is likely that he will have run up against experiences that will cause him to wonder about God's care in ways he can't ignore.

In emerging adulthood there is a deepened readiness to become more consciously aware of our assumptions about whom we trust, what to believe, and how reliable the meanings we live by actually are. Learning to assess the strengths and limits of whom and what can be trusted as authoritative is important work in the process of becoming a mature, responsible, and wise adult. In part a cognitive process, this work is an essential element in the development of the intellectual life, a vital feature of preparing for citizenship and leadership in democratic societies, and integral to the formation of mature adult faith.

Forms of Knowing

During the emerging adult and subsequent years, the relationship of the self to authority can undergo considerable transformation. Perry's study of nine shifts in students' relationship to knowledge provides an interpretive lens. Here, however, I both consolidate and elaborate them to reveal four primary positions, or "forms of knowing." Later, I will add a fifth that is particularly useful in interpreting the potential and vulnerability of emerging adults.

Forms of Knowing	Authority-bound Dualistic	→	Unqualified relativism	→	Commitment in relativism	→	Convictional commitment

Authority-Bound

The first form of knowing is oriented to Authority outside the self.[1] Within this form, what a person ultimately trusts, knows, and believes is finally based on some Authority "out there" who can know truth by reading "tablets of Truth written in the sky."[2] In some way regarded as self-evident, Authority "knows." Belenky, Clinchy, Goldberger, and Tarule described this as "received knowing."[3] In this mode of knowing it is assumed that you "get" knowledge from somewhere outside yourself. Authorities are trustworthy because they have done this—or because "we all think alike" (that is, we all see things simply as they are).

Authority may take the form of a particular person—a parent, teacher, religious leader, or the boss in the workplace. Often, however, Authority functions in diffuse but subtly powerful forms that pervade a person's conventional ethos: media (the Web, film, television, print—including all forms of advertising and the authority of name brands); culturally affirmed roles, personalities, and institutions (experts, government officials, spiritual exemplars, artists, scientists, entertainers, other celebrities, and admired peers); and custom (expected conventions of thought, feeling, and behavior, whether broadly based throughout a society or within a small subgroup). These various authorities are confirmed by the stories, symbols, and myths (traditional or contemporary) that hold the meanings of a people and their society.

This form of knowing may be characterized as "Authority-bound" (not Perry's term) and it functions in an all-powerful, determinative manner. When people compose their sense of truth in this form, they may assert deeply felt and strong opinion; but if they are asked the basis for their knowing, eventually they reveal their assumed, unexamined trust in sources of authority located outside the self. When this form of knowing prevails, people cannot stand outside of their own perspective or critique their own thought. Their knowing is inextricably bound up with the power of the trusted Authority.

Dualistic

Authority-bound knowing also tends to be dualistic. People who compose self, world, and "God" in this form tend to make clear either-or divisions between what is true and untrue, right and wrong, us and them. There is little or no tolerance for ambiguity. It is important to recognize, however, that what they hold absolute certainty about—the content of their sense of truth—varies from person to person, though they share the same cognitive structure. Thus, even though the structure of this form of knowing is quite rigid, the content that is known so absolutely may appear to be fluid. Thus one person may say, "Toleration is a sin," and another may say, "You must *always* be tolerant," yet both may be making meaning in this Authority-bound form of knowing.

In this form of knowing, even the inner self is primarily composed by others. For example, sometimes this form of knowing is heard in a young person who is working very hard to prepare for medicine, law, or another career. Listening carefully over time, we may discover that "I want to become a lawyer" actually means "My family has always expected me to become a lawyer."

Reflecting on how he felt after the first exam of his freshman year, a college senior reveals how significantly the Authority-bound form of knowing may be affected by circumstances and messages from outside of one's self:

> In terms of studying, I didn't know how I would stand in a
> class. Like I remember the first test I took was in History of
> Asia. I didn't know at all what I would get on the
> test . . . anything from a C to an A. I didn't think I had flunked
> because I had studied for it, but I didn't know quite how I
> stood. And I got the test back and I got an A. And that seemed
> to set a precedent, you know, what goals I set for myself. It's
> kind of strange. I look back, and if I'd gotten maybe a B or a C
> on that test I might have . . . set lower standards for myself.

A constructive-developmental perspective yields the recognition that this uncritical, Authority-bound, and dualistic form of knowing is characteristic, not just of children and adolescents, but also of some people throughout the whole of their biological adulthood. Further development beyond this conformist way of knowing does not inevitably occur.

Thus, some who enter higher or professional education or the workforce at whatever age arrive with this mode of making meaning very much intact. For others, this form of knowing has already begun to dissolve. In either case, the transformation that can occur (and for which higher education at its best can be a primary sponsor) is a movement from this unexamined, uncritical form of Authority-bound knowing to another form of knowing.

Disconcerting Discovery

This shift typically begins in the disconcerting discovery that established patterns of thinking do not fit lived experience. For example, while taking notes from several trusted professors, a student may begin to realize that one professor's point of view seriously conflicts with another's. The student may put them in separate compartments, thus ensuring that each point of view is sealed off from the other, conveniently obscuring the conflict. Or the student may place the two perspectives in some hierarchy of value, deciding, for example, that the sciences hold "truth" and the arts hold only "opinions," or that personal decisions can be simpler than professional decisions. As an illustration, here is a young woman's reflection on the pressures and choices in a business context:

> I'm very hard-line, straight, and level when it comes to an
> ethical choice. . . . But here we are being challenged with,
> "OK, yes, there's clear right and wrong maybe when it comes to
> a personal choice. But when it comes to a public, professional
> choice in a business decision you have other stakeholders, other
> people are involved, and you have to think about every
> segment when you're making this decision and the effects that

it will have." And so in my mind I see a lot more gray than I did before, and I find it very uncomfortable.

The discomfort reflected here is likely to persist. The validity of competing points of view is difficult to ignore and seriously undermines even heroic attempts to hold simplistic, either-or forms of true and untrue, right and wrong, whether in personal or public life. For a time, it may be possible to trust that there is still a right answer that some Authority has or will surely discover because the existence of such a right answer is still assumed. But a cataclysmic shift occurs in the revolutionary moment when the relative character of all knowledge becomes the only truth.

Unqualified Relativism

In the course of ongoing experience, as Authorities conflict or fail, awareness dawns that the human mind can compose many perceptions of reality and does not simply receive reality "as it is." The person becomes aware that if he or she had been born into a different family or society, had attended other schools, worked in another lab, or listened to other music and watched different films, any given phenomena might be perceived and known quite differently. Thus knowledge becomes relative, meaning that all knowledge is shaped by, and thus relative to, the context and relationships within which it is composed.

Slowly it dawns that even the most trusted adults (or other Authorities) must compose reality within a relativized world. Now it appears that every perception leads to a different "truth" and every opinion and judgment may be as important as any other. This form of knowing falls at midpoint in Perry's scheme,[4] and in its most substantial form it might appropriately be described as *unqualified relativism*.[5]

This shift may be precipitated by a lead from the head when, for example, a person in a stimulating seminar is introduced to a new idea that counters previous assumptions. But

Authority-bound and dualistic thinking may also come unraveled outside the classroom—the lead taken by either the head or the heart. Whenever one undergoes experience that does not fit the assumptions of one's conventional, assumed world, there is an invitation to develop critical thinking: the ability to stand outside one's own thought and wonder, *Why do I think that?*

Sometimes this happens in relatively smooth, uncomplicated, and intriguing ways. A freshman in college described what a "great roommate" she had: "I'm an athlete, and she's not. She does arts. I don't. I'm learning that what time I get up, when I shower, could be different. I've always been conscientious about my schoolwork. She says, 'That paper is only worth five points, come play.' But sometimes I say to her, 'You'd better finish that paper.' We come from different backgrounds, and living with her I realize that I value what I've been given, but the patterns I've developed don't have to stay that way."

Other times, however, as we began to see in Chapter Two, learning to wonder about familiar assumptions may happen in more difficult ways. For example, a person may be involved in a romance or some other close and emotional relationship. It is assumed to be trustworthy because it fits the myths that the person holds about life, how life works, and how life will unfold. Yet when the romantic relationship (or perhaps the career opportunity) collapses, the person may suffer not only the obvious loss, but also the loss of an assumed life script: the shipwreck of self, world, and "God." The truth of life itself feels betrayed. One may begin rather ruefully to wonder, *Why did I ever think the way I did?*

In this moment, both subject and object are recomposed. The person is no longer subject to her earlier assumptions; these assumptions may now be held as possible points of view among others as objects of reflection. This new way of seeing and knowing may offer some new power and freedom, but it is achieved at the cost of an earlier certainty. Perry describes the experience as it may be felt from the inside:

Soon I may begin to miss those tablets in the sky. If this [one possible interpretation among others] defines the truth for term papers, how about people? Principalities? Powers? How about the Deity? . . . And if this can be true of my image of the Deity, who then will cleanse my soul? And my enemies? Are they not wholly in the wrong?

I apprehend all too poignantly now that in the most fateful decisions of my life I will be the only person with a first-hand view of the really relevant data, and only part of it at that. Who will save me then from that "wrong decision" I have been told not to make lest I "regret-it-all-my-life"? Will no one tell me if I am right? Can I never be sure? Am I alone?

Then Perry observes, "It is not for nothing that the under-graduate turns metaphysician."[6]

As this realization begins to form, a person may cope by saying, "I have my truth, you have your truth, and they have their truth. It doesn't matter what you think, as long as you are sincere." "The Truth" seems to become one truth among many (giving rise to the current vernacular "whatever"). But this stance discloses, on the one hand, the hope that absolute certainty still dwells somewhere (in this case in sincerity), and on the other hand it reveals a sort of bravado defending against the increasing awareness that conventional certainty just isn't holding up very well. Doubt is further deepened when someone points out that both Martin Luther King Jr. and Adolf Hitler were in a sense "sincere."

Thus a position of unqualified relativism is difficult to sustain over time. One discovers that there is a difference between just any opinion (even one's own) and an opinion that is grounded in careful and thoughtful observation and reflection and that takes more into account. One may move into a *qualified* relativ-ism, increasingly aware that discriminations can be made between arguments based on such principles as internal coherence, the systematic relation of an argument to its own assumptions, exter-nal data, and so forth. But the dilemma remains: if thinking doesn't bring us to certainty, why think? At this juncture, unqualified relativism may be experienced (to varying degrees) as a bleak abyss where the possibility of finding meaning, purpose, and faith appears to be a futile enterprise leading to stark despair.[7] A way through may be discovered in the imperative of ongoing life.

Commitment in Relativism

Certainty may be impossible, but we still make choices that have consequences for ourselves and all that we love. Particularly in relation to important life choices, a person may begin to look for a place to stand, a way of dwelling viably in an uncertain world. He or she may begin to value those ways of composing truth and making moral choices that are more adequate than other options. This is a search for a place of commitment within relativism.

Finding a place of commitment in a relativized world requires taking self-conscious responsibility for one's own thinking and knowing. Now one becomes conscious of joining other adults in discerning what is adequate, worthy, and valuable while remaining aware of the finite nature of all judgments. Fowler describes this shift as a movement from a "tacit" form of world coherence to an "explicit system" formed in a strengthened desire to make the meaning of life coherent, as best one may. One young person expressed it this way: "I still feel my Big Picture is only so valid because so far I've only been able to look at it from a couple of angles. The more angles I have, the more valid my sense of meaning will be. But I have learned that a couple of angles are better than none and should not stop me from doing as much as I can with the limited picture I already have."

This awareness reflects the great shift that makes intellectual reflection possible and thus serves as the threshold into the conscious life of the mind. This shift into critical reflective thought is a primary facet of becoming an adult in faith and, as we shall see, a central feature of the potential of the emerging adult years.

Convictional Commitment

Because Perry focused particularly on the undergraduate years, his elaboration of forms of knowing "ends" with commitment in relativism. Fowler, however, described the development of yet another form of knowing beyond it. Along with Fowler, I believe that this form typically does not develop until well after the young adult years—indeed, not until midlife. I describe this place as *convictional commitment*. This form of knowing was expressed well by Carl Jung in a film made near the end of his life. As I recall it, when the interviewer asked, "Do you believe in God?" Jung immediately responded, "Now?" I happened to watch this film with a large university audience, mostly undergraduates, and many spontaneously laughed, assuming that of course, Jung was too sophisticated to believe in God. Jung, however, continued his response: "I don't need to believe; I know." This time, no one laughed.

Jung exemplified a quality of knowing that is quite other than the Authority-bound, dualistic knowing described earlier. Aware that all knowledge is relative, he knew that what he knew on any given day could be radically altered by something he might learn the next day. Yet he embodied a sense of deep conviction with a quality of knowing that we recognize as wisdom, whether or not we concur. This wisdom is also reflected in a statement of Oliver Wendell Holmes, who reportedly said, "I do not give a fig for the simplicity on this side of complexity. But I would give my life for the simplicity on the other side of complexity."[8]

Mature wisdom is not escape from, but rather engagement with, complexity and mystery. Our response to this form of knowing is not necessarily agreement but it does arrest our attention and compel our respect. Such knowing does not put us off the way Authority-bound and dualistic knowing may. Rather, we seek it out or sense that we are sought by it. Without abandoning the centered authority of the self and a disciplined fidelity to truth, this way of thinking represents a deepened capacity to hear the truth of another or even many others. This form of knowing can embrace paradox. This convictional knowing is a still more mature way of holding and being held in the ongoing motion of meaning-making and faith.

Reconsidering the Three-Step Model

Tracing forms of knowing in this way suggests that the movement toward mature adult faith (convictional commitment) leads from the assumed, received, tacit, conventional knowing of the adolescent (Authority-bound), through some sort of transition, wilderness or at least "sophomore slump" (unqualified relativism), to a critically aware and responsible adult faith (commitment in relativism). This three-step process—Authority-bound, then unqualified relativism, then commitment in relativism—has been the pattern generally assumed by faculty, administrators, supervisors, and others in the culture at large who in varying roles accompany the adolescent-becoming-adult. Many presume, for example, that as any young adult moves out into the world to take on increasing responsibility, he or she will bump up against naive assumptions, flounder a bit perhaps, and then take up residence in the discovery of how things really are. It has been assumed, for instance, that in four years of college one can essentially complete the first leg of the journey from Authority-bound and dualistic faith to an informed yet committed stance on the other side of discovering the relative character of all knowledge— arriving at what we have called commitment in relativism as an intellectually and socially adult place.

Constructive-developmental theories in large measure shared and reinforced these assumptions. Fowler's theory of faith development describes this first leg of the journey as a movement from "synthetic-conventional" faith (stage three) to "individuative-reflective" faith (stage four). This development he described, in part, as a shift in the locus of authority from outside the self to within, with the place in between regarded as simply "transitional." Kegan and Lahey also describe an evolution from a third order of consciousness (or the socialized mind) to a fourth order of consciousness (the self-authoring mind), the place in between likewise described as transitional.[9]

However, in my ongoing experience of teaching, counseling, and consulting, I have consistently encountered behavior that these models do not account for. It is indeed helpful to recognize the broad movement from conventional thought to a critically aware form of knowing. But I observe that the transition in between holds a kind of equilibrated integrity that itself constitutes a distinct form of faith—a developmental balance worthy of attention.

Teaching and counseling undergraduates first compelled me to notice how complex the dynamics of emerging adult faith are—that is, the faith that begins to form just beyond adolescence. Students who seemed confidently beyond Authority-bound knowing (and unqualified relativism) in their junior year often seemed more fragile in their senior year or reflected a subtle but surprisingly persistent dependence on Authority outside the self in their early years as alums.

Not wanting to be a professor who cultivated a cadre of dependent followers, I delighted in offering the well-timed push from the nest that would enable students to discover their own wings and soar away. Why, then, did the long-distance phone calls come every so many months, "just to touch base"? Though obviously distinctly different, they seemed faintly reminiscent of the way a two-year-old goes off exploring, returning periodically to touch in with the parent, only to go off again. For example, why were two former students, both of them bright, talented, and responsible, sitting at my breakfast table one morning, delaying their scheduled departure? Both had moved through the ups and downs of undergraduate years, developed critical thought, and demonstrated a confident sense of direction on graduation. One was now enrolled in a prestigious graduate program, the other was going abroad for travel and study, and both were surely about to miss the bus that would take them to their train. It was my sense that each was less confident about his or her own knowing than I had presumed and perhaps dependent in some way I didn't quite understand on the security, affirmation, and haven I represented. Yet the possible description of "regression" did not quite apply. I took them to the train myself and returned, bewildered.

These puzzling dynamics continued to confront me when I began to teach at the graduate level and perceived rather sophisticated graduate students still engaged in recomposing a place to stand on the other side of the dissolution of their received, conventional faith. As they sat in my office and talked about the questions they struggled with, the strength, suffering, richness, and compelling integrity of their meaning-making simply could not be adequately described by the adjectives *adolescent, transitional, regressive*, or *arrested*—nor by the notion of moratorium. Yet these were the only images that prevailing developmental theories offered.

What were we all failing to see? As I kept listening to both students and theorists, I "found," embedded in the place called transition, a distinct form of composing meaning, a recognizable stage. I began to see the power, promise, and vulnerability of the emerging adult soul.

Some of the clues clustered around the formation of identity and the search for a fitting role in society. To see them, we must return to adolescence and proceed slowly, paying particular attention to the shifts that occur at the thresholds first between adolescence and emerging adulthood and then between emerging adulthood and tested adult strength.

Identity—a Self-Aware Self—at the Threshold of Young Adulthood

Adolescence begins with puberty. Erikson described it as "the last stage of childhood."[10] Along with biological changes, puberty brings new cognitive possibilities: the capacity for formal operational thought and for thinking symbolically and abstractly.

This new mental power also makes third-person perspective-taking possible. This means that one can hold both one's own perceptions and those of another at the same time. Initially this leads to a new (and often painful) self-consciousness because the adolescent can for the first time see the self as perceived through the eyes of others. Thus the adolescent lives under the "tyranny of the they." The great task still ahead is the development of a self that has the strength to counter this tyranny and to mediate among the powerful images reflected in the adolescent's house of mirrors. This new strength is the power of identity. Cultivating this strength, and doing so in such a way as to also achieve recognition in the social world, is, in Erikson's view, "the adolescent ego's most important accomplishment."[11]

Whether or not the achievement of both identity and social recognition can be fully accomplished at the end of adolescence is increasingly problematic, as we shall see shortly. But what may well be achieved in adolescence is what Erikson points to as the hallmark of identity: a self-aware self. This self has enough ego strength to recognize that one can make some choices about how one becomes. With this new power comes a corresponding new quality of responsibility for the development of self. This new awareness of responsibility for self corresponds to the diminishment of a received, conventional, Authority-bound form of knowing. This is an enormous achievement. It means that one can consciously choose to differ with conventional Authority, and not merely for the sake of "pushing away from the dock." One begins to choose differently out of a responsible loyalty to one's own experience, perception, and knowledge.

This is not to say that the critically aware postadolescent necessarily speaks of composing a self. Rather, there is a conscious sense of needing to make choices and to take responsibility for their consequences for the future of self (and others). A young woman choosing a college other than the one her parents had hoped she would choose expressed this awareness: "If I went to that college it would fit the person I have been. I am choosing this college because it fits the person I am becoming."

This self-aware process often includes some struggle and acceptance of that struggle. In describing her sense of movement to a new place on the other side of the loss of an assumed world, another young woman said, "I guess . . . I'd give myself the freedom to struggle; then when I was done with a particular struggle and saw how I grew from it, . . . it was less threatening to me when other people would struggle with things—people who were really close. It wasn't like, 'Oh, no—what's gonna happen?' It was like 'Oh, yeah, this is part of growing so it's OK for them.'"

This newfound freedom to struggle for an identity and to take responsibility for it are signals that an adolescent has crossed the threshold into emerging adulthood.

Setting One's Own Heart

When we focus on the development of faith, it is significant to note that in Erikson's view the corresponding virtue developed in tandem with identity is fidelity. This suggests the development of a new capacity "to set one's heart." I propose, then, that the most profound marker of the threshold of emerging adulthood is the capacity to take self-aware responsibility for choosing the shape and path of one's own fidelity.

Thus, depending on the scope of the questions life poses, the young adult may realize, however partially at first, that one may and must take responsibility for the faith one lives by. This is sometimes a chilling recognition. Faith can now doubt itself; it is no longer possible to simply adopt the convictions of another, no matter how weighty and respected they may be. One becomes an emerging adult in faith (at whatever age) when one begins to take self-conscious responsibility for one's own knowing, becoming, and moral action, even at the level of ultimate meaning-making. This moment in the journey of faith does not typically occur until at least the age of seventeen.[12] For many people it emerges much later—or never.

What claims the heart's trust at this important threshold? By what process will this newly emerging identity locate a worthy place for itself in society? It is here that Keniston's pioneering work on the young adult era helped to clarify what other theories missed.

Seeking a Place in Society

The people Keniston described have achieved a self-aware self and individuated from their family in significant measure. This new self, however, is as yet "over-against" society or the world as it is. It is not yet a full participant in what is perceived as the adult world. Newly equipped with the power of critical reflection, the new self is aware of its own emerging identity, values, and integrity as distinguished from societal (and conventional) norms. The self-aware self is able to "sense who he or she is and thus to recognize the possibility of conflict and disparity between his or her emerging selfhood and his or her social order."[13]

In other words, Erikson described the formation of self-identity as an adolescent task that included achievement of both self-awareness and an effective social role. Keniston recognized, however, that although in earlier historical eras these two tasks might have been achieved simultaneously, now the composing of a self that is also effective in society is more likely to occur in two steps. First, the critically aware self comes to birth. But the task of integrating it into our increasingly complex society with integrity—that is, in a way that is both effective and satisfying—may well constitute an effort of its own.

What this postadolescent-not-yet-full-adult still needs to accomplish is finding a home where the integrity, promise, and power of the emerging self can dwell in sync with the perceived realities of the social world. This means that the big questions whose answers once defined adulthood remain to be settled: purpose, belonging, and vocation ("Where, why, and with whom will I dwell, love, and work?"). We might say that living these questions has become a task unto itself and is a primary characteristic of the emerging adult era.

A Pervasive Ambivalence

As noted earlier, the period of this life task has been described as "extended or prolonged adolescence"—certainly a pejorative description at best and, as we are beginning to see, inaccurate. As Keniston observed, "For, while some young men and women are indeed victims of the psychological malady of 'stretched adolescence,' many others are less impelled by juvenile grandiosity than by rather accurate analysis of the perils and injustices of the world in which they live."[14]

The emerging adult capacity for critical thought also makes possible a sense of the *ideal*. Emerging adults can dream of a better world than that which they find around them. What's more, they long to play a role in forming that world rather than simply fitting into the real world as they presently find it. At the same time, they may question whether they have the requisite power to bring their vision into being.

This new self-awareness and the emerging consciousness of an unresolved relationship between self and world was elegantly captured by Ernie Boyer Jr. When he was a young man of nineteen, he left the harbors of his good upbringing and literally went to sea. In the journal he kept as a sailor and later printed on an antique press, we can hear the postadolescent longing for a simpler world now lost, the consciousness of a new power and a new vulnerability, the awareness of composing a balance between self and world, and a clear sense of living in relationship to transcendent forces more powerful than the self alone:

I often imagine myself skippering a small sloop, out on the deck in the dark hours of morning while the small crew sleeps below. I would feel the ship beneath me slipping through the water, feel the sails above me tugging against the breeze, and dream until I fell asleep only to dream more deeply. As the wind shifted I would awaken, check the compass, and readjust the sails to put us back on course. Then I would wait for the sun to rise.

Always when I watch the sea . . . I think of the times when I would have to fight it. I realize now, after seeing the height of these waves and feeling the power of this wind, that sailing is the living of a deadly balance. At times these forces would carry and caress me. But there would be other times when forces would rise and tilt the balance against me. Then I would be struggling for my life. I might win once or twice—I might— but if I did, it would be the sea's mercy more than my skill that had saved me. I have seen the sea; I have watched its moods, and I know: it has power as absolute as death itself, and no man rides above it as long as he would like. But everything would be so simple, life in its bare energy or death, none of these squalid shades in between. I long for this life of the sailor.[15]

In "these squalid shades in between" is embedded a dynamic that strikingly illuminates our understanding of the emerging adult years: the dynamic Keniston observed as the "pervasive ambivalence toward both self and society."[16] It became apparent why this place in the journey of faith was difficult for developmental theorists to recognize as other than merely transitional. The ambivalence characteristic of this era may easily be confused with the dynamics of transition. But ambivalence, wariness, exploration, and tentativeness are the warp and woof of the tapestry woven in the emerging adult era of faith. The dynamic of ambivalence, which might best be described as a quality of searching that is steeped in a new integrity, confounded a theory looking for a stable equilibrium of the sort that Kegan and Fowler described in their formulations of postadolescent, adult meaning-making. Rooted in a healthy and fresh recognition of ambiguity, ambivalence is a central hallmark of the equilibrium of emerging adulthood.[17]

Probing Commitment

A return to Perry's nuanced description of intellectual development helps us recognize the integrity, stability, and structural power of this ambivalent emerging adult place. He identifies several positions within the discovery of relativism and the necessity of commitment: commitment foreseen, initial commitment, orientation in implications of commitment, and developing commitments.[18] Perry's observations suggested that commitment within a relativized world initially takes the form of a tentative or what I choose to term *probing commitment*. One explores many possible forms of truth—as well as work roles, relationships, and lifestyles—and assesses their fittingness to *one's own experience* of self and world.

Thus commitments formed on the other side of the encounter with the relativized character of self and world may initially last for two weeks, six months, or perhaps a few short years (a phenomenon that frustrates faculty hoping for commitment to a discipline, department, or program and discourages managers seeking to recruit solid commitment to a long-term project). In this developmental moment, even deeply felt affirmations have a tenuous, exploratory, and divided quality. Listen again to the voice of the sailor, now in the midst of a second voyage:

> What can I do? All day I have flitted from . . . one impulse, one dream to another, never mustering the resolution or sustaining the inclination to follow through my intentions. There is so much I want to do, must do, not just today, but with my life, with what time I have left. Not a second can be wasted. . . .
>
> I try for too much. I try for nothing less than a mastery of the world aesthetically, intellectually, and physically. To do this I need not only a momentous strength, but a divided self; for

each of these three is incompatible with the other, and I must
be a butcher, severing myself into three segments to be used
only one at a time while the others are shelved and forgotten.
What if I am too long with one? Will the other two die? After
spending some extra time with philosophy my aesthetic impulse
is harder to revive, and my physical impulse is all but dead. It
worries me.

It seems intolerable. And yet three is a very small number,
and life has so many more aspects, those which many would say
are its most valuable and rewarding, all of which I have
renounced. I am a man very much alone. The scope of my
choices is both infinite and far too narrow. What is the remedy?
There must be a solution, but I thought and thought about it
until that too has become frustrating. Too much to ever be
accomplished, too little for an adequate life, this is my
dilemma. What shall I do?[19]

In this account, we hear what Keniston described as the
"divided self" and the "wary probe" of both self and world. This
ambivalent and wary searching is qualitatively different from
adolescent experimentation in search of self-definition. The
probing commitment of the emerging adult is a serious, critically
aware exploration of the adult world and the potential versions
of a future that it offers (which the adolescent, in contrast,
receives uncritically), through which society's strength, vulnerability, integrity, and possibilities are assessed. A corresponding
self-probing tests the strength, vulnerability, and capacity of the
self to withstand or use what society will make, ask, and allow.[20]

Consider for a moment a twenty-five-year-old alum who
dropped by the campus ministry office just to muse out loud about
his unfolding path. He had been an economics major and in his
junior year he worked for a term with Mother Teresa. "He is,"
the campus chaplain told me later, "now working as an administrative assistant for an educational nonprofit organization and
he is also working in a coffee bar. He is living with two roommates, one of whom is getting rich in a high-tech job. For himself,

he is wondering whether he should go to work with a community that is exploring organic agriculture or seek more schooling. He isn't in a hurry, and in the meantime, he is also advising a freshman who got swept up in the heat of a political demonstration and may face a felony for destroying a sign."

This exploratory quality should in no way suggest that emerging adult commitments are always of the sort that can be redesigned at will. Many young adults are, for example, parents, a relationship that is not easily negotiable in any fundamental sense. Yet at the same time, the extension of the life span and the educational demands of a postindustrial culture have altered the assumptions by which such commitments are engaged. The phenomenon of probing commitment is affecting assumptions about the timing and meaning of "adult work," marriage and partnership, having children. These changes in the social contract with young adults are affecting their decision making and becoming features of emerging adult meaning-making.

Here a young woman shares a section from her journal from a time when she was trying to choose between two very different forms of employment:

> The question is, what balance to strike between your life now, at 23, and your life as you hope it to be at 35. Do you predict what you want (now) for yourself at 35 and sacrifice things now for your goal for yourself at 35? Or do you ignore what you think (now) you want for yourself later and just live like you want to now? But if you do the first, will you have regrets at 35 of things you should have done at 23? Or when you get to 35 and aren't where you wanted (at 23) to be (at 35), do you regret not having set yourself up and made those sacrifices?

Then she reflects:

> These are the questions I was grappling with earlier this year with a friend who has an even worse situation because his chosen career is really dependent on working your way up the

ladder and suffering through stupid starter jobs. It's hard to figure out how faith fits in—will it really all work out for the best? Is there really a master plan? Is what I'm doing now fitting into the master plan? Am I wasting time I'll regret later? Or will I regret, later, not wasting enough time when I had the luxury to? How come I can't see the master plan? It's a really frustrating feeling to have the impatient sense you should be working toward something, but not having any idea what it is, or even if you should know what it is now.

Another example of the changing cultural milieu and its effects on young adult meaning-making is reflected in the choices of a young man in his late twenties. After serving for a few years as an officer in the military, he married a recent law graduate. He then chose to go to a two-year business program rather than law school, calculating that it would require one less year of schooling. He speculated that he would then have the credentials to achieve the same level of income that his spouse would have to give up in order to pause in her career to have a child. This two-career family-in-the-making will probably negotiate their way through a great many tangles in the years ahead, sorting out what it means to be a parent, spouse, and worker in the context of new and ancient biological-cultural patterns.

Forms of Knowing Revised

I propose that this period of probing commitment characterizes the first of the two eras within the single place previously described as commitment within relativism. If we are to recognize and sponsor adult meaning-making, we need to make a distinction between the *probing commitment* of the emerging adult and what I term the *tested commitment* of the more fully adult. Tested commitment begins to take form when one can no longer be described as so divided or as simply exploring one's worldview, marriage, career commitment, lifestyle, or faith. One's form of knowing and being takes on a tested quality, a sense of fittingness, a recognition that one is willing to make one's peace and to affirm one's place in the scheme of things (though not uncritically).[21] In the period of tested commitment, the self has a deepened quality of at-homeness and centeredness—in marked contrast to the ambivalence or dividedness of the earlier period.

We are now ready to recompose our understanding of the development of cognition as it is manifest in forms of knowing:

	Adolescent/ Conventional		Emerging Adult	Tested Adult	Mature Adult
Forms of Knowing	Authority- bound Dualistic	→ Unqualified relativism	→ Probing commitment	→ Tested commitment	→ Convictional commitment

As we continue to assess whether this emerging adult stage is simply an artifact of our times and has no deeper location within human development, it is useful to explore whether altered social conditions may reveal stages that are not new but have been present also in earlier historical eras without being recognized. Brinton's analysis of Quaker journals from the seventeenth, eighteenth, and nineteenth centuries is particularly interesting when set alongside the ambivalent, probing character of the postadolescent period described here. He has identified phases in the faith journey of Quakers that appear to corroborate this pattern. The first phase is "childhood piety," which is followed by "youthful frivolity" (adolescence, when Quaker youth of that era wanted to dance and have fancy clothes). Brinton then describes a postadolescent period that he terms the "divided self." During this period, the young person struggles between Quaker values and alternative values in the wider culture. This period of division is resolved in the choice to be at one, centered in the affirmation of the image of the "Inner Light" and the adoption of Quaker ways. It is also very interesting to note that the average age at which the Quakers he studied made the decision to be "at one" was twenty-six.[22] Moreover, we are also learning from neuroscience research that brain development continues well into the second decade of life, suggesting that the development of these more complex capacities may be aligned with processes of biological maturation.[23]

Emerging Adulthood

We can begin to see that the character of making meaning during the twenty-something decade in the human story may not be so very new. But under changing historical conditions, this place between adolescence and full adulthood becomes more apparent, its particular potential and vulnerability more evident, and the work of this era all the more critical. We must note, however, that what is potential within the emerging adult era is not guaranteed. Although adolescence may end with the emergence of a self-aware self, and although society may become more tolerant of and even require an expanded period of exploration, the robust development of critical thought—the capacity for thinking in more complex, relativistic, and provisionally committed ways—may or may not be achieved during the emerging adult years, and the optimal outcome of the emerging adulthood years may not be realized. As we shall see, it all depends.

Chapter Five

It All Depends . . .

To undergo the loss of assumed certainty and to recompose what was presumed to be dependably real involves emotion as well as cognition. Cognition and affect, mind and heart are intimately interwoven in the fabric of knowing and integral to the fabric of faith. To make this epistemological journey is to be affected and moved, as captured in a conversation between Bill Perry and a young woman recounting her experience in a physics class. There was, she said, a particular apparatus, the Ames window, that appeared to revolve in a circle. However, if the light cast on it was changed, it then appeared instead only to be oscillating back and forth. This change in perception, which occurred with the flick of a light switch, catalyzed her recognition of the relative character of all perception. Might everything, seen in a different light, be recast into another perception of reality? She concluded her telling of the incident by remarking that in the midst of the experience her physics professor was very helpful to her. When Perry asked how, she said, "Well, now that I think about it, I realize that he didn't say anything. But the way he looked at me, I knew that he knew what I had lost."

When we undergo the transformation of our sense of truth, reordering "how things really are," we may feel curiosity, awe, fascination, delight, relief, or joy. But it is just as likely that along the way we will experience a sense of challenge, threat, bewilderment, frustration, anxiety, emptiness, or loss—some measure of shipwreck. In other words, observed from the outside, the transformation of an Authority-bound form of meaning-making to a more reflective, critically aware form may appear to be a merely cognitive development. Experienced from the inside, however, this is decidedly not the case. This shift in thinking affects not only cognition but also our feelings and relationships. Kegan has stated it nicely: "A change in how we are composed may be experienced as a change in our own composure."[1]

The Affective Dimensions of Meaning-Making

Indeed, as the discovery of new knowledge and meaning occurs, the whole self—body, mind, and heart—is affected.[2] Things that previously upset us are now seen in a new light; our response is consequently transformed and we may become, for example, more tolerant. Or something that heretofore we would have accepted as "how things are and always will be" may in a new light be recognized as changeable and we become less tolerant of things as they are. The evolution of meaning occurs in the dance of being affected in one's world coupled with evolving cognitive power. Thus the motion of life is manifest as "e-motion" (surprise, disappointment, pleasure, fear, dismay, or sorrow) that regularly accompanies the discovery of new insight—and changing one's mind.

For example, our growing understanding of climate instability, our ability to manipulate DNA, our capacity to create complex digital networks—all recompose our relationship to the Earth and to each other, enlarging both our power and our vulnerability, fundamentally threatening the current arrangements of those matters that ultimately concern us. We are affected. We watch the delicate relationships among peoples and nations unravel and reknit themselves in new patterns, alliances dissolve, borders are redrawn, and slumbering forces awaken with renewed strength in our global commons. We are aware of our vulnerability to economic and political tides. We know that our inner sense of a dependable universe can precariously shift on hearing tomorrow's news.

At the same time, we live with a growing awareness that more depends on us than previous generations have supposed— even as we are continually defeated in our attempts to entirely grasp, much less control, the full measure of the challenges and opportunities with which we now contend. Whether we cope by means of psychic numbing or resolute engagement with the terrors that have become our daily fare, we are moved. Individually and collectively, we long for a trustworthy, dependable steady state in a dynamic, roiling world. (This longing is one way of understanding some of the tremendous attraction of fundamentalist ideologies—scientific, political, or religious—at this time in history.)

Within this ongoing motion of life, we repeatedly reassess our felt understanding of what is ultimately dependable. We are continually moved to compose more dependable, trustworthy patterns of knowing and being. Whatever our age, we seek viable ways of making meaning and composing faith in an ongoing daily dialogue, sorting out reality. At whatever level of sophistication, how we "depend" is a matter of ultimate significance.

Because the discovery of knowledge and faith occurs in this interaction between self and world, it follows that we learn in the context of relationships. We learn in relationship to the natural, more-than-human world, and in relationship to people, texts, and institutions. We learn because we dwell in the dynamic interconnectedness of all life. Fundamentally and inescapably, we are social, interdependent beings.

Thus "depending" is an integral dimension of life. We dwell in the power of the relation of self and other. To depend means to be "held by" or "subject to," but it also means "to hold." How we hold and are held and how this may change over time affects the ongoing formation of knowledge, meaning, and faith. Whereas focusing on cognition gave us access to how a person *thinks* in her or his composing of meaning, focusing on dependence gives us access to how a person *feels*.[3]

Patricia Killen and John de Beer have observed that when "we enter our experience . . . we find it saturated with feeling. . . . Feelings are our embodied affective and intelligent responses to reality as we encounter it. . . . Feeling joins body and mind. . . . Feelings . . . are clues to the meaning of our experience. . . . They incarnate questions, values, and wisdom that we are living but which we cannot yet articulate and of which we may be unaware."[4] Killen and de Beer also observe that in the prevailing culture feelings are often viewed primarily as problems because we cannot necessarily control them (or easily align them with a rapidly changing world). But feelings are facts and they cannot be ignored in the life of meaning-making and faith. Thus dependence, which always challenges control, serves as a particularly appropriate window into the affective dimensions of making meaning. Holding, being held, depending and being depended on within the fabric of life (even in adulthood) all touch the core of the self so profoundly that elemental emotions such as trust, strength, power, and vulnerability are inevitably evoked.

Forms of Dependence

Just as our forms of cognition can transform and develop, so too can the forms of dependence. Tracing transformations in our ways of depending is one means of observing and describing especially salient features of emerging adulthood and the affective dimensions of the development of faith.

	Adolescent/ Conventional			Emerging Adult		Tested Adult		Mature Adult
Forms of Knowing	Authority-bound Dualistic	→	Unqualified relativism	→	Probing commitment	→	Tested commitment	→	Convictional commitment
Forms of Dependence	Dependent/ Counterdependent			→	Fragile inner-dependence	→	Confident inner-dependence	→	Inner-dependence

Dependent

At the time of Authority-bound knowing, it follows quite logically that a person's sense of self and world is dependent on an uncritically assumed Authority. If a person is in his thirties or beyond and still making meaning in this way, the power of his social role may mask the profound dependence that is, in fact, in place. Dwelling in this form of knowing, he may be able to give a variety of logical reasons for holding a particular point of view but, if pressed, eventually reveals an unexamined trust in Authority outside the self.

Feelings of assurance, rightness, confidence, hope, loyalty, fear, disdain, or alarm can be determined by Authority. One *depends* in a primary way on the voice of a news commentator, a political leader, a celebrity, a parent, a supervisor, a religious figure, a favorite author, or a swarm of others who serve as trusted mediators of Truth.

Kegan has described this era in development as "socially constructed" and "inter-personal," for here a person's sense of self and truth *depends* in a primary way on his or her immediate "surround"— relational and affectional ties. With equal fittingness, Fowler described this era as "conventional," for here the person uncritically accepts the conventions of group and societal norms. The boundaries of the group may be rather narrowly drawn, as in the case of "my family" or "my soccer team," or broadly construed, as in the case of a "conventional" Democrat, Marine, or investment banker. In each instance, the person's sense of reality and what is fitting and true *depends* on a shared ethos of assumed Authority unaware of the prevailing ideology that shapes it. In this form of dependence, one can participate in the unreflective high of being swept up in the joy (or terror) of the crowd, whether in a sports arena, a worshipping community, or a stock exchange.

Counterdependent

A person's feelings continue to be shaped by assumed Authority until the day there is a yearning (or the absolute necessity) to explore and test truth for oneself. This may occur in the midst of betrayal and devastation—the shipwreck of the truth one has depended on. Or it may emerge simply as restlessness or curiosity, signaling a readiness for more adequate and satisfying ways of knowing and being. A new strength can begin to take form, one that can now push away from the dock of what has been sure moorage, to move out into deep waters—exploring for oneself what is true and trustworthy. Initially, however, this move is essentially another form of dependence: counterdependence.

Counterdependence is the move in opposition to Authority; it provides momentum for the expansion of self into the still unknown horizon. It is a dimension of the earlier dependence, because the person can push against the familiar pattern of meaning-making that has been trusted but she is not yet able to perceive or create a new pattern. Thus a kind of absolute dependence remains in place. For example, after participating in a political demonstration for the first time, an eighteen-year-old woman who was arrested for trespassing said that previously she had *always* trusted the police but now she knew she could *never* trust them. Clearly, her experience was the beginning of a complex understanding of her relationship to the law and law enforcement. But she was as yet only pushing away from her earlier assumption and was caught up in the rhetoric of others as a defining, diametrically opposing interpretation, giving her a new, counterdependent, but still essentially Authority-bound stance.

In the time of counterdependence, moving apart and creating some distance is the task at hand. Yet the very need for distance obscures continuing participation in a relationship that is still (and in many instances will continue to be) quite powerful. Here, for example, are the words of a young woman from a tight ethnic community who, after an initial period of counterdependence in relation to her family, began to find a new, more inner-dependent pattern of relationship:

I was so determined to break away from my family and the entire community that I drove to college with a vengeance. The more they told me not to go out, the more I'd go out. . . . I told them this: "If you told me to go left, I'd go right." Now I realize I can't keep making decisions based on what my parents don't want me to do. I have to think of what I really want. I've had my escape for four years and it's time to return to reality. . . . In my freshman year, when I used to think about a career it was kind of exotic: It was like I'd see something in a movie . . . a picture of myself out there. Now I know I don't belong in that movie. I would feel ostracized from my community.[5]

Thus counterdependence is a vital part of the motion of life when preparing to venture out into the deep water of knowing for oneself what is dependable and trustworthy.

This move can occur in relatively nontraumatic forms if the person has access to wise parents, sponsoring teachers, effective supervisors, or others who consciously encourage or nurture it in positive ways. Little pushing-against is then necessary, because one is actually invited to explore and is supported in doing so. However, if this vital motion is misunderstood, devalued, and resisted (or, ironically, if the bonds of relationship have been particularly strong, good, and trustworthy), the person may have to push away from the dock with greater force if a new, more adult relationship is to take form.

In time, the emerging adult may begin to recompose Authority and recognize that, indeed, Authority doesn't hold ultimate truth or power. As a new interiority begins to take form, the counter-dependent pilgrim then begins to look less toward resisting outer Authority and more toward an inner authority. He or she begins to move toward inner-dependence.

Inner-Dependent Versus Independent

I use the term *inner-dependence* to signify something quite differ-ent from independence. Western culture places an extraordinary value on individuality and autonomy. In myriad ways, we signal that all should aspire to a kind of independence that implies not only a healthy strength of self but also the utter absence of an adult's practical dependence on affectional (in contrast to merely utilitarian) relationships with others in the commonwealth of being. The presumed needs of industrial societies (for example, a mobile workforce and autonomous consumers) have spawned an almost pathological fear of dependence, reinforced by Freud's insights about infantilization.[6] Thus all psychological dependence has tended to be regarded as infantile, especially those forms of dependence that claim religious justification.[7]

Reflecting the same industrial and Enlightenment influence, Protestant religious faith simultaneously has fostered a cultural ethos in which ethical reasoning focuses primarily on individual rights, the formation of the individual conscience, and individual acts perceived as independent choices. Not all forms of dependence are, however, signs of weakness, immaturity, or regression. Dependence simply affirms the relational dimension of all life. An absence of this recognition impoverishes our cultural myths and masks the loneliness of overindividualized lives—increasingly confounded by the hyperconnectivity of a technological age that fosters both a greater capacity for individual autonomy and new forms of dependency.

In contrast to the common associations we make with independence or autonomy, inner-dependence is not intended to connote standing all by oneself—a radical self-sufficiency. Rather, the developmental movement into *inner-dependence occurs when one is able to consciously include the self within the arena of authority.* In other words, other sources of authority may still hold credible power, but now one can also recognize and value the authority of one's own voice.

One young woman, reflecting on the differences between her experience of faith in high school and later in her senior year at a major public university, wrote:

As a younger person, God was more of a higher up, all wise authority figure (father figure). Now I still sense in Him this likeness, but there is an even greater sense of friendship quality. I think this may be because as I am becoming an adult, the parent role evolves into the comrade role. I think I also have a gentler sense of Him now and this may be because I have a gentler sense of myself as well. I think the two are inextricably related: my changing sense of God with my changing sense of self. . . . At this point, as I find the individual I am myself, I find that I feel much closer to God and my spiritual center, like we are getting more on the same wavelength. . . .

Here we see that responsiveness to authority outside the self is relativized but not necessarily demolished. With the term *inner-dependence*, then, I am signifying not a negation of the essential relatedness on which all human life depends but rather new consciousness of the authority of the self in the composing of truth and choice. Here a person begins to listen within, with new respect and trust for the truth of his or her "own insides." That is, the person begins to listen and be responsive to the inner self as a source of authority—and as an object of care, "a gentler sense of myself." There is greater trust in one's own experience and intuition. Again, this does not mean that sources of insight and expertise outside the self—or the claims of others for care— necessarily become irrelevant; it does mean, however, that the self can now take more conscious responsibility for adjudicating competing claims.

In this movement of the soul, there emerges the possibility of a new quality of conversation and correspondence between inner and outer realities and the potential for new bonds of rela- tion between self and world, faith and life. But the path is rarely direct or smooth.[8] Sometimes outer realities threaten to eclipse the nascent inner authority. Said one young adult, "As I developed an awakening to the material inequalities in the world, I felt like there was no point in dealing with anything else . . . [that dealing with inner or personal struggles] would be an insane privilege—who am I to think about God when people can't eat? In my mind there was a line, an orderly way of dealing with things—material, and then inner. Now I realize you can't do social work without doing inner work. I burned out, not seeing the connection between myself and the world."[9]

This awakening of the need to honor inner as well as outer demands while finding a right relationship to a wider and more complex world is often manifest in our present culture as a hunger for things "spiritual" in contrast to "religion." One young man, for whom church was "routine" when he was growing up, describes a transition he entered about age nineteen. He began to think more for himself and to formulate his own understanding of God, which transcended what he saw as hypocrisy in the religion he knew. He was reaching for a deeper congruence between his inner experience and a way of living in the world. Looking back a decade later, he said, "I had religion but no spiritual understanding. My family was so not spiritual but they are so religious." For him, being spiritual represented a postconventional form of faith in which his own inner authority began to play a stronger role.

The transition toward greater reliance on inner authority can be a time of significant vulnerability and uncertainty as discrepancies between the claims of the self and the claims of the world come into sharp relief. One may question both self and world, wondering if either the social structures of one's world or one's own resources will prove sufficient for resolving the discrepancies. Before a new relationship between self and world is created, the claims of each may threaten the other, and it is difficult to live, as Kegan and Lahey have recently put it, "out of faith" with one's surround.[10]

It is not unusual for young adults who become aware of the discrepancy between the haves and the have-nots to find themselves buffeted by competing definitions of success, asking the big question, "Can I have what will make me happy and still make a difference?" When a student who is majoring in humanities and business spoke recently with a campus minister, for instance, the student mentioned that he had that day invested $1,000 in day trading. He wondered, could he combine commitment to service with his need to be financially secure? He was actively involved on campus in a program advocating changed economic conditions on behalf of the poor worldwide and was also trying to be a good grandson by caring for his grandfather and helping with family finances. As this young man begins to claim a sense of his own inner authority, he does so within a force field of competing claims and moral ambiguity. Thus, as we have seen, emerging adult integrity can, indeed, look like ambivalence.

Once inner-dependence begins to take form, the emerging adult (being young) may at times long to return to a former kind of dependence, but the new knowing makes that difficult. One young woman, recently graduated from college, was keenly aware of the problematic character of turning back, even as she felt its allure. As she was making her way through a maze of challenges and disappointments, she recognized that she harbored a wish that at the same time she knew would not be satisfying. She said, "It's no accident that I've been reaching for something new. . . . After what this past year dealt me, I found myself wishing I were Catholic or a devotee of Santeria so I could have someone in authority just tell me which god/saint I needed to burn a candle for to change my luck."

Another said, "In high school I trusted others, the universe, to take care of me. . . . I trusted that my soul would be taken care of. Now I'm coming back to that point and it's an uphill battle. *I'm teaching myself to trust.* But when you start to learn about injustice, it's clear we aren't being taken care of—it can never be as easy again as it was in high school. Then I lived much more by instinct, versus now, I think through decisions." That is, she now has a sense of responsibility for discerning what she can and cannot trust and believe.

A New Kind of Authority

Many developmental accounts have assumed essentially a single movement in the shift of the locus of authority from an uncritical trust in assumed Authority "out there" to a critically aware sense of authority "within." Yet it seems to be more the case that this shift occurs through a two-step process. When the locus of authority shifts from outside the self inward, it does so most solidly by moving first from dependence on a *given* Authority to dependence on a *chosen* authority—still external but one that I now choose in accord with my own observations and lived experience. Having some awareness that there are other Authorities, other points of view, I nevertheless self-consciously choose this authority that has the power to beckon and draw forth my own sense of truth and emerging critical awareness.

That is, the transition into emerging adulthood occurs most gracefully and with optimum potential when the emerging self is recognized and invited into a wider arena of participation by wise and trusted adults. Thus, this is the fitting time for the presence of mentors—whether coach, guide, sponsor, professor, aunt or uncle, supervisor, author, guru, or important friend. Those who serve this mentoring function are not, however, the heroes and heroines of adolescent devotion. The mentor holds a significant degree of power, but the "fusion" usually characteristic of the adolescent hero or heroine relationship is absent. When interviewing college seniors, for example, I found that if I posed the question, "Is there someone whom you wish to be like?" the students resisted it. They typically rephrased the question in their response: "No, there is no one who is a model for me, whom I would want to be exactly like, but there are people who exemplify certain qualities that I would like to have." Then they were able to name one or several people who served as images of aspects of their emerging self.

The power of mentoring relationships is that they help anchor an intuition of the potential self. They beckon the self into being and, in so doing, help to ground a place of commitment within relativism. As such, mentors exercise both cognitive and affective appeal, offering both insight and emotional support. But the emerging adult exercises a rudimentary sense of critical choice, at least on the level of requiring correspondence with his or her own experience. Indeed, the emerging adult will make do without a mentor rather than betray the integrity of the emerging self. Alex, twenty-six years old, reflects, "I have often felt the lack of personalized guidance. . . . Sadly, I have not had this, even in college, where I tried switching faculty advisers to get the mentorship I needed. I hope to find that in the future."

Note that Alex reveals the integrity of the emerging self, and the dependence we can detect here differs from the dependence of either the adolescent or the full adult. Though the adolescent is profoundly subject to the power of the conventional milieu, the emerging adult has a larger capacity to hear those voices that draw out the still vulnerable but increasingly inner-dependent self. In a healthy mentoring relationship, the emerging adult neither worships the mentor as a hero nor needs to push off counterdependently. Rather, he or she is appropriately dependent on a chosen (self-selected) "Authority out there" to beckon and confirm the integrity emerging from within.

There do appear to be some who move to this more inner-dependent place without much outside support. Such people may say something like, "One day, I just knew that what I had been told I had to be, do, and believe, wasn't true." Yet when we look closely at their life context, we can see precursors of this moment: influences that helped prepare the mind and heart (whether in large or small ways) for this courageous, developmental moment. If the potential of this moment is to be realized, the person needs to be met in ways that enable the new voice to flourish.[11] Without such support, emerging adults are vulnerable to floundering—even to being broken.

Fragile Inner-Dependence

One might, therefore, describe the inner-dependence of the emerging adult as initially a *fragile inner-dependence*. Here *fragile* is not intended to connote weak, feeble, or puny. Rather, it is more like the fragility of a young plant as it emerges from the soil: healthy, vital, full of promise, yet vulnerable. The emerging adult may in her or his own personal style express this new inner-dependence and strength with a kind of brazen pride or a tentative, almost shy sense of new power to declare one's own sense of things and to take important initiatives. Either way, the new inner strength represents a horizon of glimmering possibility and a deepened capacity for responsible action. The emerging adult, steeped in newly gained inner-dependence, may be bewildered when her or his own opinion is not enough for a term paper. To cite "experts" may feel like going back to always just trusting Authority, when now one can see in whole new ways for oneself: "Isn't that what you wanted me to do? Think for myself?"

The feelings to which the inner-dependent young adult is therefore correspondingly vulnerable are special forms of bewilderment, loss, and being at sea. One young woman, discovering a whole new horizon of opportunity and promise for her life, spoke poignantly of a sense of loss: knowing that she "would never be at home again in the same way—with my extended family or in the place where I worked during high school." These would remain part of her life and landscape but she knew she was choosing to participate also in a wider world—cognitively, emotionally, and geographically—and that these familiar people and places would be recast within a larger frame of belonging and choice. Her ecology of depending would be reordered as she began to make meaning in new ways. This fragile inner-dependence is evident also in the young adult's own experience of ambiguity regarding being a grown-up. Blake, for example, is a twenty-four-year-old college graduate living in a major city several hundred miles from her parents. She is an outstanding teacher in a community college, where the students in her class-room are one, two, or three decades older than herself, seeking their high school diplomas. It is Blake who decides when her students are ready to take the standardized exams that for many of them determine access to adequate employment. She carries a faculty ID card but she is not paid benefits. She pays for her own household and general expenses but her parents are paying her health insurance because they feel she should not yet have to be responsible for her full support. These mixed messages about how adult she is echo a dialogue within her where "switch-ing between adulthood and childhood minute to minute, happens in little ways." It still feels kind of "weird" to buy groceries *by herself*, but "buying mundane, day-to-day things with money you earned 100 percent by yourself is a small moment of realizing you can make it on your own." Blake heard another twenty-something friend remark, "Every once in a while, like I'm standing on a subway platform dressed for my work, and I get this paralyzing feeling that I'm about to be found out. Like everyone is going to discover that I am a kid masquerading as an adult."

But there are yet deeper streams of vulnerability in emerging adult lives. When a senior at a large university was asked, "What do your friends 'count on'?" his answer revealed a complex set of vulnerabilities. Some of his friends were students who, despite their university education, seemed to be remaining in Authority-bound and dependent ways of making meaning. As he put it, "For some, God has all the answers—they will just rely on God to get them through it. Others count on whomever they can around them, which leads to their sometimes being crushed even further because no one can be completely dependable for every-thing." These students were vulnerable to an unexamined faith and the inevitable failures of present or future Authorities.

But then the student went on: "Others just don't count on much—some of these friends have a constant struggle with depression—just passively hope that some day it will be different. And a few count a lot on themselves: 'If I just do something more, it will get better somehow.'" These friends seemed to have stepped beyond counting on Authority out there but encountered new challenges for which they are not fully prepared. Steeped as these emerging adults are in cultural messages that they should be independent, they are vulnerable to a special kind of disappointment, failure, isolation, abandonment, and depression. They cannot go back, but their emerging adulthood needs to be met and welcomed by a mentoring milieu that offers steppingstones into the promise of their future.

Tested Inner-Dependence

In contrast to the experience of those just described, if the fragile inner-dependence of the emerging adult is met with encouragement and confirmation, over time a tested, confident inner-dependence can take form. The more tested adult has a deepened capacity to compose his or her sense of value and promise and has become strong enough to let the mentor be other—even to have feet of clay. The tested adult, however, does not cease to need others. Rather, others are depended on in a different way. For instance, as the emerging adult becomes more fully adult, mentors can become peers in significant ways. The nature of this transition was captured by a mentor, who said to his protégé, "My job is to accompany you until you see yourself as I see you." When this occurs, Authority previously located outside the self becomes more fully consolidated within the self. The tested adult manifests a confident inner-dependence.

The Inner Life and the Ethical Life

In today's world, this movement to inner-dependence is a critical step in deepening one's capacity for what may be described as an inner dialogue. Inner dialogue is vital to the formation of conscience and a moral, ethical life. An ethical life as it is lived out in a complex and morally ambiguous world is dependent less on the ability to do everything right the first time and more on the ability to reflect on past and potential actions and their consequences—sometimes subtle and always significant.

How this works is described by Robert Quinn in *Deep Change: Discovering the Leader Within*.[12] He recounts the story of Steve Thompson, newly working with Ron Cedrick, a man known for his command of deep-sea engineering and construction. Cedrick had a reputation for executing huge projects and completing them ahead of schedule. Steve was responsible for lowering the diving bell into the sea and bringing the divers back up on deck. The most dangerous time in this operation occurs when the diving bell is between the surface of the water and the deck. If cables snap then, divers can rarely be recovered.

As Quinn tells the story, the sea was growing rough as Thompson's first project with Cedrick neared completion. As Cedrick walked by Thompson he said, "I know that the weather's gettin' up a bit, but those boys respect you and will do what you ask—I've seen it. We need to keep that bell in the water just as long as we can before we let a little 'ole weather shut us down." Thompson continued the operation in twenty-four-foot seas and they beat the deadline without mishap.

Later, however, Thompson gave himself "the mirror test." He stood back and reflected on himself, what he had done and why. He recognized that in his overwhelming desire to succeed, he had accomplished the task but at significant cost. He had tolerated unacceptable risk and had set a poor precedent for permissible operating parameters.

This ability to reflect on past action and compose future action is dependent on the development of interiority: a dialogue within the self. The Society of Friends (Quakers) speak of listening to the "Inner-Light" or Spirit within. Jesuits speak of discernment and cultivate exercises for discovering the presence of God within. Others speak of listening for that "still, small voice." Perry was fond of saying that part of learning the art of life is to discover that there is not just a still, small voice but a whole committee of voices inside—parents, family, teachers, advertising, threats from competitors, expectations of friends and colleagues—and the challenge is to become a good chairperson! Among the gifts of the great spiritual traditions are the practices that have been honed across generations for becoming conscious of the power and processes of the inner life.

This strengthened capacity for an inner life provides a way of holding and assessing multiple points of view and the competing claims of various authorities. Thus the power of conscience can be substantially deepened by the development of the inner-dependent self in the journey into adult meaning-making, adult faith. If it does not occur (or occurs only within limited, discrete domains), the conscience is blunted. If, however, this inner life—this interiority—is well cultivated, the capacity for responsible adulthood and faithful citizenship is enlarged.

Interdependence

After inner-dependence is established and the trustworthiness of the inner self is confirmed, there is the potential for yet another development toward further maturity. This movement again expands the arena of authority and care. It does not typically occur in its fullest measure until postmidlife.

Midlife occurs at different times for different people, because it is determined primarily by an inner sense that one has probably lived half of one's life and thus the future is no longer infinitely revisable. One's sense of "lifetime" becomes more focused. This transition in consciousness is usually marked also by both physical and social changes.

In the midlife period, a person may simply move through a transition from the first half of his or her life to the second half. But just as we are beginning to see in the emerging adult years, every transition can be an occasion for transformation. The transformative potential of the midlife transition lies in the strength achieved in the formation of the inner-dependent self.

That is, further transformation of truth and faith can still occur, but only if the adult self is strong enough—willing and able to pay attention to the reemergence of what Fowler has termed the *deep self*.[13]

The deep self is composed of those buried dimensions of oneself, particularly the sufferings and joys of childhood, the unresolved issues of adolescence, and (as we shall see) the most luminous hopes of emerging adulthood. This deep self may now come to the surface to be healed and fulfilled or at least to be known and lived nondefensively. If it is not resisted, it may thus lead to deeper knowing and trust of the self and also to a yet more profound perception of one's relatedness to others.

This transformation constitutes another qualitative shift in the balance of strength, vulnerability, trust, and faith. Now more at home with both the strengths and limitations of the self, one can be at home with the truth embedded in the strengths and limitations of others. A person's center of primary trust now resides neither in the assumed Authority of another nor in the courageously claimed authority of the inner self. Rather, trust is now centered in the meeting of self and other, in the recognition of the strength and finitude of each, and in the promise of *the truth that emerges in relation*. This trust takes the form of a profound, self-aware conviction of interdependence.

When meaning-making moves into an interdependent form, it is not the fact of interdependence that is new. As we are beginning to recognize more fully, from infancy through adulthood, a person is always interdependent. What is new, however, is one's awareness of the depth and pervasiveness of the interrelatedness of all of life and the significant yet contingent strength of one's own perceptions. One now becomes increasingly angered and saddened by assertions of truth that exclude the authority of the experience of others. For example, a manager may have been tolerant of shared inquiry and decision making and even affirmed the notion—ideologically—all the while silently harboring a sense that her own inner experience, knowledge, and intuition would lead to the best decision. When she dwells in this more interdependent conviction, however, she perceives dialogue to be not merely politically expedient but also essential. Yet she can still bring to that dialogue the strength of her own capacity for discernment—a strength that is now joined with a capacity to listen to others with deepened attention and responsiveness. Dwelling in this conviction of interdependence makes it possible to depend on others without fear of losing the power of the self. There is a new freedom that can hold the paradoxes of weakness and strength, needing and giving, tenderness and assertiveness— without anxiety that in the recognition of the other the self will be diminished.

This way of making meaning enables one to dwell in the truth that the needs of nurturance, affection, and belonging extend throughout life and into every domain of being, both private and public. Interdependence can now be profoundly owned at an affective level. The person now most trusts the truth that emerges in the dialectic or, better, in the communion between self and other, self and world, self and "God." The person can recognize and know with the whole self the truth of the interdependence that we are. This knowing may involve feelings of delight, wonder, freedom, responsiveness, responsibility, and often a deep sense of the tragic dimensions of life as a consequence of the capacity to see what others cannot or will not.

Attention to the development of dependence gives us some access to the ebb and flow of feelings of trust, constraint, threat, fear, confidence, and communion. These feelings are rooted in inner experience. But the motion of affective life and its development emerges neither in a merely private inner world nor in abstract reflections on relationship, but only in the pleasures, frustrations, and transformations of relationships lived out in the everyday. The character and quality of our ways of depending and their transformations have everything to do with the forms of belonging within and through which we make meaning and seek a worthy faith.

Chapter Six

. . . On Belonging

Some years ago, I was teaching in a liberal arts college in the Northwest that encouraged off-campus study. Another colleague and I traveled with a group of students to San Francisco, where we studied the city for a month. I noted with interest that some students who had little or nothing to do with religion on campus were choosing to explore the cathedrals in San Francisco as well as other notable and diverse religious communities. Some were also asking questions about religion, again in contrast to their behavior on campus. At first, I assumed that this was simply because of a change in environment; San Francisco, after all, did offer more cathedrals and more religious diversity. Only later did I recognize another dynamic at play with us in the city: a change in the students' network of belonging.

On campus, students tended to choose patterns of affiliation that explicitly or subtly included their orientation to religion. Once these were established, any significant departure was a threat to belonging. This meant that for some, religious practice or serious inquiry was out of bounds, though for others it was more or less expected. But when they were in another social constellation, new questions and new behavior became possible.

We expected that when students returned to campus those who had not traveled would benefit from association with those who had. We discovered, however, that the travelers tended to form new patterns of affiliation. They formed community—a network of belonging—with those who had also traveled and with whom they could confirm their new ways of seeing and knowing.

Our location and social milieu (including cyberspace) play a central role in the formation of meaning, purpose, and faith. One of the distortions of many psychological, developmental, economic, political, and religious models is a focus on the individual that obscures the power of the social context in shaping personal reality. In much of Western thought sharp distinctions have been drawn between private and public, subject and object, the human and the rest of the natural environment. These overdrawn distinctions mask the growing importance of recognizing the interdependent realities of self and social context. A young woman who had been listening carefully to her friends (male and female, some who went to college and some who did not) remarked that their faith experience was "fully based on what they were going through, who they were around, and where they were living. Everyone, across the board, identified their different moments of spiritual insight and new understanding based on their experience of 'their world.'"

Networks of Belonging

An under-recognized strength of the Piagetian paradigm is its psychosocial conviction that human becoming absolutely depends on the quality of interaction between the person and his or her social world. The individual is not the sole actor in the drama of human development. No single relationship can satisfy the casting needs for the drama of our becoming. We "interlive" with many others. Just as the infant is dependent on another for confirmation of a universe of care and promise, even so everyone throughout life is dependent on a felt "network of belonging." Everyone needs a psychological home, crafted in the intricate patterns of connection and interaction between the person and his or her community. Networks of belonging provide the trustworthy holding on which all humans depend for their flourishing within the wider world and the universe it spins though. The ultimate meaning we compose is determined partly by our relationships with the many in our lives who are "those who count"[1] and partly by a host of others of whom we may be only dimly aware. Faith is a patterning, connective, relational activity embodied and shaped not within the individual alone but in the comfort and challenges of the company we keep.[2]

The Power of Tribe

We all need "tribe." The power of tribe is a strong feature of how we as human beings have made meaning throughout the ages and continue to do so throughout our lives. For most of human history, we have lived in relatively small tribal groups. We need a place or places of dependable connection, where we have a keen sense of the familiar: ways of knowing and being that anchor us in a secure sense of belonging and social cohesion.[3]

Networks of belonging take various forms. Some are manifest as an obviously present and easy-to-identify circle of face-to-face relationships confirming identity and security: families, neighborhoods, workplaces, athletic teams, religious communities, or the regulars at the local cafe. But they may also be scattered geographically or otherwise dispersed. Increasingly, many find their tribe linked by digital technologies—with only occasional direct encounters—a network of belonging stretched thin in which ironically one may feel at once both extensively connected and very much alone. Even those who choose a life of total solitude still and necessarily embody a self formed by a history of relationships with those who count, both living and dead. One could, for instance, have a strong sense of identification with a historical figure one has never met but who serves nevertheless as a touchstone for one's life and values. It is also the case that a growing ecological consciousness has reawakened many to a sense of meaningful kinship that includes animals, trees, birds, and the creatures of the sea—a felt kinship that confirms one's own sense of place in the order of things and orients meaning and purpose.

Freedom and Boundaries

The power of any truly viable network of belonging is twofold. First, the sense of connection and security it offers provides the freedom to grow and become. Second, every network of belonging has norms and boundaries that one cannot cross and still belong. Thus every network of belonging simultaneously represents freedom and constraint.[4] Social norms, for example, may manifest collective wisdom that protects and nourishes the individual, but they can also distort reality or unnecessarily limit the promise of human life.[5] Transformations in the meaning of the self, therefore, may also require transformation of the social world—a mutual recomposing.

If we recognize this power of "the surround" in the story of human becoming, we begin to see that learning to recognize a particular form of meaning-making or a new stage in human development is not a matter of diagnosis and treatment. Rather, it prompts questions, What do we now mean to each other?[6] How does the community respond to the life of a developing person? What does a person's growth mean for the life of the community? Is the relationship mutually nourishing and sustainable? Thus, embedded in the story of human development is a story about transformation in the forms of community.

Balancing Two Great Yearnings

The power of the social milieu has been reasonably well acknowledged in psychological descriptions of children and adolescents. We know that children are profoundly affected by parents, families, teachers, playmates, and schoolmates. Peer groups are well factored into the story of adolescent development. But as people move into adulthood, their relationship to community may become confused. Because the notion of independence is so powerful in Western society and in the canons of adult psychology, the need for family and community may appear to contradict the achievement of adulthood. If the mark of psychological adulthood is autonomy or self-sufficiency, and maturity is measured in terms only of degrees of individuation, the ongoing and essential role of community in adult life can become almost invisible.

The communion features of the psyche at the threshold of adulthood remain in focus, however, if we remember that the motion of meaning-making is located in the oscillation between "two great yearnings": the yearning to exercise one's own distinct agency (one's own power to affect one's world, to make a difference) and the yearning for belonging, inclusion, relationship, and intimacy. Human becoming can be partially understood as a series of temporary resolutions of the desires for differentiation and connection; every developmental era is a new solution to this universal tension.[7]

Forms of Community

Earlier we explored the development of forms of knowing (cognition) and then forms of dependence (feeling and affect). Now we are prepared to recognize the corresponding forms of community that nourish the development of human life.

	Adolescent/ Conventional		Emerging Adult	Tested Adult	Mature Adult
Forms of Knowing	Authority-bound, Dualistic (tacit)	→ Unqualified relativism	→ Probing commitment (ideological)	→ Tested commitment (systemic)	→ Convictional commitment (paradoxical)
Forms of Dependence	Dependent/ Counterdependent		→ Fragile inner-dependence	→ Confident inner-dependence	→ Inter-dependent
Forms of Community	Conventional	Diffuse	→ Mentoring community	→ Self-selected class/group	→ Open to other

Conventional Community

If meaning and faith are composed in Authority-bound, dependent forms, composing self and world takes place within a group or groups characterized primarily by some form of face-to-face relationships. These groupings (which may occur also in some virtual forums) are conventional because they are marked by uncritical conformity to cultural and subcultural norms and interests. They may be defined by loyalty to any one, or a combination, of ethnic-familial ties, social-class expectations, regional perspectives, a religious system, a technoscientific ethos, peer values, gender roles, or media-crafted attractions. Conventional community includes simply "those like us." This form of community corresponds to the Authority-bound and dualistic form of cognition, in which Authority (implicit or explicit) defines us and them.

Diffuse Community

As one begins to gain a measure of critical reflection and discovers a relativized world, it is often the conventional social assumptions that are first called into question. Discovering that someone who is "other" (someone who was previously "them") contradicts assumptions about who "we" are and who "they" are may be a first step in questioning assumed social arrangements.

As the social horizon thus expands, the form of community may shift from a well-defined set of assumed associations to a considerably more diffuse form of belonging. An exploratory, experimental, and tentative quality of relationship may prevail as one ventures into a wider sphere of belonging. One young woman recalled how when she began to discover that she was "clueless" about what the world was really about, she actively put herself in as many different social contexts as possible to challenge her assumptions. This was part of questioning her stability and security in the universe—"a major upheaval and a period of searching."

If any one truth or perspective is thought to be as good as another, there can be a corresponding sense that perhaps any sort of relationship may be as good as any other. If unqualified relativism prevails, sustaining any particular relationship may become problematic. This is not to say that relationships become a matter of indifference. Quite the contrary may be the case as the person, now feeling a bit at sea, has both a new freedom to explore the widening horizon of life and a new vulnerability to the power of every possible relationship. Thus (and somewhat ironically) the person awash in the sea of unqualified relativism may be sustained by the subjective experience of human connectedness, letting it take what forms it may for good or ill—a spar to cling to when the shipwreck of certainty dumps us into a seemingly meaningless world.

Because, as we recognized earlier, unqualified relativism is difficult to sustain in the real world of choices and consequences, most will begin to seek a more adequate pattern of meaning—a place of commitment within a relativized world. It is here that access to an appropriate network of belonging plays a key role because it serves to confirm a new sense of self and supports the composing of a new (and sometimes hard-won) faith. Fowler described this form of social awareness as a "self-selected class or group," but here again we can discern two forms: one that is characteristic of the emerging adult era and another that signals a more tested adulthood.

Mentoring Community

For the emerging adult, community finds its most powerful form in a mentoring community. As we have seen, the growth of a critically aware and inner-dependent self should in no way suggest that the need for a network of belonging disappears. Rather, there is a readiness for a new kind of belonging. Young adulthood is nurtured into being and its promise is most powerfully realized through participation in a community that embodies a trustworthy alternative to earlier Authority-bound knowing. A mentoring community offers hospitality to the potential of the emerging adult self, poses challenging questions, and provides access to worthy dreams of self and world.

A critical, cognitive perspective is typically not enough to precipitate a significant transformation of self, world, and "God." Critical awareness in dialogue with a single mentoring figure, though influential, may still be insufficient to reorder faith itself. Rather, it is the combination of the developmental stance of the emerging adult with the challenge and encouragement of a mentor, *grounded in belonging to a compatible social group* that ignites the transforming power of the emerging adult era. A *mentoring community* can confirm the hope that meaning can be reconstituted beyond the Abyss—there will be a new home.

A viable network of belonging is key. If a person becomes critically aware and begins to take responsibility for his reappraisal of faith, then recomposing truth must necessarily include reassessing his own sense of trust and power. In such moments, the recognition, presence, and faith of others can make all the difference. The person can begin to move in new ways in the adult world of responsibility for discerning the nature of life itself, making judgments, and choosing actions—in the intellectual life, in the world of work, and within one's family, community, and the wider commons.

Thus it is particularly useful here to remember the value of thinking less in terms of developmental journeys and more in terms of transformations in one's sense of home. Imagine a series of concentric circles. The innermost is the family of origin; the next, the neighborhood; the next, the larger community; then the world of first adult work; and so on. The person, remaining at the center yet transcending each new threshold, experiences a growing sphere of belonging and participation. Becoming an emerging adult with an enlarged capacity for critical, inner-dependent thought and developing the kind of inner-dependence that grounds responsible participation within this expansion of reality does not happen easily or all at once. The emerging, still fragile inner-dependence of an emerging adult self remains significantly vulnerable to the prevailing social milieu, on both sides of the new threshold. The emerging adult has gained a new strength yet is also vulnerable in new ways. She will have her antennae out and be highly attuned to what will be asked and allowed. The social milieu, therefore, retains significant power.

In the second year of a professional degree program at a prestigious school, a twenty-six-year-old reflects on the first year:

> Everyone who gets here is such a strong individual, and then you really give up a lot of that individuality, I think, and sort of succumb to all these group pressures and learn in the way that the school wants you to learn, and the whole group thing is very powerful. It's incredibly strong, and you find yourself succumbing to these norms that you might not necessarily believe in.
>
> I think in the beginning I felt like, "Oh, that's the way it is, and I have to fit into this in order to be here," because I don't think I have the confidence to say, "Well, I feel differently than all of the seventy other people in this classroom." I think it's hard to get out of the mind frame that there's *an* answer, there's *a* way of analyzing, there's *a* way of thinking. . . .
>
> You have to . . . realize that there are many more people out there like you, and you just have to find them . . . but when you are only in the second month, you don't have that kind of perspective.

Notice that this emerging adult does not search for a way to transcend the need for a compatible community; rather, she seeks a network of belonging in which the yet fragile self can flourish with integrity.

Thus the character of the social context to which the emerging adult has access may be the most crucial element in transforming what an emerging adult "knows." Indeed, John Henry

Newman was so convinced of the power of the social environment to train, mold, and enlarge the mind that he proposed that
if he had to choose between a school without residence hall life
and one with only the life of the residence hall, he would choose
the latter, where "the conversation of all is a series of lectures to
each."[8] Moreover, Damon contends that in the formation of
purpose two conditions must apply: (1) forward movement
toward a fulfilling purpose and (2) *a structure of social support
consistent with that effort.*[9]

Again, it is useful to remember that the emerging adult is
attracted to a social context that appears to be compatible with
his or her inner truth or at least with some very important part
of that truth. Simply wanting to belong is no longer enough.
The emerging adult self depends on and responds to those individuals and groups that express patterns of meaning resonant
with the experience and the new critical awareness of the still
fragile, inner-dependent self. There is, however, profound recep-
tiveness to any network of belonging that appears to promise a
place of nurture for the potential self, even (and sometimes
especially) if its forms are demanding, calling forth the new
strength. A place that recognizes the gifts and potential competence of the emerging adult requires only as much inner-
dependent strength as the young adult yet has and provides
room for exploration, meets the yearning for power and communion in their emerging adult forms. A mentoring community
does just that. It offers a network of belonging in which emerging adults feel recognized as both who they are and who they are
yet becoming.

Inevitably Ideological

As the emerging adult recomposes meaning with fresh, critical
self-awareness, shifting from an Authority-bound, tacit, interpersonal orientation to an explicit, systemic mode, a new "ideological" quality appears. By *ideology* I mean structured and largely

rational attempts to understand self and world and to prescribe corrections and directions. By this definition, it may, of course, be argued that all structures of meaning are ideological. Ideology, however, tends to connote modes of thinking and holding ideas that are at once speculative and ideal. A kind of zealotry may occur because the new revelatory meaning that the young adult has had the courage to step out on must be affirmed with great tenacity, for the new meaning must hold a new and still fragile self. That is, the emerging adult must sometimes hold new meanings most fiercely when working up the gumption to make the passage off a once-stalwart (but now seemingly leaking and inadequate) ship that has hitherto held the self and onto a promising but yet unknown new shore. Hence the appeal of an ideological stance that offers a kind of clarity and purity of vision (the ideal), whether the issues are large or small. Thus the tentativeness and ambivalence of emerging adult meaning-making renders it inevitably ideological.

The emerging adult most thrives when there is access to a mentoring network of belonging centered in the strength of worthy meanings that impart some degree of distance from the conventions of his past and from the larger society with which he must still negotiate terms of entry. This is why Keniston described the affiliations of this period as having an over-against quality.[10] This quality is, however, distinguishable from the simple counterdependence described previously. The emerging adult is over-against the world as it is, but in a mode that is more discerning and dialogical than simply pushing away from the dock.

This dialogue between self and world may initially take the form of a fairly strong dichotomy. As we have seen, when one begins to take responsibility for one's own meaning-making there are unavoidable tensions among competing values and life choices: freedom to travel versus getting ahead, carrying on family traditions versus going one's own way, guaranteed financial security versus a riskier option, stress versus leisure. These are dichotomies, however, that allow for shades of gray, in contrast to the stark polarities of the Authority-bound and dualistic mode of the previous era. Nevertheless, in a premature bid for clarity and confidence, the emerging adult is vulnerable to collapsing the tensions of felt dichotomies.

In contrast to the tested adult, the emerging adult does not yet have much practice in holding a full range of complex feeling and thought that a more mature adulthood requires. And it is precisely the awareness that all perspectives are relative that may energize a fierce, sometimes tenacious reach for a place to stand within the anxiety of that reality (although the fragile, inner-dependent stance can in some measure recognize its ideology as a choice, unlike the embedded adolescent or conventional adult). Shelly, an undergrad student in her final two years of college, suffered a very strong sense of dichotomized tensions, which she described as follows:

parents	vs.	self
religion	vs.	agnosticism
sweet	vs.	sassy
God	vs.	empiricism
believer	vs.	psychologist
helping others	vs.	materialism
values (control)	vs.	experience (emotion)

In the midst of these tensions, she did, on numerous occasions, land on one side or the other. If the voice of a boyfriend prevailed, she abandoned her more feminist perspective; if anxiety over her mother's health became too great, she tried to return to an earlier faith; if the study of behavioral psychology was compelling, she dismissed "God" for empiricism. Then she told us:

> I worked with [the dean] in an internship and we talked about religion . . . and . . . just lately people have been really reaching out to me. [A psychology professor] and I are in similar places.

So we've spent time talking . . . again the hot issues, and I'm open to being a believer but . . . I'm comfortable and aware now that whatever I come up with will not be the traditional, and that's OK. It can still be bona fide even though I know everyone doesn't agree with it . . . and I don't have to fit into a niche. So I'm sorting it through and it feels comfortable and it feels like it'll come. . . . And it's also very freeing. . . . I am a deviant. I'm way off the scale as a deviant and I feel very good about that, in fact I'm . . . probably proud of it more than anything else, and I know I'll get flak from my parents. They've taken awhile to adjust to my being a Ph.D., which has not happened yet, but I'm on the road, and they know it. . . . They wanted me to get married, maybe get a master's degree but . . . I want to go to an environment where I'll really be tested. It seems I haven't needed a God, and I think maybe in Chicago I'll need one.

In Shelly's description of this push-and-pull, there seems to be a good deal of pushing away from the dock. Yet when she describes her resolution of these tensions, she seems not to stand in a place of simple opposition. Rather, she seems to find a certain relief in describing herself as "deviant." It is a strong word, but it seems to reflect both the freedom of her emerging inner-dependence and a way of naming herself that is able to accept, articulate, and affirm a sense of engaged choice and struggle. She strengthens this new emerging voice by seeking alliances with those who buttress this new stance.

In the company of good mentors, Shelly accepts deviance, tentativeness, and testing as a place to stand apart from previously held patterns of meaning and affiliation. She remains, as do the rest of us, in significant measure dependent on the forms of belonging available in any given context. But now there is an enlarged awareness of "who I belong with," a diminished desire to fit in no matter what and less sense of being utterly at the mercy of the social expectations within which the self happens to be located.

In a similar fashion, we hear a young man with growing inner-dependent strength questioning earlier assumptions and, in the context of networks of belonging, recomposing his sense of self, meaning, purpose, and faith.

Raised in a conventional and secular home, Brad tells us his family celebrated Christmas and Easter, but rarely went to church. As a teen-ager,

> I adopted my father's point of view and declared myself an atheist. My first couple of years at the university were no different in terms of religious faith. I found myself in the same conversations about religion—agreeing with my fellow atheists about the absurdity of God, while challenging the believers about the possibility of God. It was not until a conversation with a close friend's father and sister that I altered my view on the topic of faith. I was visiting my friend and his family in Munich. Only because I didn't know them well enough to voice my opinion, I decided only to listen to a conversation they had about religion. There were three major players—the sister (religious/Christian type), the father (agnostic/philosopher type), and the friend's other friend (violent atheist type). I listened long and hard. By the end, I realized how ridiculous I had been sounding. The father convinced me to at least consider myself an agnostic, because when it came down to it, I really didn't have any good proof that God didn't exist. I decided, however, that the sister didn't have any solid evidence for the existence of God either.
>
> But this is when I promised myself that I would try and be more open-minded. And this is what I practice now— open-mindedness with a little bit of research.
>
> So, when I was offered a job planting trees for the summer with a Christian group, I took it. This was another turning point. I attended their church services regularly and did my best to open my mind fully to the possibility of Jesus as a savior and the Christian faith on the whole. I thought, "so many million people can't be wrong," so I attempted to learn and accept. I remember wanting to believe in what the rest of them believed in. They seemed so at peace, sure of themselves and sure of

each other. I was envious of their comfort level. I loved the sense of community—everyone helped everyone else, selfishness was at a minimum, and the general air of the camp was just so positive.

By the end of the planting season, however, I decided that they were too sure of themselves and of each other. And God was thrown around too loosely—doing too many things for too many people. If he exists, I felt they trivialized his existence. Their comfort level was too high and their tolerance of nonbelievers was more like pity. . . . There was not enough doubting for my liking. But I still do like the sense of community and cooperation they/we were able to establish— something I still envy organized religion for. (I also learned from them a small sense of global responsibility that has grown in me since that time.)

So! I came out thinking that Christianity by itself, and probably all of the other religions by themselves, couldn't answer all of my questions on their own. So I continue to learn as much as I can.

Self-Selected Class or Group

In the ongoing development of meaning-making and faith, such learning can settle into a tested adult faith over time. The tested adult can maintain the tension of earlier dichotomies, especially between self and the larger social world. As one becomes more confident, having composed a meaning and a voice of one's own that is less threatened by every competing point of view, fiercely ideological and over-against modes can be relinquished. The world can be more readily engaged as well as critiqued. The form of community of this confident adult self is not the ideologically compatible and mentoring community on which the emerging adult is dependent in a primary way. Rather, the tested adult values a self-selected class or group that shares the meanings that are now consolidated within the self.[11]

This new capacity for a confident sense of authority within, and thus a more relaxed engagement with others in the world as it is, is both strengthened and made vulnerable by a corresponding willingness to make pragmatic accommodations that no longer appear to threaten the essential integrity of the self. Adult faith can sustain respectful awareness of communities other than its own and it can tolerate, if not embrace, the felt tensions between inevitable choices.

Yet this form of faith also has its limitations as well as its strengths in terms of its adequacy to align the self with reality. In this era of development, though having the capacity for critical thought, we may still remain significantly tribal, keeping company with those like us. Hence, though one's new network of belonging may be, indeed, more "self-selected" and much more diverse in some respects, its members may nevertheless hold similar political, religious, and philosophical views and share the loyalties and interests of, for example, a particular economic class. Even the most cosmopolitan and liberal of mind often discover, on close examination of their own network of belonging, that those who count are also in significant respects of like mind.

Toward Greater Complexity and Inclusion

In *Beyond Our Tribal Gods*, Ronald Marstin was the first to forcefully elaborate the essential linkages between the development of faith and the capacity to move beyond provincial perceptions and narrowly tribal forms of community. He boldly affirmed that implicit in developmental theory is the perception that each succeeding stage, era, or form of consciousness *is* better in that each represents a capacity to account for more, to handle greater complexity, and thus the potential for greater inclusivity.[12] Marstin's boldness was not rooted in arrogant elitism but was rather a sober assessment of the competencies of mind and soul that social-environmental justice requires. In other words, if justice is a matter of who and what is included or excluded, then just as complex perspective-taking is essential to adequate moral reasoning so too the character of one's composition of the whole of reality (one's faith) determines what one finds tolerable and intolerable.

Marstin understood that human beings develop "because we *need* to."[13] We recompose meaning, purpose, and faith when we encounter the "other" (other people, other knowledge, other experience) in such a way that "we are left with no other choice, short of blocking out what we can no longer block out with any degree of honesty."[14] When human development happens well, we embrace a new way of interpreting the world because it can account for things that the old way no longer could. We can acknowledge considerations previously ignored, take more facts into account, and extend hospitality to questions that earlier we could not entertain.

This developmental perspective celebrates the promise for human life inherent in the ongoing encounter with a world inhabited by other selves and other beings with their own needs, an encounter that requires incessant recomposing of what is true for the self in relationship to a world of others. As Marstin grasped, cognitive development surely requires relativizing the tribal gods—recognition of the limitations of one's provincial ultimacy and a subsequent recomposition of one's faith. He was, however, keenly aware that for many, leaving their tribal gods appears to lead only to adopting a new set of tribal gods. (This occurs, for example, whenever people settle into a self-selected class or group that offers an easy pluralism, the leisure to experiment that creates merely a private truth—while those who suffer throughout the world remain unrecognized.[15])

In other words, critical awareness that prompts movement to a self-selected class or group represents a more adequate *structure* of knowing, but it may not represent an advance in the *content* of knowing unless it yields a larger inclusiveness, which in turn can lead to a greater measure of social and ecological justice. Those of critical but like mind may even represent diminished concern for others, if critical awareness leads only to forming a network of belonging that harbors fateful distortions and new loyalties too narrowly drawn.

Open to the Other

Just as an encounter with a person, community, or idea that is initially perceived as "other" may prompt the development of the critical thought of the emerging adult, similarly the tested adult may also undergo further transformation, prompted by a deepening receptivity to "otherness." If one continues to bump up against those who are significantly different from one's self, and listens to differing and compelling points of view that one recognizes as more adequate, one's tested, inner-dependent self begins to discover how we are never finished in the work of comprehending the Mystery we all share. In the ongoing dialogue with the other, still more adequate intimations of truth may emerge. The fundamental yearning for a fitting network of belonging may finally yield a still more profound understanding and practice of inclusiveness, because it is truer. Ongoing meaning-making necessarily leads to challenging the system that protects some while neglecting others: "Issues of social justice," says Marstin, "are essentially about who is to be cared for and who neglected, who is to be included in our community of concern and who excluded, whose point of view is to be taken seriously and whose ignored."[16] As meaning-making in its most comprehensive dimensions—that is, faith—grows more mature, it challenges all the established answers to these questions.

This challenge becomes embodied in a form of community that recognizes the other as "truly other" yet part of a complex and differentiated whole. This form of community appears in its strongest form in the postmidlife period. It is characterized by a longing for communion with those who are profoundly other than the self, not as a matter of mere political correctness, or ideology, or ethical commitment, but as a longing in the soul for an embodied faithfulness to the interdependence that we are.

The Value of Recognizing the Emerging Adult Era

By combining the three dimensions of development we have described—thinking-knowing, feeling-dependence, and belonging-community—we are able to portray the place and role of the emerging adult era in the development of a mature adult faith. This model suggests a series of transformations by which we may become more fittingly at home in the universe, moving from Authority-bound forms of meaning-making anchored in conventional assumed community, through the wilderness of counterdependence and unqualified relativism, to a committed, inner-dependent mode of composing meaning, initially fragile and later tested. It challenges notions of adulthood that are cast in an Authority-bound form of faith by inviting attention to the possibility of further movement toward a still more mature faith—an engaged wisdom grounded in the conviction of inter-dependence, seeking communion with those who are profoundly other than the self.

This portrayal is but one way of telling a story that could be woven with other elements, other perspectives, and in other proportions—each conveying additional facets of human meaning-making. One of the most serious limitations of this model is the possible implication (and not infrequent charge) that the activity of faith is represented as linear and fixed rather than as the dynamic, multidimensional, creative process that it is in reality. Again, a spiral model with a recentering process, for instance, might capture elements that this portrayal does not.

The critical feature this portrayal does reveal, however, is a place of integrity in the journey toward mature adult faith that is distinctively characteristic of emerging adulthood. It brings into the foreground of our awareness a mode of meaning-making that theorists and institutional structures overlook at our collective peril. Accurate naming is an act of creation. Naming the power, vulnerability, inherent ambivalence, and the vital tasks of emerging adult faith helps us recognize it when it arises in our midst. If we understand its articulate nature and special hunger for mentors and mentoring communities, we are better able to respond. There is much at stake—for emerging adults and for the life of the commons—in whether or not we do this well. Never before in the human life cycle (and never again) is there the same developmental readiness for asking big questions and forming worthy dreams. In every generation, the renewal of human life is dependent in significant measure on the questions that are posed during this era in our meaning-making. The dreams those questions may seed yield the promise of our shared future.

By what alchemy do powerful questions yield worthy dreams? Shifting our focus from the forms of meaning-making to the contents, we turn to an exploration of the role of images and the imagination in the development of meaning, purpose, and faith.

Chapter Seven

Imagination

The Core of Learning and the Heart of Leadership

Scott Russell Sanders was trying to break his son's sullen silence following their quarrel as they bounced along a rutted road on what was supposed to be a father-and-son hiking trip. As he recalls the moment in *Hunting for Hope: A Father's Journeys*, Scott demanded of his son:

> "So what are my hang-ups? . . . How do I ruin everything?"
> "You don't want to know," he said.
> "I want to know . . ."
> "You wouldn't understand," he said.
> "Try me."
> He cut a look at me, shrugged, then stared back through the
>   windshield.
> "You're just so out of touch."
> "With what?"
> "With my whole world. You hate everything that's fun. You
>   hate television and movies and video games. You hate my
>   music."
> "I like some of your music. I just don't like it loud."
> "You hate advertising," he said quickly, rolling now. "You hate
>   billboards and lotteries and developers and logging
>   companies and big corporations. You hate snowmobiles
>   and jet skis. You hate malls and fashions and cars."
> "You're still on my case because I won't buy a Jeep?" I said,
>   harking back to another old argument.
> "Forget Jeeps. You look at any car and all you think is
>   pollution, traffic, roadside crap. You say fast-food's

134

poisoning our bodies and TV's poisoning our minds. You
think the Internet is just another scam for selling stuff.
You think business is a conspiracy to rape the earth."

"None of that bothers you?"

"Of course it does. But that's the world. That's where we've
got to live. It's not going to go away just because you
don't approve. What's the good of spitting on it?"

"I don't spit on it. I grieve over it."

He was still for a moment, then resumed quietly. "What's the
good of grieving if you can't change anything?"

"Who says you can't change anything?"

"You do. Maybe not with your mouth, but with your
eyes. . . . Your view of things is totally dark. It bums me
out. You make me feel the planet's dying and people are
to blame and nothing can be done about it. There's no
room for hope. Maybe you can get by without hope, but I
can't. I've got a lot of living still to do. I have to believe
there's a way we can get out of this mess. Otherwise
what's the point? Why study, why work—why do anything
if it's all going to hell?"[1]

This son is not just frustrated with his father. He is struggling
to make meaning. He is asking the big question, "Why?" He is
searching for purpose. He is reaching for hope. He is seeking a
faith to live by. He is claiming the possibility of an alternative
imagination to the one his father seems to offer.

Now capable of critical reflection on his father's thinking as
well as his own, this emerging adult is moving into an inner-
dependent but still fragile mode of meaning-making, appropriately dependent on the images and narratives available to him.
He is keenly aware of some of the most significant challenges of
our time. He is willing to work and study but he also wants to
have some fun in this life. He wants to believe that things can
be changed and that "there's a way we can get out of this mess."
He is poised on a threshold of both learning and leadership.

Threshold Existence

As human beings, we find ourselves again and again on the thresholds of time, space, and the unseen. Despite the massive evidence of the mundane, the ugly, and the fearful in our experience, at the core of the human spirit lies an amazingly resilient intuition that there is more for us to live into, embrace, and be embraced by. We sense that we participate in possibilities wider and deeper than we have yet realized: the creative work of our own lives, a more just society, and a more profound knowing and loving of life in its manifold forms. Time and the world of space and sense awaken and beckon our longing for enhanced participation in a coherent and sacred universe.

As we have begun to see, emerging adulthood is a time for becoming more conscious of this "threshold existence"[2]—an awareness that we do not dwell in static assumptions but live always on the verge, on the borderland of something more. With abstract, hypothetical thought well established, and critical thought and an inner-dependent sense of authority taking form, the emerging adult is ripe for developing an informed passion for the ideal. This is the time for initiation into the powers of imagination and for learning to "self-superintend"[3] this power and its consequences.

Imagination Versus Fantasy

In Western culture, imagination is often equated with fantasy. Imagination and fantasy, are, however, *not* the same thing. *Fanciful* in its common usage connotes "the unreal." Indeed, Samuel Taylor Coleridge identified "fancy" as having a function quite other than the imagination. Fancy, he explained, takes images already in the memory and arranges and rearranges them associatively or aggregatively.[4] Fancy, for example, can associate talking and mice, composing a Mickey Mouse to reign over Fantasyland. This is not to say that fantasy is necessarily trivial.

Free association can play a significant role in exploring possibility in the quest for adequate truth. Fantasy alone, however, cannot finally compose truth. In contrast, the work of the imagination is to compose the real.[5]

Imagination: A Composing and Shaping Activity

At least since Immanuel Kant, we have been aware that all of our learning and knowing is a composing activity.[6] The human mind does not receive the world-as-it-is in itself. Rather, we act on the world to compose reality (or better, we interact with it in a mutual composing). As Suzanne Langer expressed so well, the human mind is "not merely a great transmitter, a super switchboard [or computer]; it is better likened to a great transformer. The current of experience that passes through it undergoes a change in character, . . . [as] it is sucked into [a particular] stream of symbols which constitutes a human mind."[7]

Following on Kant, Coleridge also identified imagination as the composing activity of the mind, but he extended its significance. Coleridge was intrigued with the German word for imagination, *Einbildungskraft*. *Kraft* denotes power; *bildung*, shaping; and *ein*, one. Imagination is "the power of shaping into one."[8] Coleridge made visible the indivisible bond between imagination and faith: understanding that faith is the place of experience and the imagination—the process of composing a coherent and trustworthy pattern of meaning from the disparate elements of our experience.[9]

Imagination: The Highest Power of the Knowing Mind

Coleridge described imagination as the highest power of Reason, which includes all of the powers of the mind (sense, perception, understanding, and so on). That is, imagination serves as the living power and the prime agent of all human perception; it dissolves to re-create, struggles to unify, is essentially vital, and is a repetition in the finite mind of the eternal act of creation.[10]

When Coleridge describes imagination as the primary agent shaping all perception, this does not imply that people simply imagine the world into being, as though the world does not exist and the human imagination merely conjures it up. Rather, we compose that which we find.[11] The imagination thus orients perception (one notices and chooses certain details over countless others) and informs how one makes sense of discrete elements, forming a distinctive pattern. In other words, the imagination works as a filter and then a lens. It is in these ways that our perceptions are created by means of the imagination.

Moreover, although this process of imagination goes on without our conscious awareness, it can, to some degree, become conscious. We can reflect on our own experience of learning, and we can observe the process of imagination as it "dissolves to re-create" and "struggles to unify." We can feel that it is essentially "vital"—alive and dynamic. In moments, we glimpse how the motion of creation moves in and through us—our imagination participating—as Coleridge would have it—in the activity of Spirit, the ongoing motion of life.

Thus for Coleridge, Reason includes but is more than analysis and logic narrowly construed. Reason is the highest and most complete power of the mind, and its completing, unifying, transcending activity is wrought by means of the imagination—"the breath of the power of God." Imagination—the power of shaping into one—is the power by which meaning-making in its most comprehensive dimensions—faith—is composed.[12] Therefore, if it matters how we think, it matters that we understand the role of imagination in human intelligence.

Imagination—for Good and for Ill

As we are keenly aware, the human imagination works for both good and ill. Thus a crucial insight for our purposes is the

Enlightenment and postmodern insistence that if human beings are to awaken to the fulfillment of our own humanity, we must become critically aware of and responsible for the powers of imagination. The human being is most mature when the powers of imagination are fully awake, alive to the deep motion of the universe and to the power of persons to participate in this motion of life to create (and to distort) self and world.

Imagination: Process, Content, Action

Three dimensions of the activity of imagination are essential to understanding the formation of meaning, purpose, and faith. First, imagination is a *process*. It is the process through which our most profound learning occurs, the power by which our worldview can be recast, the power by which we move from faith to faith. The transformations of the forms of faith that we have described (such as the movement from assumed Authority-bound faith to the emergence of an inner-dependent, probing commitment) occur by means of the transformative process of imagination.

Second, embedded in the process of imagination is the power to give form to our knowing—the power of naming—the *content* of feeling and thought. By employing images, we name self and world and conceive ideas and the ideal, the worthy, the good—as well as recognize what is false and toxic. Images are the content that the underlying structures of thought, feeling, and belonging hold. Images lend their form to hold and name our experience and thus render it meaningful. *Images give form to faith.* For example, two years out of college and talking with a friend, twenty-four-year-old Stacy grapples with how she can and can't name her understanding of ultimate reality:

> I believe that the universe is organized and interconnected. For me, it's not a question of God as a single entity running the whole show. I have a big problem with the personification of

God. God is not human—and more importantly not male. The word "God" seems to imply that Universal Presence has an ego, and I have a problematic relationship with that idea. I prefer "The Force" or something that is egoless. I believe there is a plan or pattern, and the daily struggle for myself, and for people in general, is to figure out one's place in that plan. I don't know who it is or how it works, but people call that "God."

Like Sanders's son, Stacy is living the process of making meaning and doing the hard work of theology: seeking understanding, experimenting, sifting and sorting out images by which to name and respond to reality as she perceives it. Unless they are consistently distracted or otherwise numbed to these big questions, emerging adults who develop the capacity for critical thought begin to do this work for themselves, sorting out reality on the largest canvas they can conceive—an ongoing act of imagination. As Stacy seems to recognize, it makes a difference, for example, whether we name ultimate reality Father, Mother, Nothingness, the Tao, a unified field, the Force, the Holy One, the Universe, the Abyss, or Mystery. It makes a difference whether one feels and names the character of ultimate reality as loving, indifferent, hostile, or however the reader might name it, might imagine it.

Third, imagination is an act of creativity that matters because it manifests as embodied *action* in the world. Human beings participate in the ongoing creation of life itself, for better and for worse, continually birthing our shared reality. Our imaginations of life move or inhibit the mind, heart, and hand. We create forms of governance and economic life, produce communication technologies, design new feats of architecture, develop religious ritual, envision medications, compose music, discern theories of the origins of the universe, and invent ways of playing and ways of making war. It is by means of the imagination that we entertain the great questions of our time and craft the fears and dreams we live by. Imagination is more than mental activity narrowly understood. Imagination is embodied and drives our actions.

Learning and Leadership

As we can begin to see, imagination may be understood as the core process by which transformative learning occurs, the process by which we "change our mind." We may also begin to recognize that an understanding of the human imagination is a vital pathway into understanding the art and practice of leadership. Moreover, as emerging adults are the stewards of our shared future, every college, university, corporate, and military recruiter claims to be preparing tomorrow's leadership. What kind of learning does this require? We do well to recognize that in a dramatically changing world, both the process of learning and the practice of leadership that are now required are illumined by a robust understanding of the human imagination.

Adaptive Leadership

As recognized in Chapter One, we live at one of those great hinge points in history when our institutions and our social covenants are under review. In this context, our assumptions about the purpose and practice of leadership are also being reconsidered. Ronald Heifetz, author of *Leadership Without Easy Answers*, has with his colleagues at Harvard's Center for Public Leadership developed an approach to understanding the art and practice of leadership (and a way of teaching it) that is a response to this task.[13]

This approach makes two useful distinctions: (1) Although leadership tends to be equated with positional authority (assuming the boss, dean, president, CEO, captain, and so on is also the "leader"), Heifetz, however, distinguishes the practice of *authority* from the practice of *leadership*. Authority functions to maintain a steady state within the social group. Leadership, in contrast, is understood as *the ability to mobilize people to face their toughest challenges*, that is, leadership helps people move from the current pattern of organization through the swamp of the unknown to a more adequate pattern. Leadership enables a group, community, or society to reimagine what is and imagine into what can be. (2) A corresponding distinction is drawn between *technical problems*—problems that are amenable to routine management and expertise already in hand—and *adaptive challenges*—challenges that require innovation and new learning (and often include loss and grief).[14] Although even very difficult problems can sometimes yield to answers already in hand, an adaptive challenge, by contrast, signals dramatically new conditions that require a creative response.

Here the word *adaptive* does not suggest mere accommodation. Rather, the art and practice of leadership requires the capacity for a kind of social-political artistry—the ability to reimagine and orchestrate a learning process within a group, organization, community, or society that must undergo transformation into new ways of life. In this view, leadership can be practiced from "wherever you sit," as everyone is a part of the pattern that must undergo change and can have an affect within the field of action. The art and skill of adaptive leadership is centered in learning how to intervene in complex systems to catalyze the collective imagination and encourage adaptive learning.

Adaptive Learning

In *Leadership Can Be Taught: A Bold Approach for a Complex World*, I describe, interpret, and assess the Heifetz theory and pedagogy[15] and suggest that one of biggest questions of our time is, "What will it be important to know for citizenship and leadership in the twenty-first century?" Are we preparing people for a world that isn't going to be there? [16] These questions invite us to consider the call in our time for transformative, adaptive learning, and the practice of an "anticipatory imagination."[17]

A Paradigm—a Grammar of Transformation and Learning

The work of James Loder (an educator and clinical psychologist) and John Paul Lederach (a mediator in places of persistent, cyclical violence) combine to provide a grammar of transformation that serves as a paradigm for how the process of imagination works. It charts the core process of adaptive learning, illuminating the heart of adaptive leadership. Loder identifies five critical elements in the process of imagination as they bear on human development, learning, and meaning-making.[18] It is helpful to think of them as five "moments" within the act of imagination (and the reader may recognize this sequence named in other ways[19]).

1. Conscious conflict
2. Pause
3. Image or insight
4. Repatterning
5. Interpretation[20]

It is by moving through the ebb and flow of these five moments that we, as individuals and groups, come to new horizons of insight, knowledge, meaning, faith, and new ways of living in the world.

Conscious Conflict—Paradoxical Curiosity

Whether or not we hold a formal theory of growth and change, we know from our own experience that insight, transformation, and new patterns of life often arise out of conflicting circumstances that may be, initially at least, confusing, disturbing, even devastating. Other times conflict arises from becoming intrigued or dazzled by wonder. In any case, the moment of conscious conflict occurs when something doesn't seem to fit our previous experience and the meanings we have made, and we are set at odds with our usual perceptions of things. Conflict may be present in an unconscious or preconscious sense, but it does not become available for recomposing meaning and the transformation of faith until it becomes conscious. Good teaching and good leadership seek ways to recognize or evoke a real question that fosters this kind of dissonance in the mind and heart of the learner. In the practice of leadership, one is attentive to the hidden issues, the conflicts just below the surface of business as usual, that are waiting to be artfully surfaced and worked in the life of the group.

Doubt. Conscious conflict may foster doubt. Doubt is often viewed as a threat to faith. But viewed as a manifestation of conscious conflict, we may see it in quite a different light. Doubt can serve the development of meaning and faith.[21] Doubt may emerge in the form of the collapse of previous assumptions, vague restlessness, intense weariness with things as they are, interpersonal or social conflict, or simply the discovery of intellectual dissonance. A familiar pattern no longer holds.

Conscious conflict may be prompted by questions and it spawns questions. The development of emerging adult faith is often precipitated either by the questions that arise from one's own life experience or those that are posed to the emerging adult by others. Emerging adult faith is steeped in questions. Often they come unbidden and inconvenient. Sometimes they are stimulating attractors.

The conflicts that doubt and questions create present a threefold task. First, the conflict must be allowed, felt, and made fully conscious. Second, it must be wrestled into clarity: What is really amiss? That is, the moment of conflict cannot serve the process of transformation as long as there is only a contradiction of vague generalities. One must enter into the particulars of the puzzlement, tugging unruly thoughts and feelings into view. Third, the conflict must be tolerated with openness to a solution—no matter how remote it seems. That is, the conflict must neither be glossed over nor otherwise suppressed. Thus the moment of conscious conflict requires rigorous and disciplined care for thought. And digging into a new complexity to face the specter of a new truth may require a measure of courage.

Perils. The perils of this moment of conscious conflict are two: overdistancing and overwhelming anxiety. For the conflict to be engaged in the hope of resolution, the elements of the conflict need to be put at right distance—putting the conflict, so to speak, out of gear with our self and thereby looking at it in a new way.[22] Overdistancing, however—separating oneself too far from the task—breaks the connection with one's own field of affective receptivity and with Spirit. It breaks the tension of conscious conflict by dividing the conflicted self from the rest of the self. The essence of the self becomes disengaged and unaffected. This may be as common as "deciding never to get hurt again" after a heartbreak or as stark as cold indifference to the interminable suffering of a refugee population.

Alternatively, if the conflict is going to nourish the development of self and society, meaning and faith—whether in the neighborhood or the research lab—it must be endured as a baffling and sometimes agonizing struggle with irreconcilable factors that can lead to anxiety and overwhelm. Questions of faith ("Who and what can we trust and depend on? Who and what matters?") are rarely small—or if they begin so, they tend to balloon and may appear increasingly irresolvable. Whatever the factors, they generally represent a tension between established patterns of meaning—deeply rooted in mind and heart—and new conditions. This evokes a longing for both preservation and transformation. This is, therefore, typically a moment of trying to figure out and name what's wrong, while at the same time feeling some resistance to finding out.

The emerging adult is particularly vulnerable to escaping the conflict either in false security of a premature resolution ("I'll never try that again") or in facing the dichotomy of the conflict as stark and absolute ("It would be a great opportunity but I'm sure they would never select me"). Having had little experience of hope in the face of radical uncertainty (whether personal or professional), the emerging adult may assume the conflict is ultimate—a recipe for armoring, despair, and depression.

Coleridge held with great conviction that this moment of conscious conflict must not lead to ultimate separation. Rather, we separate to distinguish and clarify, never to divide. To divide is to destroy the underlying and ultimate unity. Thus thought distinguishes but is essentially connective.[23]

Hence, the moment of conscious conflict can suggest new possibility. At the same time, however, it is also the location of much of the suffering dimension of faith, and the temptation to avoid this moment is understandable.

Paradoxical Curiosity and a Context of Hope. One of the most common ways we seek to avoid the suffering is to reduce a complex story into dualistic polarities: we are right, they are wrong; you are either with us or against us. The transformative work moves beyond such polarities to a paradox in which we hold together seemingly contradictory truths in order to locate a greater truth. What we need, says Lederach, is a stance of attentiveness and continual inquiry that he calls *paradoxical curiosity.*[24] Paradoxical curiosity approaches personal and social realities with an abiding respect for complexity, an inquisitiveness about the possibility of a greater whole, refusing the pressures of forced dualisms and narrow definitions of reality, seeking something beyond what is initially visible. One emerging adult described this moment as "squinting into the fog of not knowing." This stance, Lederach writes, "is built fundamentally on a capacity to mobilize the imagination."[25]

Loder insists that the moment of conscious conflict, therefore, must be held in a "context of rapport"—a sustaining network of belonging and hope to avoid excessive distancing, overwhelming anxiety, and sheer avoidance.[26] Indeed, when self and world—even faith itself—are being recomposed, a network of belonging is crucial: friendships, a mentoring relationship, a sturdy community that can include, sustain, and even encourage constructive conflict—intellectual, emotional, and spiritual. A part of the arts of learning and leadership is the formation of communities that can remain resilient in a swirl of discord and doubt. Such communities and organizations serve the processes of imagination and thus the development of new knowledge and faith. They embody an informed hope, and emerging adults appropriately require them.

In the struggled conversation between father and son at the opening of this chapter, we hear an emerging adult aching for a "context of rapport," some form of relationship and community—a network of belonging—that can share his despair and at the same time buoy his hope. Such holding environments honor the inner momentum that arises from conscious conflict and drives toward resolution. Momentum of this kind can be ignored, thwarted, or submerged only at the great cost of betraying and diminishing the potential self and consequently impoverishing the human community.

Pause

Once the conflict has been clarified, it is no longer fruitful to try to keep sorting it out or otherwise work at it. Rather, it is time for the second moment in the recomposing process of imagination, the moment of *pause* or incubation, an "interlude for scanning."[27] Here the conflict is moved out of consciousness but not out of mind. This is not denial but relaxed attention. In the pause the conscious mind is passive, or better, permissive. Here, the mind is asleep, but "the soul keeps watch with no tension, calmed and active."[28] Coleridge described this moment with the images of the waterbug and the snake—images incorporating pause as a factor of locomotion.[29]

Coleridge also described this moment as "connected with master-currents below the surface."[30] The motion of the master currents beneath the calm surface may be likened to scanning for images and integrative patterns. Lederach writes about how critical it is "to provide space" for the creative act. When Heifetz teaches adaptive leadership, he models the importance of tolerating and using silence.[31] The Tao Te Ching asks, "Do you have the patience to wait till your mud settles and the water is clear? Can you remain unmoving till the right action arises by itself?"[32]

Humankind has formalized modes of giving itself over to the deep master currents of the soul. The power of pause is embodied in a host of contemplative traditions. One finds it, for example, in Buddhist meditation practices, in the Jewish observance of Sabbath, in the discipline of Islamic devotions, in Native American vision quests, and in the practice of Quaker silence. Contemplative pause is integral to the intellectual life, and to the formation of trustworthy meaning—the life of faith.

The contemplative moment is under siege in contemporary society, where life is shaped by the unexamined demands of an economy running on digital and brittle time. Nevertheless, the deep need of the spirit for pause relentlessly makes its claim, sometimes in mundane forms. We discover ourselves lingering, even when we know we should be speeding on our way. Something shifts in us, even though we are just staring into space. "Let me put it on the back burner for a while," we say, or "I'll sleep on it."

Recounting the experience of Barbara McClintock, a pioneering genetic biologist and a Nobel Prize recipient, Evelyn Fox Keller describes the experience of pause in the intellectual life:

By her own account, her confidence had begun to fail. . . . "I was really quite petrified that maybe I was taking on more than I could really do." She went, set up the microscope, and proceeded to work, but after about three days, found she wasn't getting anywhere. "I got very discouraged—something was quite seriously wrong. I wasn't seeing things, I wasn't integrating, I wasn't getting things right at all. I was lost." Realizing she had to "do something" with herself, she set out for a walk.

A long winding driveway on the Stanford campus is framed by two rows of giant eucalyptus trees. Beneath these trees, she found a bench where she could sit and think. She sat for half an hour. "Suddenly I jumped up, I couldn't wait to get back to the laboratory. I knew I was going to solve it—everything was going to be all right."

She doesn't know quite what she did as she sat under those trees. She remembers she "let the tears roll a little," but mainly, "I must have done this very intense, subconscious thinking. And suddenly I knew everything was going to be just fine." It was. In five days, she had everything solved. . . .

Her principal success lay in being able to pick out the chromosomes clearly enough to track them through the entire meiotic cycle. . . . Seven days after coming out from under the eucalyptus trees, she gave a seminar on the meiotic cycle of Neurospora. In addition to the five days of actual work, many years of experience went into those observations. But above all, she felt it was "what happened under the eucalyptus trees" that was crucial. She had brought about a change in herself that enabled her to see more clearly, "reorienting" herself in such a way that she could immediately "integrate" what she saw.

That experience taught her an important lesson. "The point is that when these things happen—when you get desperate about something and you have to solve it. . . . You find out what's wrong, why you are failing—but you don't ask yourself that. I don't know what I asked myself; all I knew was that I had to go out under those eucalyptus trees and solve what was causing me to fail."[33]

This moment of pause may require only a few seconds or many years. But if emerging adults are going to learn to self-superintend the power of imagination, they need to be initiated into the power and practice of pause—the strength of the contemplative mind.

The gift of pause in the process of imagination and the re-formation of faith is a unifying image or insight, a gift that, no matter how intense the struggle that precedes it, always "takes awareness by surprise."[34]

Image (or Insight)

The moment of pause has completed its work when an *image* (or insight) emerges that simplifies and unifies the conflict that seemed to be unresolvable. The image recasts the conflict into a single pattern, a unified and coherent whole. This is the individual or collective moment of "ah-ha!" "eureka!" breakthrough and revelation. Seemingly unrelated frames of reference converge to create a wholly new outlook, a new take on reality. The image that works creatively simplifies and unifies the disarray of the conflict, shaping it into one. The imagination depends on the images that are available to it—and a part of the teaching and learning process (and an act of leadership) is to make images (content) available that can serve in this way.

Image as Revelation. In the re-formation of faith, as it is in all learning, this moment of image or insight is the revelatory moment. Revelation is that part of the inner experience of a person or people that "illuminates the rest of it."[35] Revelation is the event that offers an integrative, unifying image of meaning. H. Richard Niebuhr wrote:

> By revelation in our history . . . we mean that special occasion
> which provides us with an image by means of which all the
> occasions of personal and common life become
> intelligible. . . . Whatever else revelation means it does
> mean an event in our history which brings rationality and
> wholeness into the confused joys and sorrows of personal

existence and allows us to discern order in the brawl of communal histories.[36]

Niebuhr likens such revelatory images to a luminous sentence in a difficult book "from which we can go forward and backward and so attain some understanding of the whole."[37] The new image or insight enables us to see the whole of life in ways that previously eluded us. Occasions of just such revelatory insight are the motivating purpose of all truly liberal education, and it is this moment in which the purposes of education and the formation of faith are most inextricably linked. As Niebuhr expressed it, "When we speak of revelation we mean that moment when we are given a new faith"[38]—when we make meaning at the level of ultimacy in a new way.

Image as Metaphor. The image in itself, however, is simply an object or act of the sensible world. In the service of the imagination, it becomes an "outward form that carries an inward sense."[39] That is, when we wish to express a thought, emotion, or intuition that cannot be simply pointed to or physically demonstrated, we must use objects and acts of the sensible world as mediators. To convey our meaning, we point to an object or act, not as a one-to-one correspondence but as metaphor. The image then loses its own gross material quality, so to speak, and lends its form as a vehicle to convey the spirit of an inner meaning. Thinking is the handling of thoughts by their forms.[40] For instance, the word *sincerity* is rooted in "*sine*, without, and *cera*, wax; the practice of the Roman potters was to rub wax into the flaws of their unsound vessels when they sent them to market. A sincere (without-wax) vessel was the same as a sound vessel, one that had no . . . flaw."[41]

In the process of teaching and learning the practice of adaptive leadership, a metaphor that has proved to be particularly potent is "getting on the balcony." Imagine dancing in a grand ballroom. There are some things you will never know about the dance unless you are dancing. But there are other things you will never know about the dance unless you go to the balcony to observe the larger patterns and other features of the scene. After you go to the balcony you may reenter the dance, but you will have more choices and you even may intervene to change the dance—the system—itself. We are all vulnerable metaphorically to "getting swept up in the dance." But the art of life and leadership requires us to resist getting swept up and to seek a larger, more adequate perspective about "what is really going on here." Notice that this is a particularly useful metaphor for cultivating the capacity to move from conventional to critical and systemic thought.[42]

Image as Symbol. As we now see, human beings give form to their meaning-making by using images. If an image serves as a key to a whole pattern of relationships, the image becomes a symbol. Because the task of faith is to shape into one the whole force field of life, whenever an image functions to give form to meaning at the level of faith, it necessarily engages a degree of complexity held only by symbol. Its form may be, for example, a concept (Love your neighbor as yourself), a person (Muhammad), an event (Passover), things (bread and wine), a mathematical formula ($E = mc^2$), or a gesture (kneeling). The function of the symbol is to grasp and shape into one a fitting conviction of reality.

Perceiving the distinctive activity of the human being to be the act of symbolization, Suzanne Langer wrote, "I believe there is a primary need in human beings which other creatures probably do not have, and which accentuates all . . . apparently unzoological aims, . . . wistful fancies, . . . consciousness of value, . . . utterly impractical enthusiasms, and . . . awareness of a 'Beyond' filled with holiness. . . . This basic need, which certainly is obvious in any person, is the need of symbolization."[43] Symbols serve as the architecture of our thoughts and affections.[44]

Writing an essay for her college application, a young athlete reveals how "an act of the sensible world"—in this case, running—serves as a symbol, a key to a whole pattern of meaning, anchoring her sense of being at home in the universe. Running in perfect sync with her sister through the "cold crisp air" of a November afternoon, she feels her way ahead into what it will mean to leave her childhood home and move out into the world of college.

Here, on the trails I know so well, it is hardly necessary for me to look at the ground. Each turn is anticipated, each dip as natural to me as cracks in the sidewalk are to city-dwellers. It was here that I first started running and it is on these trails that I still feel the most at home. . . . Running always seems to intensify the connection that I feel to my Island dwelling place and today is no exception. Here, surrounded by fir trees and wild huckleberries, time warps; I no longer need to worry about work schedules, term papers, or scholarship applications. For a brief moment each day I am free to merely exist. Each breath is invigorating, each step healing. Even the musty smell of the forest comforts me. It promises the continual cycle of the seasons and stability in my ever-evolving existence. On these trails I can believe in myself like nowhere else in the world. Here, any dream seems within my reach and there is a solution to every problem. I know that eventually these trails will be nothing more than a haunt of my youth, but today they are everything to me. Today these trails are my home. . . .

We speak of life and the world, of the inconsequential details of daily life. Nothing is too grand a topic for this place, nothing too slight. The words drip off our tongues like juice off popsicle sticks in the summer. Our relationship as sisters is secure.

It is at moments like this that I know I am truly blessed. I won't always be able to run these trails while I discuss life with my sister and let the cool breeze play with my dreams, yet the essence of this place will remain with me always. In every corner of the world I will be able to believe in dreams and solve impossible problems by merely letting my mind wander while my feet find the familiar rhythm of speed. And I know that no matter how far I stray from the waters surrounding Whidbey Island, I will always be able to come home with no more than a pair of Nike tennis shoes, a dirt trail, and a healthy batch of nostalgia.[45]

Having recognized how an image as metaphor can symbolize a whole pattern of meaning in the life of an individual, we are now prepared to recognize that images as metaphors function "religiously" when they serve as symbols that orient a community to the whole of life.[46] Religion, at its best, provides a dynamic distillation of images (symbols, stories, smells, sounds, songs, and gestures—what Tom Beaudoin describes functioning in many emerging adult lives as "sacramentals"[47]) powerful enough to shape into one the chaos of existence—powerful enough to name a community's conviction of the character of the whole of reality that its members experience as both ultimate and intimate. The religions of the world survive as systems of symbols—metanarratives—only when countless people are able to confirm, "Yes, life is like that."

Strengths and Limits of Images. Images and symbols can carry us into communion with the sublime, and they can also get us into trouble. Understanding the power of image in its use as metaphor and symbol leads us to the crucial insight that all images functioning as bearers of meaning are at once true and untrue. Images are merely forms we employ to handle reality. Consequently, the image is simultaneously like and unlike the intuition, concept, or feeling it mediates. Thus, there is inevitably some distortion in every image and therefore in every expression of truth.

Their deception—their untruth—lies partly in their tendency, as earthen vessels in which truth is borne, to offer their mere pottery as being truth itself. If the earthen vessel is regarded as truth itself (rather than a conveyance), we lapse into idolatry. Such idolatry is deepened when we fail to recognize that any image used to grasp, name, and give form to unseen reality is always peculiar to the individual or group that selects it. Every image, therefore, carries particular associations—social, political, and psychological. Thus the same image may bear quite another meaning—or no meaning—for another person or for a different group. This is true even of those images that have become "sacred"—be they economic, political, or religious.

When a compelling image or insight emerges that does appear to resolve the earlier conflict and offer a new window into reality, we move into the next moment in the process of imagination: repatterning.

Repatterning

The new image or insight prompts a necessary *repatterning* of reality as we have previously known it. The mind and heart have found an easier way—are learning—to hold all the aspects of the conflict.[48] In this moment, vast reaches of one's knowing and being may be reordered in light of the new insight, as we repattern the connections among things—or, as it were, "connect the dots." From the point of the insight, there is a rippling effect that recomposes the former pattern into a new way of seeing the whole. This moment in the imagination process requires its own time.

It took Barbara McClintock five days of intense work to lay out the new pattern of connections that arose from a single insight. Others may require a period that feels like ongoing reflection, a debriefing in which the new experience and insight is plumbed for its meaning. In the experience of meeting adaptive challenges, a community may have to run numerous experiments to figure out a viable repatterning of their organization and its practices in light of the new insight. The new insight requires us to turn back to see where we have been and to live into where we are now arriving. Repatterning may be understood as part of the process of creating a new home place for the mind and soul of an individual or a community.

One emerging adult who had recently "found faith" remarked, "Finding faith is not enough. The key is to find connections between faith and life. My period of revelations was a honeymoon period. Now it's figuring out how to make things work— period." Educators sometimes describe this moment as "teaching for transference." This happens, for example, when one assists another in seeing that what is discovered within a scientific experiment has implications for public policy. Discerning the fitting connections deepens associations and enriches awareness, making new power available. The consequence is a feeling of enlargement and a new quality of relationship between self and world. Above all, there is a sense of having achieved a more adequate orientation to reality. Imagination, again, is the power of realization: to make real.[49] Thus faith as the activity meaning-making and realization is indeed something quite other than wishful thinking or mere assent to irrelevant dogma of whatever kind.

Interpretation: Testimony and Confirmation

The act of imagination is incomplete until the image—no matter how compelling the repatterning it constellates may appear—is fully owned and tested. The new insight must "come to voice" and find a place of confirmation within a wider public life.

Testimony. We do not seem to fully grasp the new insight and we are not entirely at ease with it until we can ratify it within our self, express it in our own terms, embody it with confidence. This is the moment "when potentiality moves from the realm of possibility to the world of the tangible."[50]

In this act, we are, once again, dependent on a community of others. As social beings, we seek assurance of correspondence, coherence, and connection among the original conflict, the new image, and a concerned or interested public. Sometimes we do this through verbal or written communication. But the new insight may also be demonstrated through scientific analysis and replication or artistic expression. Whatever the form of testimony may be, bringing our insight to "voice" in dialogue with a wider communal life is crucial to a trustworthy formation of our inner confidence in what we are learning.

Earlier, we recognized the perils embedded in the work of the imagination, and again in this completing moment we must honor both how strong and how precarious the process is. That so much depends on the search for fitting and right images and that our access to images is so conditioned by context should put us on alert. Northrop Frye has said that the use of metaphor can seem "like crossing a deep gorge on a rope bridge: we may put all our trust in its ability to get us across, but there will be moments when we wish we hadn't."[51]

We most wish we hadn't when haunted by questions such as "How do I know I'm not just making all this up?" or "How do I know I'm not crazy?" Once we have developed the capacity for critical thought, we know that sometimes even the most attractive images and insights nevertheless seriously distort and lead away from truth—a crucial point of consciousness for the practices of citizenship and leadership in today's world.

Images may be held, for example, with deep feeling, but depth is no guarantor of truth. Recognizing the "seduction of the depths," Loder writes, "The depths are as capable of error and distortion, seduction, and corruption as are the routinized patterns of behavior that others use to keep them from ever exploring matters of depth. The creative process surely has a depth dimension but is not validated thereby."[52]

If we compose our knowing and are formed in faith by means of the imagination, how do we account for, and how are we saved from, what H. Richard Niebuhr describes as "an evil imagination of the heart"?[53] Is it not the case that though we have been following Coleridge's perception of imagination as the act of Reason—the divine in the human—nevertheless imagination persists in common usage as a "slippery term designating a power that penetrates the inner meaning of reality but also a power that creates substitutes for reality"?[54]

Similarly, Coleridge also recognized an "evil imagination." He understood it to be the isolated imagination, divided from the unity of the "One Life" and therefore cut off from its Source.[55] Thus if the imagination of an individual, a small group, a community, or a nation becomes isolated, whether as a result of ignorance or arrogance, depression or oppression, that imagination becomes vulnerable to the distorting features of its own metaphors.

Communities of Confirmation and Contradiction

All images must, therefore, be brought to the test of "repeated, critical, and common experience."[56] We are saved from the distortions of our own subjectivity within a community of others who are also seeking truth (a primary function of the academy at its best and integral to the hard work of political life in every context). Formally or informally, we must test our new insight in the forum of common experience that alone can confirm or refute the capacity of the image to grasp the real because "which 'gods' [images of defining and unifying power] are dependable, which of them can be counted on day after day and which are idols—products of an erroneous imagination—cannot be known save through the experiences of . . . history."[57] Thus a community assessing the work of the imagination must serve as *a community of confirmation and contradiction*. Emancipation from distorting subjectivity and narrow faith is dependent on a community that distinguishes between inadequate images—those that distort and diminish selves and communities—and life-bearing, truthful, worthy images. (This is one of the primary

functions of a mentoring network of belonging on which emerging adults depend.)

We must not, however, too easily endorse the power of finite
communities to serve the search for truth. Even a cursory review
of the history of human communities, including those of religious
faith, abounds with examples of the failure to serve the process
in which insights and symbols are discerned. Too often, inadequate images are greeted with acclaim, whereas the true prophet
is rarely popular. Moreover, in today's world, so riddled with new
media technologies dispensing vast streams of images into the
everyday environment of all of us, any community of discernment is in some measure overwhelmed and vulnerable to being
swept up in the rapid flow of the prevailing discourse. The adequacy of communities of confirmation and contradiction must be
assessed in the context of the long-term historical experience of
both particular communities and, increasingly, the whole Earth
community.

Imagination and the Moral Life

What I am describing here is another way of understanding the
deep motion of life as it is manifest in human experience, a
process that is integral to learning, development, creativity,
transformation, ethics, politics, the spiritual life, and "faithing."
As H. Richard Niebuhr saw so clearly, "The heart must reason,"
and "The participating self cannot escape the necessity of looking
for pattern and meaning in its life and relations. It cannot make
a choice between reason and imagination but only between reasoning on the basis of adequate images and thinking with the aid
of evil imaginations." Thus "anyone who affirms the irrationality
of the moral and religious life simply abandons the effort to discipline this life, to find right images by means of which to understand oneself, one's sorrows and joys."[58] Or as physicist Arthur
Zajonc has stated, "Knowledge is an event, not an object. . . .

Once we appreciate knowing as personal epiphany, the way is opened up for a reconciliation between facts and values, between science and spirituality."[59]

The search for "right images" is a compelling way of thinking about this kind of reconciliation in the formation of emerging adult faith in a rapidly changing world—a world of adaptive challenges calling for adaptive learning and practices of adaptive leadership. Today's emerging adults swim in a vast sea of images calculated to recruit their allegiance. One of the perils of an advertising, opinion-saturated society is that so many false images are offered in highly sophisticated ways to resolve questions of meaning, purpose, and significance.[60] There are too few networks of belonging in which emerging adults are encouraged to critically and contemplatively reflect on the images, symbols, and narratives that shape their souls and their society. Yet a strong, empathic, moral imagination is increasingly critical to the practice of citizenship and leadership and to the vocation of a faithful adulthood in a world marked by social-political-economic-religious conflict, and the growing recognition that our most vexing challenges cannot be addressed by any single sector alone.

Relationship and Risk

In the quest for a practice of a worthy and practical imagination, Lederach observes, "Time and again, where in small or large ways the shackles of violence are broken, we find a singular tap root that gives life to the moral imagination: the capacity of individuals and communities to imagine themselves in a web or relationship, even with their enemies."[61] As my colleagues and I found also in our study, *Common Fire*, the moral imagination is grounded in a recognition of the interdependent web of life, and that in today's new commons, ultimately the quality of my life is dependent on the quality of the life of others.[62] To act from this place requires what Lederach describes as a key discipline of the moral imagination: the willingness to take a risk—to step into the unknown without any guarantee of success or even safety—a practice of a courageous imagination. The moral imagination, therefore, depends on the practice of an imagination "that carries people toward a new, though mysterious, and often unexpected shore."[63] Similarly, Heifetz observes that in adaptive territory, often one can lead "with only good questions in hand," and in the absence of a map into the unknown future, only a clarity of deep purpose can provide orientation. Moreover, when people are being asked to change—to reimagine—in ways that involve loss and grief, there are very real dangers. Citizenship and leadership of this sort requires the skill of learning "how to walk the razor's edge without getting your feet too cut up."[64] Emerging adults can learn to walk that edge.

To Mend a World

Graduating as a twenty-something master's student in religion, Mary Moschella gave a baccalaureate address, excerpts of which illustrate features of the process of imagination as the power of shaping into one—meaning-making at work in emerging adulthood:

> Many of us might admit that we . . . were drawn to this place by the modest desire to learn to see everything clearly. Though it sounds presumptuous, we who have spent two or more years here, dissecting holy Scriptures, comparing world religions, constructing and deconstructing the concept of God, cannot pretend any lack of ambition. We did not come here to satisfy cool academic curiosities, but rather to learn how to see everything—the whole picture of life—clearly. We came to explore the very mysteries of God, to expand our view of the world, and to discern what it is that the universe demands of us.
>
> After being here for a while, we have discovered that the process of learning to see religiously is a difficult, if not

overwhelming, endeavor. For in delving into questions of ultimate meaning, we have learned how blurred is our vision, how tentative and partial our . . . insight. In this, we are like the blind man from Bethsaida, who even with a miracle, could only slowly and gradually learn how to see. . . .

Our studies and our common life have bombarded us with more . . . than we know how to manage. For our study . . . has caused us to examine our own faith and values: to decide what it is that we treasure . . . and what is essential to human be-ing.

Thus we have been involved in the process of naming our Gods. This process has demanded not only that we clarify issues of personal faith and belief, but also that we regard anew some of the global issues of human struggle. It is not that horrors such as world hunger have just recently come into being. But somehow before we hadn't quite seen (or faced) the magnitude of suffering involved, or the ethical challenges that such suffering present.

So in the process of naming the gods, we have been naming some demons too. We have seen and named the terrifying demons of militarism, racism, and sexism in our world. These appear to us as horrifying patches of darkness, frightening shadows that make us want to shut our eyes tightly and return to the comforts of our former blindness. . . .

Last summer I was in Israel, working on an archaeological dig. At the site of the ancient city of Dor, each day as I swung my pick into the age-old soil, I was inwardly chipping away at just these sorts of issues. I expended a good deal of energy cursing the facts of human suffering in the world, and trying to imagine some kind of hope of restoration.

Excavating at the level of the Iron Age can be rather tedious; only rarely did we turn up any precious small finds. Most of the time was spent staring at dirt walls and broken pottery shards. In my square, not even one whole vessel was uncovered all season—just so many broken pieces, scraps of ancient civilization. All of the brokenness appeared to me as an accurate metaphor for understanding the world. Broken and crushed, every piece of it; broken with small personal pains, as

well as with overwhelmingly large human struggles. Yet as the
summer went on, and I kept staring at the pottery, I slowly
started to notice something more than just the brokenness.
Some of the pieces of clay, however broken, were really quite
beautiful.

Later in the summer, I found out about the business of
pottery mending. This tedious work goes on year-round in a
cathedral-like building not far from the tel. Here ancient
vessels have been slowly and carefully reconstructed. I
remember being completely amazed at seeing those huge
restored jugs for the first time. How could anyone have possibly
managed to piece together so many small nondescript chips
of clay?

Seeing those restored vessels encouraged me to imagine
perhaps that at least some of the world's brokenness could be
overcome. I began to picture myself in a kind of vocation of
mending, of repairing some of the world's brokenness. To mend
the world. To proclaim a radical vision of social transformation
that would prevent future brokenness from occurring. These
are the tasks that I perceived the world to be demanding
of me.[65]

In Moschella's account, we hear the emergent self-aware
inner-dependent commitment and the conscious, self-
superintending imagination of the emerging adult. We hear how
the imagination seeks a grip on reality through an adequate
enough image (broken shards). We also hear the power of imagination to envision possibility and purpose: a mended world,
social transformation "that would prevent future brokenness
from occurring"; "the tasks I perceived the world to be demanding of me."

Not simply to the study of religion but to every discipline,
professional school, corporation, or other workplace, emerging
adults come seeking initiation into the powers of the imagination
and into vitalizing, fitting, and right images. The emerging adult
has a unique capacity to receive and to create images that can
lend themselves to the formation of worthy dreams and kindle

the passions of a generation to heal and transform a world. By intention or default, the environments in which emerging adults dwell become communities of imagination—mentoring environments—with the power to shape or misshape the promise of emerging adulthood.

Chapter Eight

The Gifts of Mentorship and a Mentoring Environment

Mentoring, in its classic sense, is an intentional and appropriately reciprocal relationship between two individuals, a younger adult and an older, wiser figure who assists the younger person in learning the ways of life. A venerable term, it is grounded in Homer's *Odyssey* and laden with expectations of a tradition of guiding wisdom. It has been popularly captured in such figures as Yoda in George Lucas's *Star Wars* trilogy, Gandalf in *The Lord of the Rings*, and more recently Dumbledore in the *Harry Potter* series. Interestingly, it is said that although George Lucas allows a good deal of exploitation of other characters for commercial purposes, there have been special protections on Yoda. Apparently there is some recognition that a good deal is at stake in the little wizened figure of dependable wisdom—an anchoring value amid the feeding frenzy of global media economics.

Indeed, good mentors play a vital role in stewarding the promise of a worthy future. As emerging adults are beginning to think critically about self and world, mentors provide crucial forms of recognition, support, and challenge. Mentors also care about your soul—they inspire. Whatever the immediate challenge or subject matter, good mentors know that all knowledge has a moral dimension, and learning that matters is ultimately transforming, affecting the whole person and intimately linked with the whole of life.

Mentors convey inspiration for the long haul. They are accountable and do not simply recruit people to serve their own agenda. Though true mentors are never perfect, they know that the emerging adult has a future beyond the imagination of the mentor and they try to hold their own commitments and the promise of the emerging adult life in fruitful tension.

Mentors offer good company as emerging adults cross the threshold of critical thought into new questions and possibilities. They respect the growing competence of the emerging adult and at the same time they are present to invite still richer and more profound learning. Mentors do not abandon emerging adults to their own devices, rather, they are willing to be part of the emerging adult's initiation into a practical and worthy adult imagination of self, other, world, and "God."

Overuse of the Term *Mentor*

Mentor is an overused word in contemporary culture. It is used to describe relationships across the entire life span, serving objectives both profound and superficial. Perhaps this is because the term *mentor* connotes a relationship that is more than instrumental, and in today's societies so much of human interaction requires a financial transaction. In contrast, although you can hire a professor, counselor, physician, coach, therapist, advisor, supervisor, or consultant, you can't really hire a mentor. There is a giving of self on the part of the mentor, an intent and response on the part of the protégé, and a vulnerability experienced (through differentially) by both that transcends the other categories of relationship—no matter how genuinely helpful they may be. Surely sponsors, role models, teachers, heroes and heroines, colleagues and helpful friends all play their parts, but the term *mentor* is best reserved for a distinctive role in the story of human becoming.

Mentors appear when a person is discovering critical thought and must begin to take greater responsibility for both oneself and others. Mentors give you confidence that you will make it through this transition. Emerging adults appropriately depend on mentors for authoritative guidance at the time of the developmental move from Authority-bound faith to a more inner-dependent form of meaning-making. As we have seen, this may occur in a person's twenties but it may also occur a bit earlier or later—or never.[1] When the time is right, mentors provide five key gifts: *recognition*, *support*, *challenge*, and *inspiration*—in ways that are *accountable* to the life of the emerging adult.

Recognition

If we want to learn about the formation of a person's life, a helpful question to pose is, "Who saw you?" As human beings, we all have a need to be "seen" throughout the life span but in a particular way as an emerging adult. One young woman in her early twenties was living away from home, still sketching her sense of her future. In a phone call home, she told how wonderful it was to have a couple who had been family friends for many years declare, credibly and thoughtfully, that she was very smart and capable and that she could be—and already was—worthy of respect in her chosen field. When her parents responded that they had been saying the same thing, she said, "But you're my parents and of course you think of me that way."

Clearly, parents can play aspects of the mentoring role (see the Coda) but quite understandably the emerging adult seeks recognition in a wider world of adult roles and responsibilities. As respected voices from beyond the parental sphere, mentors can confer recognition in powerful and practical terms.

Support

Support is one form of recognition. Supportive mentors are well known in the world of adult work: in corporations, the professions, the arts, and in other fields of practical skill. As a young adult is moving into the labyrinth of the corporation, through a combination of showing and telling, mentors may assist the protégé in finding a way into the arenas of power and finally up the corporate ladder. This is not merely a matter of the protégé doing what he or she is told or merely copying the mentor's own pattern. The good mentor simply recognizes that the younger adult is still dependent in substantial ways on Authority outside the self, and at the same time the mentor is a champion of the competence and potential the younger life represents.

Thus the mentor extends support, in part by consistent recognition and affirmation of every manifestation of that potential. Reflecting on her experience of having a mentor in a business context, one young executive said simply, "I had to live up to being terrific!"[2] A mentor is supportive in a host of ways, including serving as an advocate, a guide to resources, a source of protection and comfort, and sometimes a source of healing.

Mentors sometimes function unawares. A campus chaplain spoke movingly of a young student in her second year of college who came from a city two thousand miles away. She had been abused and neglected by her family but she had a good therapist who helped her make her way to college. There, she sought out a campus chaplain, who in turn, referred her to a therapist nearby. Staying in regular contact with both the therapist and the chaplain, she took classes. She did well—especially demonstrating real intellectual talent in philosophy—while every day still asking herself, "Do I want to live or do I want to die?"

As the chaplain told me this story, I will always remember the way he looked directly at me across the lunch table and quietly said, "The faculty in the philosophy department have no idea what a gift they are giving this young woman every time they tell her that she is doing excellent work and shows great promise."

Challenge

Mentors dance an intricate two-step as they practice the art of supporting and challenging more or less simultaneously. While

giving the well-timed push into a new area of potential competence, the mentor may also provide essential counsel when a
protégé is in well over his head. All the while, the mentor assures
him that there is solid, challenging, and meaningful work to
do—adult work that invites and tests the growing strength of the
emerging adult. Emerging adults welcome rightly timed challenges. The art of mentoring is located, in part, in assessing the
readiness of the protégé to recognize and creatively respond to
heretofore unseen opportunities, ideas, dangers, relationships,
and solutions. Good mentors almost always practice a kind of
tough love.

You may notice and may resist an implied hierarchy in the
mentor-protégé relationship. But remember that mentors do not
necessarily represent a hierarchical relationship as generally
conceived. Sometimes the mentor is decidedly senior, but often
mentors are peers with a bit more experience in a particular
domain. Many mentors of whatever age or gender have the
capacity to work shoulder to shoulder with the emerging adult.
This capacity is often a distinguishing feature of the mentor's
strength because it is so honoring of the gifts and promise of the
emerging adult. Thus, although a mentor brings some larger
realm of experience or talent to the relationship, great mentors
nevertheless also learn from their protégés through a process of
mutual challenge and discovery. Mentoring relationships are
most alive when both the mentor and protégé are working on
the edge of new knowing.

Inspiration

Above all, the mentor is conscious of the challenges the emerging adult confronts in the process of learning to practice critical
thought in a complex world—to stand outside or apart from
things as they are on behalf of strengthening perception, understanding, and potential insight. In the midst of this sometimes
rocky, sometimes exhilarating learning, the mentor serves as

a steady, inspiring point of orientation, beckoning toward the possibility of meaningful commitment on the other side of the achievement of critical thought. To varying degrees and in differing forms, mentors worthy of the name embody and inspire the possibility of committed and meaningful adulthood. In the formation of tough-minded critical awareness, a good mentor can be an antidote to floundering in unqualified relativism, cynicism, or despair.[3]

In Dialogue

There is a subtext embedded within the recognizing, supporting, challenging, and inspiring role of the mentor. The mentor becomes significant only if he or she "makes sense" in terms of the emerging adult's own experience. Although the protégé is still appropriately dependent on the authority of the mentor, he discovers that his own voice is increasingly included in the arena of authority. The good mentor is recruited to (but not overwhelmed by) the emerging adult's dialogue between fear and trust, power and powerlessness, alienation and belonging, doubt and belief, hope and hopelessness, as he becomes more at home in a larger world.

The task at hand is to search for ways to strengthen and confirm the still fragile emerging adult self and its integrity while the emerging adult finds a place of contribution and significance in the world of adult work and relationships. The dialogue between mentors and protégés is marked by mutual respect. At their best, mentors keep finding ways to call forth the kind of dialogue in which the protégé's own experience and the distinctive voice it may birth can learn to speak with integrity and power in the force field of life. In a festschrift for his mentor, Gary Whited writes candidly about this hard learning:

> I remember many afternoons sitting with Henry [Bugbee] while he guided me through my study of Marcel's . . . *The Mystery of*

Being. . . . We would begin with whatever end of a thread presented itself to us, and follow where it led, weaving in and out of war stories, fishing stories, reflections on other philosophers' writing, and often hearkening back to the *Bhagavad Gita* or *The Book of Tao*, from our earlier work together. As I look back on these conversations now, I see that I was being mentored. . . . I was being initiated into a style of philosophic reflection grounded in experience, in recollection, and in trust. . . .

I learned a hard lesson about trusting my own voice when . . . I went to graduate school in the East. I was drawn to the work of the pre-Socratics, Parmenides and Heraclitus in particular. The sense that all things are interconnected, often in ways invisible to us, but nonetheless always so, grew directly out of my prairie experience—and it is this sense that drew me to the central theme of unity in Parmenides' poem. The first draft of my dissertation was to design a dialogue between Parmenides' poem and a phenomenology of my early experience on the prairie. In the course of rewriting, however, I lost faith in the enterprise. Perhaps I was too self-conscious to use all that recollected material from my past, or perhaps I thought I needed to speak in a more acceptable "philosophical" voice. In any case, in the final draft, I dropped most of the recollections, which I believe Henry had liked very much in his reading of the first draft.

Shortly after Henry read the final version, I returned to the University of Montana to teach. I'll never forget that first meeting upon my return. Henry was standing in his home office holding my dissertation in his hand, the usual smoking pipe clasped between his teeth. In a pensive tone he asked simply, "What happened?"

At the time I do not think I took in the full import of Henry's short question. Over the years what he meant has slowly, and somewhat painfully, dawned on me. What Henry saw was that I had suppressed my own voice, and with it, my trust in the ground I stood on as a source for philosophic reflection.[4]

Mentors are like that: posing questions that go straight to the heart and the heart of the matter. Their power lies in the protégé's growing awareness that the mentor knows that each life has a distinctive contribution to make to our common life, and if this contribution is not made, a life is diminished and the commons is impoverished.

This does not mean that the mentor regards everything that comes from the protégé as golden. Rather, the mentor is allied with the potential of the emerging adult life and, as we see in Henry Bugbee, works to develop within the protégé the capacity for discerning what is true, worthy, and life-bearing, serving as a community of both confirmation and contradiction.

Mentoring relationships do not always take the form of face-to-face relationships sustained over time. Sometimes mentors are quite mindful of their role; other times, they play a powerful role with little or no awareness that their life is being watched and "speaking volumes."[5] There are people who perform some elements of what mentors do, while failing altogether in other elements. There are "mentoring moments"—brief yet powerful encounters that make a difference. Sometimes a mentor is a favorite author or historical figure, known only from afar. One emerging adult put it simply: "Books can be good mentors." Long ago, Coleridge wrote that the writings of George Fox, Jacob Behmen, and William Law "during my wanderings through the wilderness of doubt, . . . enabled me to skirt, without crossing, the sandy deserts of utter unbelief."[6]

If books can be good mentors, so can the Internet. Digital technologies can serve as a conduit for exploration and a vehicle for some aspects of a mentoring dialogue. Just as a mentoring book offers the imagination something far more than information alone, digital technologies also serve the potential of the mentoring relationship only to the degree that they mediate some aspects of the central gifts of mentoring, beginning with recognition, support, challenge, and inspiration. Because these functions of mentoring tend to occur most significantly through the elusive quality we call *presence*—including gestures both grand and subtle—mentoring may happen best when digital communication augments rather than replaces face-to-face encounter.

Accountable—Mentors and Clay Feet

Though the mentor may represent considerable expertise, in the alchemy of mentoring the talents, smarts, skills, and best intuitions of the protégé combine with the mentor's experience to forge new realities that neither could create alone. Although initially either may seek out the other, the relationship comes about finally through mutual attraction toward similar aims. When the relationship works, the meaning and satisfactions that it yields are gifts to both the protégé and the mentor.

Moreover, as laudable as the mentor's role is, few mentors manage to get it right all the time. A mentor is in every case a finite human being, and the relationship can go awry. The false mentor may attract the engagement of emerging adults for any number of self-aggrandizing reasons, and mentors are sometimes threatened by the growing competence of the protégé or in other ways allow shadow factors to take the upper hand. Precisely because good mentors bring a quality of commitment and passion to the work, they are vulnerable to assimilating the protégé's vision and potential into their own vision rather than honoring the distinctive gifts and callings of the protégé.[7]

One woman, now a pediatrician working with infants born to mothers addicted to crack, revealed how the mentoring relationship may be costly to both: "We've maintained a close relationship even though I didn't follow the path that she [the mentor] would have liked. She would have liked to see me in research. She respects what I do, particularly now that I've had some successes. But when I first started out, it wasn't OK. I think she was very disappointed."

Mentoring Communities

The bulk of mentoring research and writing since the 1970s has focused on this model: one mentor, one protégé. But a form of mentoring that can diffuse some of the pitfalls I have just described, while also deepening the formative influence of a mentor, is a mentoring community. In the Harvard Assessment Seminars, students revealed that often their most positive learning experiences were *not only* in one-on-one learning contexts, where, for example, an individual student might work with a professor in an office or laboratory. Highly valued learning occurred also with a teacher and a *small group* of students.[8]

In an age when mentoring has reappeared as a significant—and scarce—relationship, this is good news for faculty and other potential mentors. Pressured by the growing demands of financially stressed institutions, many professionals understandably wilt when the call to mentorship is added to a long list of musts. Thus, it is vital to recognize that a network of belonging that serves emerging adults as a *mentoring community* may offer a more powerful learning and social milieu and play a critical role in the formation of meaning, purpose, and faith.

Indeed, if an emerging adult is going to be initiated into a profession, organization, or corporation as it is presently defined and practiced, a mentor who guides the way is enough. But if one is going to be initiated into a profession, organization, or corporation and the societies they serve *as they could become*, then only a mentoring community will do. Because we are social beings, if each new generation is to contribute to the ongoing creation and renewal of life and culture, emerging adults need to know they will not be alone—or alone with "just my mentor." If they are going to have the courage to take the road less traveled and wade into adaptive challenges because they represent a more worthy truth, then emerging adults must discover that in doing so there will be a new sociality. Ideas and possibilities take hold in the imagination of the emerging adult in the most profound ways when he or she is met by more than a mentor alone—that is, by a mentoring community.

Mentoring environments are created by a mentor (or a team of mentors) who provide a context in which a new, more adequate imagination of life and work can be explored, created, and anchored in a sense of *we*. As one effective mentor has put it, what is needed is "a container, a community, and a conversation (content)."[9] Similarly, Heifetz and Linsky describe the importance of creating "a container"—a "holding environment" or a "crucible" that will help hold people in the hard work of adaptive learning and the formation of leadership, such as an off-site meeting, a course, or a task group requiring sustained engagement.[10]

Mary Jo Bona, Jane Rinehart, and Rose Mary Volbrecht have elegantly described the special benefits of *co-mentoring*, by which they mean the formation of a learning environment in which the leadership team models mutual support and challenge among each other. This evokes comparable relationships among the students, creating a mentoring community that is characterized by a heightened degree of trust and enhanced capacity for engaging and challenging everyone.[11]

In the study for *Common Fire*, it became apparent that although people in later adult life may appear to sustain significant commitments to the common good with little or no support, courageously going against the tide, in fact they often carry within them a deep sense of *we*. This conviction is often forged in the emerging adult years in association with a group of others who share inspiring ways of thinking and working in the world. Even if they do not maintain direct contact with the others who shared their particular experience of a mentoring community, the confidence of participation in a commonwealth of aspiration and commitment is sustained.[12]

Features of a Mentoring Environment

Mentoring communities play their essential role by offering the gifts of recognition, support, challenge, and inspiration and incorporating certain features that distinctively honor and animate the potential of emerging adult lives. These include a network of belonging, big-enough questions, encounters with otherness, vital habits of mind, worthy dreams, and access to images (content) and practices.

A Network of Belonging

A mentoring community is a network of belonging that constitutes a spacious home for the potential and vulnerability of the emerging adult imagination in practical, tangible terms. It offers a sociality that works (at least well enough) physically, emotionally, intellectually, and spiritually as the emerging adult becomes more fully at home in the universe. A mentoring network of belonging may be sustained for only a relatively brief but influential period of time, or it may extend for several years.

Although the emerging adult is reimagining self and world on the other side of critical thought, a trustworthy network of belonging serves as the community of confirmation and contradiction that is so essential to the practice of a faithful imagination. Jonathan participated in an annual summer program for college students. The program builds an interfaith mentoring community. On his return to the program the second summer, he described the role of enduring friendships:

> Over this past year, any time I had a problem or something that
> I didn't think that any of my friends at college would
> understand, I knew I could always sit down at the computer
> and send someone a long e-mail . . . and they would reply back.
> And I knew that even though we weren't all together, I still
> had the support system—it was just a little bit further
> away. . . . But it was still the same people, and I knew that they

would understand, and that they could help me through it, or give me a suggestion, or at least say, "You're crazy, don't make such a big deal of it," or whatever. It was very reassuring.

Another in the same program said, "We had this great experience and then everyone leaves, but you know that there's some kind of web or connection out there. You don't just leave it behind. You stretch it out. So that gives me hope, and actually it gives everyone else hope." The way this works was captured by still another emerging adult, who said:

> If something wasn't going right, or if a program I was putting together just didn't seem like it was happening, then I could look back, and it was an inner strength in a lot of ways. I know someone else in this program who's doing something like what I'm doing, and we made a commitment to each other to do this together, and I can't let my part of the commitment down, so I need to step up and be strong here.[13]

In these accounts, we glimpse how a mentoring community as a meaningful network of belonging serves both to reassure and to encourage the development of inner-dependence, honoring both the potential and the vulnerability of the emerging adult.

Big-Enough Questions

Mentoring communities that serve the recomposition of meaning, purpose, and faith in the emerging adult years extend hospitality to big questions. If the process of imagination and ongoing development is prompted, in part, by conscious conflict, then big-enough questions play a vital role.

Why big? Because faith is the dynamic composing of meaning in the most comprehensive dimensions, questions of little consequence or those that only skim the surface of things can distract and preoccupy us while a larger field of consciousness remains assumed and unexamined. Over time, one's earlier faith can become stagnant and insufficient and begin to disintegrate. By contrast, big questions stretch us. They reveal the gaps in our knowledge, in our social arrangements, in our ambitions and aspirations. Big questions are meaning-full questions, ones that ultimately matter. Big questions may take us to places we didn't plan to go. What are some of the big questions emerging adults ask?

Who am I and why am I here?

Why is the world the way it is?

Who do I really want to become?

How do I work toward something when I don't even know what it is?

Am I lovable?

Will anyone be there for me?

What are the values and limitations of my culture?

Who am I as a sexual being?

Do my actions make any real difference in the bigger scheme of things?

Do I want friendship, partnership, marriage? If so, why? With whom?

What is my society, or life, or God, asking of me? Anything?

What is the meaning of money? How much is enough?

Am I wasting time I'll regret later?

What constitutes meaningful work?

How have I been wounded? Will I ever really heal?

What do I want the future to look like—for me, for others, for my planet?

What is my religion? Do I need one?

What are my talents, preferences, skills, and longings?

What are my fears?

Will I be able to get a real job?

When do I feel most alive?

Where can I be creative?

Why is suffering so pervasive?

How am I complicit in patterns of injustice?

Will I always be stereotyped?

What do I really want to learn?

Do I want to bring children into the world?

How do I discern what is trustworthy?

Where do I want to put my stake in the ground and invest my life?

These are questions of meaning, purpose, and faith; they are rightly asked in every generation, in emerging adulthood, and throughout adult life.

There are also big questions particular to our time in history or to certain domains of inquiry. For example, Why is there a growing gap between the wealthy and the poor? Why is the prison population growing in the United States? Why are anti-depressants being prescribed for increasing numbers of children? What are the reasons for climate change? What is my role in the economic-political process—nationally and globally?

All of these questions are about the relationship of self and world. When we are younger, we can defer these questions to others, but becoming adult means increasing capability and responsibility for our own participation in the life of the commons, our own knowledge and action. These are questions of consequence that can't be simply ducked as irrelevant or "not my concern."

Yet it is my observation that many emerging adults, even and sometimes especially those who are regarded as privileged, are being cheated in a primary way. *They are not being asked big-enough questions.* They are not being invited to entertain the greatest questions of their own lives or their times. They are moving through their emerging adult years on default settings—often busy and stressed but distracted from matters worthy of their interest, concern, and practical engagement.

Some are swept up in what I have described elsewhere as the flow of success. Responding to a prevailing cultural narrative of presumed expectations, they are simply jumping the next hurdle. They are at once highly sophisticated in their capacity to calculate certain opportunity costs while remaining naive about the wider context in which their career choices, for example, are being made. As a consequence, they seek power but have little awareness of the reach of their own agency in truly shaping their lives and their world. They are functioning within various systems on which they have very little if any critical purchase. That is, they may have the capacity for critical thought but they use it only within certain limited frames—unable to question the frame (the narrative) itself.[14]

A very bright young businessperson, asked to comment on an investment decision by a health care chain, suggested that certain risks were acceptable "because a community hospital is, after all, simply a piece of real estate that could be liquidated if necessary." This emerging adult had not been initiated into the complex social, political, and moral terrain of the commons and the big questions that lurk there.

These and other less-privileged emerging adults are, like the rest of us, increasingly distracted by the lures of an entertained, consumerist, and anxious society, making their way as best they can, trying to enjoy what life has to offer, stressed but keeping up—or trying to. For many, the big questions somehow just don't come up, get set aside, or are more or less not worth it because the experts seem to disagree on what the questions are. Or (more cynically), as one young man put it, "It is better not to care than to care and have to deal with the fact that others don't."

In a mentoring environment that nourishes the formation of a worthy adult faith, others do care. There is a place for asking the questions that begin to arise in the imagination of the young adult, from the inside, from that emerging inner authority. There is a willingness to tolerate the conflict (along with both the zest and the anguish) that such questions may raise, in the trust that it may lead to a more faithful imagination. In return, mentoring environments pose questions that the emerging adult would otherwise not have the privilege of engaging. The mix of questions arising from within and posed from without can create great questions that launch the worthy investment of a lifetime because "questions marry the intellect's passion for inquiry with the heart's affinity for the unknown."[15]

Encounters with Otherness

In the interviews that informed *Common Fire*, my colleagues and I discovered that encounters with otherness are the most powerful sources of vital, transforming questions that unsettle unexamined assumptions, foster adaptive learning, and spur the formation of commitment to the common good. By "otherness" we mean encounters with those outside one's own tribe, those generally regarded as *them* instead of *us*.[16]

It has been said that in the life of faith, "God is always revising our boundaries outward."[17] This occurs through an encounter with the other in which an empathic bond is established that transcends *us* and *them*, creating a new *we*. This grounds commitment to the common good rather than just to me and mine.

In a constructive encounter with otherness, an empathic bond arises from recognizing that the other suffers in the same way as we, having the same capacity for hope, longing, love, joy, and pain. These are the undergirding features of our humanity that link us with the vast commonwealth of being. The ability to imagine the experience of the other by drawing on our own well of experience and blending it with the particular features of the other's experience makes it possible to see through another's eyes, to feel through another's heart, to know something of another's understanding. What one knows of another's experience is always partial. But one of the most significant features of the human adventure is the capacity to take the perspective of another and to be compelled thereby to recompose one's own perspective.

This kind of perspective-taking gives rise to compassion (the capacity to suffer with). Compassion in turn gives rise to a conviction of possibility, the sense that there has to be a better way. This conviction of possibility fosters the courage to risk on behalf of more than mere self-interest, recognizing that my well-being and the well-being of the other are linked.

We can hear the beginnings of this kind of transformation in the reflection of a young African American who had grown up in a suburb of a major American midwestern city. As he told it, through his high school years he assumed that any young person of color in this society who worked hard could have the same access to the privileges and comforts of upper-middle-class society that he had. It was not until he was in college and began to tutor a young African American boy in the inner city that he had his first conscious encounter with otherness. He discovered that without the same resources and encouragement that he had known, it would be much more difficult than he presumed. As the living image of the young boy in the inner city took up lodging in his imagination, he had to recompose both self and other, becoming a different *I* because of a reconfigured *you*.

Emerging adulthood is a time of special readiness for this expansion of mind and heart. Loosening the bonds of conventional belonging (which is fostered by critical thought) and developing inner-dependence (with a consequent openness to wondering and exploration) conspire to set in place a ripeness for meeting and hearing "the other" in a new way.

Just home for the Christmas holiday, a freshman reflected on her experience of a camping trip during her college orientation week. She remembered especially meeting other freshmen "who were into the 'hard-core alternative scene' and in high school I would have thought of them as just that. But on the camping trip, there we were, all coping with the rain and the mud, and I discovered that one of them had a cat they hated to leave behind and another had a mom he liked to cook with. I learned to see them for who they are, not what they are."

This doesn't mean that it is necessarily automatic or easy for emerging adults to entertain unpopular and challenging perspectives within a field of study or other social contexts. Young adult inner-dependence is fragile, and Authority—though more chosen—remains located outside the self. Emerging adults remain vulnerable to needs for recognition and inclusion and hence are vulnerable to the norms of the networks of belonging to which they have access.[18]

Cast in this light, a recent research report is particularly disturbing. Sara Konrath has found that college students today are 40 percent less empathetic than those of thirty years ago, with the numbers plunging primarily after 2000—a finding reflected in other studies. Empathy includes perspective-taking and the ability to identity with another's distress, and thus the implications for society at large are significant. "'We don't actually know what the causes are at this point,' Dr. Konrath said. But the authors speculate a millennial mixture of video games, social media, reality TV and hyper-competition have left young people self-involved, shallow and unfettered in their individualism and ambition."[19] To these observations we must add economic trends that erode opportunities for emerging adults to secure education and meaningful work.

At the same time, we are expecting colleges, universities, and the military—institutions with significant emerging adult populations—to be primary testing grounds for discovering how we will all learn to dwell together within the small planet home we share. In these settings, emerging adults representing a very broad range of social-cultural perspectives are cast in close proximity. We expect that they can manage it—and to some degree they often can, precisely because of the emerging adult readiness I have described. When we must bridge vast cultural differences, however, while there is power in proximity, proximity alone is often not enough.

Talking with a young graduate of a prestigious university who was embarking on a master's degree in business, I asked him if he could tell me when, if ever, he had experienced encounters with people significantly different from himself. He felt he had not, but he hoped it would happen in the school in which he was now enrolled, where there was an obvious diversity of American ethnic and international students. He recalled, "At the university where I was an undergraduate, there were a lot of different people, but we all sat in our own section of the dining hall." This experience is common, as all of us tend to seek out our own comfort zone, our own tribe. In a related fashion, some faculty report that increasing numbers of emerging adults, even the bright and informed, are reluctant to disagree openly with one another, whether in informal or classroom contexts, because the terms of belonging (increasingly fragile in our society as a whole) are set too much at risk by the free exploration of ideas around matters of real consequence.[20]

Constructive, transforming encounters with otherness and true exchange of ideas are facilitated in those mentoring communities where hospitality to otherness is prized and practiced. Such communities can be created in the workplace, the neighborhood, a classroom, on the playing field, and in religious communities. In most social environments today, however, there are many forms of otherness in addition to ethnicity, culture, gender, sexual orientation, and economic class. In almost every context, it is useful to take an "otherness inventory" to assess the many divides waiting for creative abrasion. Transforming encounters across any significant divide set at the soul's core the knowledge that every assumption may be potentially transformed by an encounter with otherness. Faith develops at the boundary with otherness when one becomes vulnerable to the consciousness of another and thus vulnerable to reimagining self, other, world, and "God." This quality of engagement with otherness is dependent, however, on key habits of mind.

Vital Habits of Mind

One of the gifts of a mentoring context is initiation into the habits of mind that make it possible for emerging adults to hold diversity and complexity, to wrestle with moral ambiguity, and to develop deeper wells of meaning, purpose, and faith.

They assist in creating habits of discourse and inclusion that invite genuine dialogue, strengthen critical thought, encourage connective-holistic awareness, and develop the contemplative mind.[21]

Dialogue. Dialogue is not just talk. It is a way of being in conversation with others that involves a good deal of listening, desire to understand, and willingness to be affected—to be moved, informed, and to change one's mind. In a sound-bite world, the art and practice of dialogue is relentlessly at risk. Dialogue requires time and space and it has to be learned.

Diana Eck, professor and director of the Pluralism Project at Harvard University, has provided significant leadership in opening pathways into the multireligious reality of today's societies:

> Dialogue in which we listen as well as speak may seem so commonsensical it is scarcely worth making a fuss over. And yet dialogue, whether between women and men, black and white, Christian and Hindu, has not been our common practice as an approach to bridging differences with understanding. Power and prestige make some voices louder, give some more airtime, and give the powerful the privilege of setting the terms for communication. . . . Today the language of dialogue has come to express the kind of two-way discourse that is essential to relationship, not domination. One might call it mutual witness. . . .[22]

Unless they have become too wary, armored, or cynical, emerging adults are particularly open to cultivating the art of dialogue because it is a satisfying means of honoring one's growing curiosity about self and world. When one speaks and then is heard—but not quite, and therefore tries to speak yet more clearly—and then listens to the other—and understands, but not quite, and listens again—one becomes actively engaged in sorting out what is true and dependable within oneself and about one's world. How one makes meaning is composed and recomposed in this process. This can occur in a wide variety of contexts when mentors embody and establish norms of discourse that foster genuine encounter and engagement.

When models and expectations of this kind of conversation are nourished and there is support for learning its forms and rhythms, more than dialogue can be learned. Dialogue tills the soil for the growth of critical thought and inner-dependence.

Critical Thought. As described previously, critical thought is the capacity to step outside of one's own thought and reflect on it as object. It is the ability to recognize multiple perspectives and the relativized character of one's own experience. This is the vital capacity that marks becoming an emerging adult in faith. Mentoring environments that serve the formation of adult faith extend hospitality to critical thought and invite its further development.

Nourished by compelling questions, critical thought flourishes when emerging adults are encouraged to test their responses (their mental and practical powers) in a supportive and challenging milieu of differing perspectives. But to lead to viable commitment rather than mere unqualified relativism and combative individualism, they must be met in ways that sustain a deepening, refining dialogue. Renee Lertzman has written:

> It was the day after our professor, Carlos Norena, lectured on Kant that I felt something slipping away from me. I was in my dorm room, looking out the window at the redwoods, and the view of the Pacific Ocean beyond the knoll. I suddenly had the

sense that I had no idea what was real and what wasn't and how to tell the difference. Under this new gaze, the chair, the table, the cup, all became questionable entities in the universe, each containing their own subjectivity, truth, and meaning. Coherency was elusive and beyond my grasp. How was I to know what was going on here? How could I continue to live—buy groceries, run errands, call friends—if I did not know?

I went to Carlos's office that day, and told him, "I don't know what is real and what isn't. I am thinking of dropping out of school to do organic farming. At least I know that growing carrots is real. . . . " He laughed and said to me in his thick Spanish accent, "Let's not do anything too drastic here. I suggest you take up swimming."

Since that day in my freshman year in college, I have felt a sort of "waking up" from sleepwalking through life. . . . I was perplexed by my own catapult into wanting to know what life was about. . . . Why was no one talking about this?

It was when I left college midway for an eight-week field study in the Sierra Nevada Mountains studying "nature philosophy and religion" that I began to locate this inquiry in the larger context of how we live among others—humans and non-human species. For two months, we lived in various wilderness areas. We walked between worlds; drinking the cold clear waters of the mountains while making plans to return to the streets, lamps, steel and glass. To step into wilderness is to see how complex our relationship with the ecological world is, and to see more clearly what we have determined as "meaningful." . . .

The questions I was asking that first year in college did not go away; they only deepened, found new contexts and arenas. I had a professor once who jokingly called me "ontologically insecure" like the people on the "Star Trek" holodeck. It is as if to question reality and living deeply . . . can actually unhinge one's attachment to normative reality, so as to occupy a space of "always looking in." This sense of being ontologically insecure, I have come to see, is where I draw my strength; . . . I have also come to see that to question and investigate life, on the deepest levels possible, is to walk on a rim of sorts. . . . For me, the life worth living is to have the courage to be on the rim, and tolerate the space of not knowing, and honor what is known.

The people I look to as role models and teachers are those who live contemplatively, ask keen questions, and tolerate uncertainty. They thrive on the rim. Their minds are like diamonds, glittering with inquiry and beauty . . . deeply engaged with the world of the living.[23]

Connective-Systemic-Holistic Thought. In an increasingly complex world, however, critical thought alone is insufficient. The capacity to make distinctions must be joined with the capacity to discover the systemic and dynamic connections among things. This is a critical feature of an adult faith that can stand the test of time and support positive, effective action.

An international student in graduate school, making the transition from Authority-bound ways of knowing to a critical-systemic perspective described his experience this way:

> I don't know whether it's good or bad, but the way my brain works now has changed a lot. It's like a large flywheel which has been spun, and you can't stop it anymore. Before it was kind of an unstructured approach to the surrounding environment. You saw facts around you, but you weren't able to select and structure them—to place them on a kind of shelf in your brain. But now it's more like you are inclined to analyze all the facts of life and try to structure them and place them on different tiers in your brain. This actually is my concern because now there is a brain inclination of using the tools [systemic ways of seeing and the new theoretical perspectives in his profession] maybe not on relevant events in my life, even on the way the world is working. It's a stress . . . because you can't do it; you can't apply this to the whole world around you.

This emerging adult has the capacity for critical thought; he can think about his own thinking. In addition, we hear his growing capacity for connective-systemic thought: the ability to structure the facts, placing them in relationship to one another. We hear also a question of faith: "Can I apply this to the whole world?" His answer seems to be no. Any particular theory may interpret some aspects of life, and though powerful and compelling, may not be adequate to interpreting the whole of life. Mentoring environments that serve the formation of adequate faith not only assist in understanding discrete aspects of life but also welcome and encourage grappling with how these understandings relate to the whole of life.

A Contemplative Mind. Big questions can activate the reimagination of meaning, purpose, and faith. But for this to happen well requires, as we have seen in Chapter Seven, the moment of *pause—contemplation.* Particularly because busy-ness has become so pervasive and time for contemplative pause is crowded out, mentoring contexts that most profoundly serve the formation of the intellectual life and adult meaning-making do not underestimate the power of pause.

When decision makers and others do not have time for and are unpracticed in the power of contemplation, we are in peril. As evidence of this concern, a nonprofit organization, The Contemplative Mind in Society, has been opening new pathways for contemplative practice in undergraduate education, professional schools, corporations, and even in prisons—places where emerging adults and their mentors can learn the power of pause.[24] Practices of contemplation encourage the cultivation of the inner life, honor the emerging inner authority of young adults, and confirm that they participate in a larger motion of life that sometimes transcends their own efforts to manage and control it. The place of pause in the process of imagination is the place where one learns both to endure and to resolve the apparently irreconcilable tensions that constitute life's biggest questions. Initiation into the power of pause at once strengthens and chastens the imagination of the emerging adult and can be one of the greatest gifts of a mentoring environment.

Worthy Dreams

Transformative dialogues with otherness, critical and connective thought, and the practice of contemplation can yield the gift of *a worthy dream*—intimately linked to a deep and satisfying sense of purpose. Daniel Levinson was the first developmental theorist to recognize the significance of the Dream as an orienting vision for one's life, and that it takes form in the "novice" phase of adulthood. With Judy Levinson, he has contended that the most crucial function of a mentoring relationship is to develop and articulate the Dream. The Dream, with a capital *D*, is something more than night dreams, casual daydreams, pure fantasy, or a fully designed plan.[25] A Dream is more than a goal, and it is shaped by questions such as, Does this Dream make me feel truly alive? Does it align with my values and contribute to the lives of others? Will it honor my full potential? Will I require help from outside myself? Can I step out on it—or is it mere illusion?

A worthy Dream coalesces a relationship between self and world that recognizes the reality and needs of the world and honors the authentic potential of the emerging adult in practical and purposeful terms, yielding a sense of meaningful aspiration. It might be said that the formation of critical-connective thought is the threshold achievement of emerging adulthood and that the formation of a worthy Dream is the central work of emerging adulthood.

A Reach for the Ideal.   Dreams come in all shapes and sizes, from conventional to radical. But the Dreams that most profoundly serve the composing of a faith to live by stem for the most part from a particular capacity of the emerging adult: the capacity to envision the ideal. With the capacity for critical-connective thought, emerging adults have the ability to critique self and world and also to imagine how it might become. Thus, although emerging adults are often accused of youthful idealism, we might better understand emerging adulthood as the potential birthplace of purposes and aspirations worthy of the promise of emerging adult lives—a time for composing a Dream of a worthy adulthood.

The emerging adult has struggled to push away from the safe but constraining harbor of conventional knowing in order to achieve an initial sense of self-aware integrity. Yet he or she is not yet embedded in the full range of adult commitments. These circumstances create a certain freedom and a unique capacity to critically conceptualize the ideal. By *ideal* the young adult means that which is pure, consistent, authentic, and congruent. The emerging adult's quest for the ideal is a potent element in the search for what will most adequately ground and orient the integrity, commitment, and investment of the emerging self.

We know, however, that in attempting to address what they consider adult "hypocrisy," and seeking to resolve what they construe as a tension between the "ideal" and "reality," they may settle for easy cynicism or shallow hedonism—a kind of pseudo-integrity. The sobering fact is that once the young person has seen relativism and seeks a new integrity in which to stand, even hedonism or a comparable variant may appear as a viable faith. In this fragile time, whatever content (or ideology) appears to be at least consistent and authentic may appear to fit the young adult's hunger for the ideal, as long as it is liberated from the "hypocrisy" of the conventional (and the inconsistent).

Seeing this pattern among some of her interviewees, Carol Gilligan observed, however, that those students most able to move through the mire of superficial relativism and grapple responsibly with moral issues seemed to be those "whose concept of morality . . . entailed an obligation to relieve human misery and suffering if possible."[26] This sense of *appropriate obligation* arises from recognizing one's intrinsic connection with the "other" and can give rise to a worthy Dream and ultimately a sense of vocation.

Vocation. Understood through the eyes of the great traditions of faith across time, a worthy Dream is more than imagining a job or career or profession narrowly understood. The Dream in its fullest and most profound sense is a sense of vocation. *Vocation* conveys "calling." It is a relational sensibility in which I recognize that what I do with my time, talents, and treasure is most meaningfully conceived not as a matter of only personal passion and preference but in relationship to the whole of life. Vocation arises from a deepening understanding of the suffering and wonder of both self and world—and a sense that who you are is in sync with your place in the scheme of things, your "calling," your niche in the ecology of life. More poetically, vocation is the place where the heart's deep gladness meets the world's deep hunger,[27] the double-strand helix in the DNA in the seed of vocation.

Access to Key Images

Forming a worthy Dream depends, in significant measure, on access to fitting, vital images, narratives of worthy possibilities. Certain kinds of images are especially important in the formation of emerging adult faith, including images of truth, transformation, positive images of self and of the other, and images of interrelatedness.

Images of Truth: A World of Suffering and Wonder.   Forming a viable faith depends on serious engagement with the truth of the world, the universe as it is, including "things that should not be so."[28] This means that though we can never fully comprehend Truth, the emerging adult may learn to apprehend something of the wholeness of life—the infinite complexity of the social and more-than-human world—and particularly in the dimensions of both suffering and wonder.

It is not surprising that one of the most ancient and venerable stories about the formation of human faith concerns a young person who went into a wider world and discovered the realities of suffering. Just as the Buddha came to grapple with suffering as a feature of enlightenment, any adult faith must do the same in some form. Emerging adulthood can be a time of coming to terms with suffering, often one's own and sometimes that of others who suffer far more than the emerging adult may heretofore have imagined. As the quest for Truth expands, emerging adults grow increasingly vulnerable to a raw awareness of the stark and tragic dimensions of suffering. The pervasive injustice of some forms of suffering as a primary feature of the fabric of life itself is among the irreducible facts with which mature faith must contend.

The paradox is that as integral to life as suffering is, it is matched by wonder—the awe and reverence invoked in those moments when we come alive to the intricate luminosity, beauty, power, and vast grandeur of the universe and the amazement we feel that we are in any measure privileged to behold it. By wonder I mean also the sense of Mystery that cannot be exhausted even by our most magnificent forms of knowing, including the awe-full ambiguity that arises from any reasonable assessment of the complex, dynamic, and confounding character of life. Emerging adults have a readiness for soaking up such wonder, especially if it is distinguished from the various forms of artificial high that exploit this readiness. This dimension of wonder, too, is a fact that any worthy faith must be able to enfold.

Ironically, in today's society we have greater access to the suffering and wonder of life and on a larger scale than the generations before us—and also myriad ways to be insulated from both. Mentoring environments do well to recognize that the citizenship and leadership needed for the twenty-first century is best schooled at the crossroads of suffering and wonder.[29] There, at that crossroads, contradiction and dissonance proliferate, raising big questions and activating the imagination in its search for purpose and faith. Joan Baez once remarked "I do not know whether it is worse to bring a child into this world and submit him or her to the disease we call society, or to refuse to bring a child into this world and thus rob him or her of one glorious red sunset." If emerging adults are steeped in images that grasp both the suffering and wonder of their time, they may gain a faith, a way of making meaning that can be sustained because in a certain sense it cannot be surprised. A great mentoring environment skirts neither suffering nor wonder; rather, it holds them in that dynamic "paradoxical curiosity" that Lederach describes.

Images of Interrelatedness and Wholeness. Wading into the suffering and wonder of the world can yield images of interrelatedness recognized earlier as foundational to the moral imagination and the formation of worthy Dreams. As we all emerge into a more profound ecological and global consciousness spurred in part by new technologies that daily destroy any illusion that our actions in one place do not have unexpected consequences everywhere else, we can feel overwhelmed and powerless. Consciousness of "our small part" can, however, become a positive source of inner confidence if that small part is seen as *participating in*, and thus affecting, the larger whole. Thus the search for right images in our time needs to include images that enable us to grasp an intuitive sense of the whole in ways that link the particular and the universal, holding each accountable to the other.

In their appropriate dependence on the images available to them in their environment, emerging adults are especially vulnerable to partialities. By confusing a part with the whole, they may move toward a faith that consequently works "here" but not "there." Access to images, symbols, insights, theorists, and narratives that create durable, enlarging, and open-ended patterns of thought and meaning enlarge the mind and expand the heart. They enable emerging adults to compose and recenter themselves in an increasingly trustworthy faith that, in spite of immediate circumstances, makes it possible to become at home in the universe.

Images of Transformation—Seeking a Posture of Hope.
Suffering and wonder appear to be opposing realities. They are
resolved in the human soul only in the sensibility we call hope.
Authentic hope is no mere bromide. It is grounded in the facts
of things as they are, taking into account the known and
unknown—the glory and anguish of reality.

Initiation into a conversation with truth and hope embraces
the complex, composing character of the motion of life and its
transformations. Emerging adults must be met in their dialogue
with possibility: the dialogue between despair and hope, shipwreck and gladness, bondage and freedom, death and life, stasis
and the incessant transformation of all things. Accordingly, mentoring communities serve well when they nurture an imaginal
complex of integrating symbols that grasp the dynamic of dissolution and recomposition. A recognition of the finite nature of all
constructions of knowledge and the possibility of their ongoing
reconstruction toward more adequate knowing is a crucial feature
of an adulthood that fosters hope. In this context, "hope" signals
a posture in the world rather than a confidence in guaranteed
outcomes. Without being either naive or glib, it is grounded in
a recognition of the master currents of ongoing transformation
that always yield some measure of the unexpected.[30]

Rosemary Radford Ruether, a noted Roman Catholic theologian, recounts her discovery of this central dynamic through
the teaching of Robert Palmer, a classicist:

> Palmer was . . . more than faintly contemptuous of
> Christianity. . . . [It was] Palmer, the believing pagan, who first
> taught me to think theologically or, as he would have called it,
> "mythopoetically." Through him I discovered the meaning of
> religious symbols, not as intrinsic doctrines, but as living
> metaphors of human existence. I still remember the great
> excitement I felt in freshman Humanities when he said
> something that made me realize that "death and resurrection"
> was not some peculiar statement about something that was
> supposed to have happened to someone 2,000 years ago, with

no particular connection to anyone else's life. Rather it was a metaphor for inner transformation and rebirth, the mystery of renewed life. He happened to be talking about Attis or Dionysos, not about Jesus. For the first time I understood a new orientation to Christian symbols that eleven years of Catholic education had never suggested to me. That was the beginning of my being interested in religious ideas in a new way.[31]

If emerging adults discover this dynamic of dissolution and recomposition at the core of life, they become attuned to the motion at the heart of the universe, which may be named in humanist, naturalist, or spiritual-religious terms.

Positive Images of Self. The formation of a worthy Dream that fuels a sense of purpose must be intimately linked with positive images of self. Although awards and grades provide some measure of affirmation, a mentoring community can provide a larger gift. The emerging adult needs to be seen in ways that convey a fitting correspondence between his own aspirations and positive reflection in the eyes of others who are valued and trusted. Being seen in this way can yield an imagination of a positive adulthood, especially when there is access to images of adults who are living purposeful and joyful lives that counter the perception that the delights of life are left behind when one becomes truly adult. This is the power of attraction and confirmation that mentoring communities hold when the adult self is still in formation.

Reminding us that mentoring can be practiced by those who are still emerging adults themselves, Moses, a young Kenyan, tells a story. After completing a Jesuit education in Kenya, he came to the United States for study in a small college. Unprepared for the racism in this culture, he came close to despair and almost shut down as a way of coping. Then a Caucasian American student whom he admired, Krista, only slightly older than himself, said to him one day, "It isn't your problem that they have a problem with you, it's their problem." It was a turning point. It was an insight that made sense of his experience, and it provided a reframed, positive image of himself. In time, he became the first international student to be elected as student body president in that college.

Emerging adults hunger for images of self that promise authenticity along with a mix of competence, excellence, and the finest qualities of life. Such images need not minimize the struggle inherent in claiming these qualities. One young woman reflecting on her experience as an athlete in track said:

> I had one really terrific coach. He was much more interested in personal bests and the effort produced than actual placings. I wanted to train really hard to prove to myself and to him what I was capable of. This desire came out of a set of personal goals rather than feeling over-pressured by him. He helped me keep the goals realistic and always provided positive feedback. After both years of track season, there were other athletes that set more outstanding records. I accomplished good performances and was above average but did not have the same outstanding overall results. And yet, after both seasons, I was awarded the female track MVP by my track coach, based on my personal achievements, extensive improvements, and intensive training and effort I had put in on a daily basis. The qualities and characteristics he most respected in an athlete were ones that he evoked through his attitude and words, and that I had developed to a fair extent. Many of those qualities were further strengthened in me because of his apparent respect for such characteristics.

Images of self that encourage high aspiration in meaningful terms (in contrast to mere success) enable the emerging adult to see beyond self and world as they presently are and to discern the world as it ought to be and the self as it might become.

Communities of Practice

Mentoring environments are communities of imagination *and practice*. *Practices*, as we use the term here, are ways of life—

things that people do with and for each other to make and keep life human.[32] Among the many that might be identified as significant in the emerging adult years, there are three in particular that all mentoring environments might strategically recover to serve the formation of emerging adult meaning-making: the practices of hearth, table, and commons.

The Practice of Hearth. Hearth places have the power to draw and hold us because they are places offering an exquisite balance of stability and motion. Hearth places are where we are warmed in both body and soul, are made comfortable, and tend to linger. Indoors or out, hearth places invite pause, reflection, and conversation: fireplace or campfire, the ocean shore, an inland vista, a bench set at the edge of an active park or plaza. These are places for lingering.

Hearth places invite reflection within and among. As we have seen, emerging adult faith is forged in contemplative dialogue that occurs both within the self and among an available network of belonging in interaction with the wider world. The dialogue of which we speak—between power and powerlessness, success and failure, alienation and belonging, right and wrong, despair and hope—cannot usually be accomplished in fleeting sound bites. It requires something more like a hearthside conversation.

Because dialogue does not mean two people talking, but rather "talking through," time and places for talking through are essential in forming critically aware, inner-dependent, and worthily committed faith. An understanding of the courage and costs inherent in the formation of an adult faith asks educator-mentors and their institutions to acknowledge in their everyday practices that when truth is being recomposed in the most comprehensive dimensions of self, world, and "God," then necessarily the soul suffers disequilibrium in the service of a larger, more adequate knowing. Opportunities for key practices—ways of being—that support and nourish a new and worthy imagination need to be consistently present and viable.

Young adult shipwreck and the search for a new shore occur often in inconvenient, untimely forms: trauma in a romantic relationship, raising fundamental questions about the nature and worthiness of the self; a tumble into issues of social justice, disordering one's notions of the character of the world; an unwanted pregnancy, a divorce, or a death that shatters expectations of both past and future; or an encounter with new knowledge, leading to an intellectual impasse that swamps an earlier faith and its hope, replacing them with a sense of futility that no lecture can cure but that an afternoon with a mentoring professor might comfort and inform. These are hearth-sized conversations.

In some colleges, business settings, and elsewhere, one can still find vestiges of the traditional hearthside. Interestingly, they are reappearing in some new educational and corporate structures, though often in rather cold forms designed more to suggest an elegant ambiance than to invite lingering conversation. Students do not want simply more office hours. Coworkers and colleagues do not want an appointment. There is a hunger, however, for hearth and for conversation that begins as it happens and concludes whenever.

The practice of the hearth place can be recovered in a variety of forms and throughout a wide range of organizations and institutions. We know the difference between offices and homes that are at least sometimes willing to run on hearth time and those that cannot or will not. Mentoring environments find a way to practice hearth time.

The Practice of the Table. It has been said that in the practice of the table you know there will be a place for you, what is on the table will be shared, and you will be placed under obligation. In every culture, human beings have eaten together. It has been said also that a group has become a community when someone brings food. The practice of the table prepares us for civitas. In the practice of the table we learn to share, to wait, to accommodate, and to be grateful. The table is emblematic of economic, political, and spiritual realities. At the table, we learn delayed gratification, belonging, commitment, and ritual. The table is another kind of hearth place; likewise, it is a place where we may share conversation and become practiced in dialogue. It has served many as a place for learning how we can disagree yet remain deeply aware of our common bonds.

In an overindividualized, consumerist culture, however, the microwave oven easily becomes a primary saboteur of the family dinner table, ensuring warm food for all whether or not they are home for dinner "on time." We are not only consumers of "fast food," but there are also "stand-up gourmet restaurants" in which people eat sophisticated cuisine on the run and alone. The typical marketplace design serving emerging adults in schools or work-places focuses more on infinite individual options than on arrangements and aesthetics that encourage shared, lingering conversation. The practice of the table shrinks under the pressures of efficiencies and choice.

Yet we hunger; yet we eat. Emerging adults are drawn to those places that nourish them: places that in very practical terms recognize that the body, the heart, and the intellect are intimately interrelated and the whole is nourished. The practice of the table can play a significant role in creating meaningful and mentoring networks of belonging that serve the formation of adulthood in often subtle but significant ways.[33] The practice of the table foreshadows the practice of the commons.

The Practice of the Commons. Just as the table serves as a micro expression of civitas, so does the practice of the commons. The commons, as described in Chapter One, is the image that stands behind the concept of the common good. It is a place where people meet by happenstance and intention and have a sense of a shared, interdependent life within a manageable frame.

The commons affords practices of interrelatedness, belonging, and learning how to stand—and stand with—each other over time.

Many organizations and communities have a commons: the common room, the quad, the coffee shop, the park, the baseball stadium, the square, the local theatre, a chat room, a place of shared meditation, prayer, or worship. Whether the commons is inside or out, an active practice of the commons can bring together in fruitful tension and celebration the disparate elements of a community. It is a place within which to confirm a common, connected life, and in combination with various forms of story and ritual it can become a center of shared faith and grounded hope. A practice of the commons sets at the heart's core an imagination of *we* and weaves a way of life that conveys meaning and orients purpose and commitment.[34]

When parking lots create a centrifugal pulling away from the center, when there is no common time for gathering, when common space is shaped exclusively by commercial interests (as in a shopping mall), the commons ceases to serve an imagination of community and becomes fragmented, used only serially by various parochial interests, if at all. Emerging adults become vulnerable to dreams that represent only the interest of self and tribe rather than building Dreams that embrace and serve a wider life.

I am persuaded that if emerging adults are to become at home in the universe in ways that prepare them for citizenship and leadership in what has now become a global commons, they need to be grounded in meaning-making shaped, in part, by a micro experience of the commons—an embodied image and practice that nourishes the possibility of shared participation in creating the common good. The lived practice of hearth, table, and commons is a threefold gift by which a mentoring environment may nourish the emerging adult's imagination of purpose and faith in a changing, complex, diverse, and dangerous world.

Gaston Bachelard has written that the chief function of the house is to protect the dreamer.[35] It is the purpose of mentoring environments to provide a place within which emerging adults may discover themselves becoming more at home in the universe. Through many means, including the practices of hearth, table, and commons, mentoring environments create a context of recognition, support, challenge, and inspiration. They foster dialogue, critical and connective thought, and initiation into the power of the contemplative life. As networks of belonging, they invoke and offer hospitality to big questions. They serve as communities of imagination that distinctively honor and protect emerging adult meaning-making and the formation of worthy Dreams.

Chapter Nine

Higher Education as Mentor

A panel of university students is asked when and where they have conversations about "big questions." After quite a bit of discussion, one observant student responds, "We're numb to those issues." Further discussion reveals that this is not exactly a consequence of either apathy or skepticism but rather a lifestyle that has no room for such questions.

At its best, higher education is distinctive in its capacity to serve as a mentoring environment in the formation of critical, inner-dependent adult meaning-making—the formation of the consciousness, conscience, and competence needed in today's world. As society grows more complex, extended education becomes increasingly necessary as both a personal and a public good. The privileges and duties of citizenship and leadership require a well-informed, broad, multicultural perspective combined with practices of critical, connected, and contemplative thought to meet the needs of both the commons at large and the workplace in particular. The academy is uniquely positioned to promote optimal development during the emerging adult years— exposing people to ideas and experiences that challenge their expectations and worldviews in ways that honor both their potential and vulnerability.[1] Higher education can be vital space for the exploration and learning that is the heart and essence of the twenty-something decade and a preferred institution for the formation of adulthood.

Optimal learning and development depends on access to a mentoring environment, and higher education functions best when there is a clear understanding of this critical role: how the academy is composed of multiple mentoring communities, each providing in appropriate and accountable ways the recognition, support, challenge, and inspiration so vital for emerging adult lives. Mentoring communities—by intention or default—are formed within or across academic departments and professional schools, a particular course, a program of study, a scientific research project, an athletic team, a music or theatre arts group, a residence hall, a service-community learning project, internships and assistantships, campus religious life, and student clubs. These mentoring communities are shaped in turn by the four generally recognized subcultures of college life—"collegiate, vocational, academic, and rebel" that are woven throughout the whole life of the campus, and their significance as mentoring realities should not be underestimated.[2]

When we recognize the academy as a mentoring community serving the formation of meaning, purpose, and faith, we are in contested territory. Yet it is increasingly recognized that if "faith" is defined as meaning-making in its most comprehensive dimensions, it is naive to presume that higher education is a disinterested party. Moreover, it is primarily to this institution that young (and older) adults come to be initiated into critical thought, and on the other side of that discovery to make meaning and perhaps discern new purposes. Thus it is not too much to say that every institution of higher education serves in at least some measure as a community of imagination in which every professor is potentially a spiritual guide and every syllabus a confession of faith. To understand how this may be appropriately understood, it is useful to acknowledge and reflect on the epistemological assumptions of the academy.

Epistemological Assumptions

Since the nineteenth century, and particularly with the development of the research university, higher education has been

increasingly dominated by a particular interpretation of academic objectivity that over time has appeared to preclude questions of value and meaning. As a result, commitment to the true
has been divorced from the question of the good. Responsible
teaching has seemed to require only the dispassionate presentation of value-neutral fact or the presentation of multiple points
of view. Teachers, individually and collectively, are more inclined
to say, "The data show . . ." than "I have found . . . ," "We
contend . . . ," or "I believe. . . ."[3]

Correspondingly, the academy tends to perceive students
either as independent thinkers prepared to make objective judgments among competing alternatives or as conventional, dependent neophytes in need of being awakened to the complex and
relative character of all knowledge. These assumptions and this
ambivalence have extended to residence hall and extracurricular
life, where *in loco parentis* once prevailed but where now students
are regarded as rational adults on the one hand and presumed to
be in a process of development on the other. If, however, the
realities of cognitive-affective-social-moral development are recognized, in many instances they are no longer seen as the direct
concern of the faculty per se, nor are they regarded as germane
to the primary purposes of the college or university. As a consequence, on most campuses the work of the faculty and the work
of the student affairs professionals have been polarized and their
separation reified at the expense of students as whole persons.

These norms of academic life are rooted in the history of
Western epistemology—understandings about what we can know
and how we come to know it. The nineteenth-century influence
of a Kantian perspective (discussed in Chapter Seven) still pervades today's academy. Its members register considerable discomfort in engaging subjects that cannot readily be submitted to
empirical investigation. That is, following Kant, we have sharply
distinguished the knowing of the empirical world (pure reason)
from the world of meaning or ultimate truth (practical reason).
This distinction has had considerable power to limit the

discourse of the academy and to determine the focus of our collective attention. The academy is dedicated to knowledge. The
phenomenal can be known but noumenal reality cannot. And if
it cannot, the reasoning goes, then questions of meaning, morality, ultimacy, and faith—although surely important—stand
outside the realm of "knowledge" and are beyond (or irrelevant
to) the work of the academy.

In other words, the domain of knowledge has been reduced
to the domain of objective reality (understood as empirical fact
and theoretical analysis abstracted from fact). The knowledge of
the object that is known became divorced from its relationship
to the experience of the subject who knows, thus diminishing
the significance of emotion, intuition, the personal, the moral,
and full engagement with the complexity emerging from lived
experience. Reason and knowledge, thus defined, are reduced to
certain limited analytical processes that can be produced and
controlled—even bought and sold. As a consequence, whether
one traces the origins of the academy to the monastery or to
Athens, the academy's complex relationship to truth has been
diminished and within this framework the university is vulnerable to becoming a "knowledge industry."[4]

This shift in our claims for knowledge was initially a great
relief. A more adequate recognition of the limits of the human
mind required a more modest stance in relationship to claims of
ultimate truth. The academy relinquished some forms of hypocrisy, elite moralism, and un-self-critical assertions of truth.
Scholarship has made vital progress as a result of its now more
self-conscious methodologies. Still, whenever a strict dichotomy
between the objective and the subjective has been practiced, we
have become vulnerable to exchanging wisdom for knowledge
and moral commitment for method. Moreover, professors have
been vulnerable to functioning as less-than-whole persons, the
vocation of higher education has been impoverished, and students concerned with exploring questions of ultimate meaning—a
faith to live by—have been abandoned by faculty and others in

the academy who are distinctively positioned to serve the formation of a critical and worthy adult faith. Emerging adults are bereft of mentors they need, professors are too often reduced to mere technicians of knowledge, higher education fails to articulate an orienting vision or offer leadership toward a coherent unity, and discrete academic disciplines disclose only isolated (and thus distorted) aspects of truth. As a consequence, some of the most significant questions of the contemporary world are difficult to address within the prevailing rubrics of the academy.

Increasingly, this stance has been challenged by voices at the margins of the academy that make the claim for perspectives outside the privileged norms. These perspectives, many rooted in the particulars of place, ethnicity, gender, sexual orientation, and economic class, are typically grounded in personal or communal experience, both immediate and historical.

Thus, though the role of higher education in the formation of purpose and faith remains contested, a shift is taking place. There is a growing recognition emerging also from the sciences that an enriched epistemology is now required that takes into account the role of experience in all knowledge, the interdependence of all knowing, and the integrity of the whole person.

Along with a growing number of others, Arthur Zajonc, a physicist at Amherst College, has effectively made the case:

> Within the unfolding multiplicity of viewpoints posited by the new physics is a hidden harmony between the knowledge of one observer and all others that weaves the universe together into a dynamic whole whose faces are many but whose core is single. The new physics is no mere language game, but it does urge us to recognize our place in the genesis of a life-world, which is our world of experience. . . . We are thus called back to the centrality of human experience in all its forms. The implications of this ontological shift for education are profound . . . because each domain has equal standing, inasmuch as they are based equally on experience and reason. Whole organism biology and ecology have equal standing with

molecular genetics if their observations are of comparable quality and scope. Likewise psychology has as much legitimacy as neuroscience. . . . The predominance of the hard science approach has been based on a metaphysical precommitment. Now we know that that commitment is flawed, and what matters is the care and range of the observations within a field of inquiry and the quality of thought that has been applied to the field. . . . What distinguishes the hard sciences from the softer sciences is not the subject of study (neurons versus emotions, for example) but the reliability of the data. When observations are variable and uncertain, then knowledge is likewise insecure. The challenge to the soft sciences, which depend on qualitative assessment, is to ensure that their observations are accurate and reproducible. In my view, all data is in some measure "subjective"; the challenge is to make the subjective something we can count on.[5]

Recognizing that knowledge is an event in the life of the knower, Zajonc calls for a more contemplative form of inquiry as an essential modality of study complementary to the analytic methods that currently dominate every field and respect for "the elusive human capacity of imagination so central to a vital and genuine university."[6]

This enriched epistemology recognizes that every perspective is relative to particular personal, social, and cultural conditions. Yet because each incomplete perspective is, nevertheless, an attempt to comprehend the one reality there is, it is possible to make judgments about their validity as multiple perspectives mutually inform and correct each other. The boundary between the knower and "the one reality there is" becomes permeable, setting in its place an ongoing, dynamic process between the knower and the real, between the whole knower and the whole of life—the process Coleridge identified as Reason, with imagination as its highest power.

This way of understanding our search for truth invites a reconsideration of the relationship of the academy to issues of transcendent meaning. The reified boundary between empirical truth and questions of value, meaning, and faith that has characterized (if not tyrannized) the academy is, in principle, dismantled and the whole of reality becomes the concern of the academy in its commitment to truth. Certainly this perspective does not negate the responsibility of the academy to facilitate the learner's encounter with the relative character of all knowledge; indeed, it affirms that responsibility. But this perspective also frees the academy first to recognize that a value-free course has yet to be taught and second to serve emerging adults by assisting in composing critically aware and worthy commitments within a relativized world. As Michael Waggoner and his colleagues in *Sacred and Secular Tensions in Higher Education* have recognized, the academy is being asked to host the high stakes "tournament of world views" that is now underway.[7]

In a wide range of settings throughout the academy, therefore, there is growing evidence of considerable attention being paid to exploring alternative epistemologies that give voice not only to ethnic, gendered, and class perspectives that have been marginalized by the prevailing norms but also to perspectives that contend with questions of ethics and meaning and incorporate a recognition of the spiritual dimensions of knowing.[8] This coincides with a profound reordering of the academy taking place as a consequence of the development of new technologies and with growing concern about how the academy has become beholden to economic interests.[9]

This set of conditions means that on the one hand there is a fresh opening within the academy to consider the big questions of its own purpose and vocation, but on the other hand there is an erosion of the relative freedom of the academy to grapple with such questions on behalf of the wider culture. As a consequence, we are seeing bright emerging adults who have had so-called privileged educations, yet they have not been initiated into some of the great questions of this time in our cultural history. It is within this complex milieu that faculty, therefore and nevertheless, have significant opportunities to create mentoring communities responsive to a reassessment of the deep purposes and "lifestyle" of the academy.

The Syllabus: A Confession of Faith

Harvey Cox observed:

> When I ask my students to read something for a class, they want to know why. And when they ask why, they want me to tell them about the person who wrote it, why he or she wrote it and, most of all, why I find it important. They want especially to know what in my experience leads me to think they should bother to read it.
>
> Students will not sit still anymore while I argue that anyone who wants to be familiar with the "field" should know this book. They are drowning in things they "ought to know," as we all are. They sense already what it took me years to discover—that they will never know all the things somebody thinks they ought to know. Like me, they stagger under the daily surfeit of words we call the "information overload crisis." They wisely suspect that much of what they are supposed to "know" is useless information that has been magically transformed into awesome lore by those who control educational institutions and career advancement. But they do not want lore, they want testimony. . . .
>
> What my students are saying, sometimes incoherently, is, "I don't want to master a field, nor do I want to leave all the decisions to experts and pros. What will help me survive, choose, fight back, grow, learn, keep alive? That I'll read or think about: anything else can wait."
>
> These sentiments are not those of mere intellectual vagabonds growing up to be dilettantes. We are evolving a new way of organizing the life of the mind, and contrary to the criticisms, it does have a principle of selection and order. These students want to learn whatever will help them make sense of the world as they experience it and enable them to work for the changes they believe are needed. They will also gladly read

something they know has made a real difference to someone they respect, be he or she faculty, student or anyone else.[10]

Cox wrote this in 1973. If it sounds current, it is because early on he was attuned to the realities of an information age, to the careerism that increasingly shapes the expectations of emerging adults, and the desire on the part of many students to make a difference and shape the future. It has always been the case that some students, seemingly motivated only by utilitarian concerns, simply never consider or abandon the hope of finding meaning and purpose that is truly satisfying. They need initiation into critical thought, in part so that they may reflect on the careerism to which they have become subject. For others, the question looms large: "Can self and world be composed into a meaningful and viable future?"

Once we recognize the academy as a community of imagination in recomposing knowledge and faith, it appropriately follows that a syllabus functions as a professor's "testimony," as a "confession of faith." That is, in preparing a syllabus, educators declare what they believe to be of value: questions, images, insights, concepts, theories, sources, and methods of inquiry that they have found to lead toward a worthy apprehension of truth. In an interdependent universe in which all aspects of knowledge participate in the one reality there is, we may say that each theory, course, and discipline discloses some aspect of this one reality. Nancy Malone, a Roman Catholic educator, writes that "in a sacramental universe, to teach and study mathematics can be, and in fact is, as holy as to teach and study the Bible."[11]

It does not surprise me that, in my experience, the most effective educators are those who engage in their discipline (or administrative responsibilities) because in the work they do, they have found at least some access to transcendent meaning. In a world in which there is evidence in almost every news broadcast that matters of scientific fact are also matters of moral concern, reflective learners are intrigued by and grateful for access to the connections professors have seen between the subjects they teach and life lived in the complexity, wonder, and terror of the everyday world.

Students may rightly intuit that it is not incidental that educators have given the energy of their lives to the particular disciplines they teach. They have done so because, to some significant degree, they find their discipline to be a worthy investment in their own meaning-making—even in the composing of faith. Thus, the syllabus reflects only a portion of the professor's truth if it includes nothing more than a confession of some aspect of meaning (such as the technical aspects of study) and fails to include the educator's understanding of the relationships between his or her discipline and the quest for meaning and purpose in a complex world.

Big-Enough Questions

Every generation of scholars, therefore, must consider, To what questions do we lend our intellect and discipline? What is the work, the deep purpose, of higher education in today's world? Do we serve the formation and practice of adequate truth? In what ways do we affect who our students become? Such questions draw our attention to the moral power of the academy to teach critical thought, awaken the imagination, and encourage development of the inner authority and the potential leadership of emerging adults—in part by creating conscious conflict and sustaining the tension of restless opposites. The academy may bring together with real power and seriousness those subjects that are at the present time thought to be major aspects of reality, no matter how threatening their mutual contradiction. The quest here is for a quality of "deeper learning"—"a commitment to foster a level of learning that pushes us so deeply into our own questions that the conclusions are unforgettable."[12]

In a time of dramatic social and technological transition, the art of the syllabus and the curriculum as a whole dwells in the questions that give them life. For example, in today's world, should students be able to graduate from a university if they have not learned to live with those around them? Do we have a functional cosmology—a "common sense"—that respects insights from the new sciences, appropriately assesses new technologies, and addresses our radically changing cultural circumstances? Do we need a new economic imagination? Can we continue to prepare people to extend human dominion over the more-than-human world without preparing them for intimate presence and responsible participation within it?[13] Can the resources of the university become increasingly sophisticated while the neighborhoods on the university's doorstep deteriorate? These kinds of questions stretch the imagination of all and reorder the syllabus and the wider curriculum. Such inquiry invites the academy to reexamine its own meaning, purpose, and faith.

The Professor as Spiritual Guide

Mentoring communities are composed of more than mentors, but apart from mentors they do not exist. Many people within the academy may serve in mentoring roles: faculty, administrators, student affairs, other professional and technical staff, and often students themselves. It is, however, the faculty-student relationship that forms the backbone of any educational institution, and it may be said that the true professor serves, inevitably, as a spiritual guide.

Again, we must acknowledge that to speak of the professor as a spiritual guide may well make any number of teachers and administrators uneasy. It may appear especially problematic for public institutions in a culture committed to separation of church and state. R. Eugene Rice has helpfully recognized the finitude of the image: "*Guide* is a strong word," he writes, "and for me it crosses a professional boundary that needs to be acknowledged and respected." Though he does not offer a direct alternative, he rightfully seeks a way of recognizing both the inevitable and appropriate role of faculty in relationship to the meaning-making and spiritual lives of students that avoids any suggestion of arrogance or indoctrination and conveys a sufficient measure of humility balanced with a kind of necessary courage.[14] The image of "guide" is not intended to violate that boundary but rather to recognize the unity of all knowledge, the inevitable and appropriate influence of faculty in students' lives, and to emancipate professors from an inappropriate separation of self from truth.

A professor is an educator (from the Latin *educare*, to lead out or draw out), one who has the responsibility of guiding toward "right" imagination. The practice of right imagination is, as Coleridge saw, participation in the motion of life itself, the activity of Spirit, a process that faculty do not ultimately control but that they do participate in and influence. Further, because the emerging adult (in whatever field of study or endeavor) is still appropriately dependent on authority outside the self, one way in which the professor leads out is by responsibly beckoning the spirit—the animating essence—of the student. Hence, the encounter of student and teacher that serves a recomposing of truth—affecting the meaning of the whole of life—is a meeting of spirit with spirit.

A reexamination of the word *professor* is instructive. A professor (at an earlier time, this meant "church member") is, in the primary definition, a person who professes something, especially one who openly declares his or her sentiments, religious belief, subject, and so on. Therefore, an educator-professor is one who leads out toward truth by professing his or her intuitions, apprehensions, and convictions of truth *in a manner that encourages dialogue with the emerging inner authority of the student.*

Cheryl Keen, a professor in education, has recognized the vital role that such professing can play in the learning process. A competent student first asked for a more challenging assignment and then for more time to complete the paper. When she finally arrived, with a completed paper describing her own educational philosophy, the student didn't feel it was finished. There were kernels of ideas drawn from her recent teaching experience in the community, but she was in pain because writing the paper had reminded her of how critical she was of the present school system, and she was questioning whether or not she could be a teacher anyway. Keen writes:

> In the face of her frustration, I can feel myself shift to a deeper plane. I want to be honest, to partner with her as she asks essential questions. She is pulling from me the best I have to offer. I'm surprised it has taken this long for me to share explicitly my own philosophy of education. I tell her, "I try to speak to that of God in every person. I work to make my classrooms, my assignments, and my conversations with students reflect this approach. I trust that our relationships matter a great deal. I worry just as much about the whole learning environment we are working in as I do about my own classroom. This means I want to know people as individuals, . . . to design assignments that provoke thought and connections between ideas and with the 'other' . . . and to give the other person the benefit of the doubt, trusting that people are trying to do their best and hoping to give them the space their inner spirit requires. I have to listen closely and pay attention or I may not see the flickering of a hopeful spirit or an awakening mind. Time has taught me to trust my intuitions. I assume that class discussions, conversations, and counseling sessions . . . help . . . toward a sense of what really matters and, ultimately toward their vocation."

The gratitude of the student confirmed in Keen a sense of that meeting of spirit with spirit.[15]

Again, this is not to suggest in any way that the educator is given license to impose idiosyncratic or private truth on the student. Andrew Delbanco has well recognized that "the *laissez-faire* norm of the modern university is a great achievement and should not be lightly discarded or even slightly modified." By that he suggests that the role of the professor is to identify worthy texts "that place the Big Questions front and center, and let the discussion begin. In small groups. Led by sympathetic but rigorous teachers who know something about the texts and their genealogies and applications. An occasional lecture from someone who knows a lot about the texts can be helpful too."[16]

Such teaching reflects scholarship as a disciplined engagement with sources that both include and go beyond one's own personal experience and perspective. An intellectual community not only consists of its living members but also extends to include its forebears and a critical reappraisal of their legacies. Thus, the responsible professor is, among other things, a bearer of tradition, participating with the student in a community's ongoing composing of wisdom. Goethe said that a tradition is not inherited; rather, one must earn it. It is earned if tradition is set in rigorous dialogue with the living community as known in the present and as anticipated in the future.

The mentoring professor, therefore, must convene and mediate among multiple perspectives, composing a trustworthy community of imagination—a community of confirmation and contradiction. This disciplined wrestling with multiple perspectives is the practice of objectivity in a reformed sense: that is, a community's commitment to the shared discernment of truth, understood as that on which all minds can agree. A graduating master's student reflected on the process this way: "I think probably 30 percent of the learning in the first year was done in preparation for class, and 70 percent came out of the discussion, because there was a lot of controversy, a lot of different perspectives that I hadn't even dreamed of."

Passion

For the emerging adult to be drawn into full participation in the academy as a community of imagination, he or she must be led out by scholarship that is animated by passion. The revitalization of both the act of teaching and the curriculum itself is being addressed in many quarters. All seek new or renewed passion, authenticity, and wholeness in the dialogue among teachers and learners, sharing a search for truth that honors the fullness of what is at stake for the meaning, purpose, and vocation of higher education itself.[17] Wholesome passion is rare in American life, however, as Keniston observed:

> Passion is usually placed "out there"—in others, in the movies, in uncivilized countries, or even "out there" in some far corner of our psyches for which we feel neither kinship nor responsibility. . . . The changed meaning of the word "passion" itself illustrates this disavowal: in colloquial speech, "passion" has become virtually synonymous with sexual excitation, and rarely means deep or ennobling feeling.
>
> Of all the forces of human life, however, passion . . . is the least amenable to repression and the most prone to reassert itself in some other form. Pushed down, it springs up; denied in one form, it reappears in disguise; refused, it still makes its claim and exacts its price. When denied a central and conscious place alongside of intelligence, it becomes ugly and degenerates into mere instinct.[18]

Many instructors do not share their passion and commitment because in their own formation as educators their vision was so disallowed that it has lost its voice. Others conscientiously resist having "too much influence." Indeed, the responsible professor does not seek a cult following built around his or her personality. Rather, and again, the emerging adult (in contrast to the adolescent) does not seek a hero but a mentor, and in the mentoring relationship it is the passion and the inner-dependent potential of the student that is finally what the relationship is all about. In the mentoring relationship, the tested commitments of the educator and the potential, emerging commitments of the protégé coincide—at least for a while.[19]

Coleridge grasped the role of passion in the process of learning and knowing when he described the poetic imagination—the infusion of the image with the poet's own spirit. Only then does the imagination become vital—full of life—and awaken those truths "that lie slumbering in the dormitory of the soul." The poet remains "faithful to nature" (honoring objectivity), while employing images and modifying them by a "predominant passion"—the poet's own spirit and apprehension of truth.[20] This understanding of the poetic imagination suggests that all educators are in this sense poets. Coleridge contended that "to contemplate the Ancient of days . . . with feelings as fresh, as if all had sprung forth at the first creative fiat, characterizes the mind that feels the riddle of the world and may help to unravel it."[21]

If the vocation of higher education is to feel "the riddle of the world and help to unravel it," mentoring educators are invited to serve as poets—awakeners of imagination, professors whose spirits so infuse their subject matter that the spirit of the student is beckoned out and discovers fitting forms in which to dwell.

Images become fitting forms only when they are resonant with the experience and spirit of the one who imagines. An image that can shape a new faith must fit the truth of both mind and heart. This is to say that truth for anyone, at least ultimate truth, is that which engages his or her whole being. If an image is going to anchor the composing of a new reality, it must resonate in the feelings, history, and anticipated future of the emerging adult; it must have the capacity to affect, to touch, and finally to lock into the being of the person. This asks the educator to draw, in part, on the reservoir of images already planted in the experience of the learner or to give the learner an experience of an image that brings the whole person into an encounter with the images (the content) the educator deems worthy. Jacques Barzun has stated it well:

> How do you pour a little bit of what you feel and think and know into another's mind? In the act of teaching it is done by raising the ghost of an object, idea, or fact, and holding it in full view of the class, turning it this way and that, describing it—demonstrating it like a new car or a vacuum cleaner. The

public has an excellent name for this: "making the subject come to life." The student must see the point, must re-create Lincoln, must feel like Wordsworth at Tintern Abbey, must visualize the pressure of the atmosphere on a column of mercury. The "subject" should become an "object" present before the class, halfway between them and the teacher, concrete, convincing, unforgettable. This is why teachers tend so naturally to use physical devices—maps, charts, diagrams. They write words on the board, they gesture, admonish, and orate. Hence the fatigue and hence the rule which I heard a Dean enunciate, that good teaching is a matter of basal metabolism.[22]

Listen to how two people describe mentoring professors who invited them to deepen their own sense of inner authority, encouraged their power to question, and helped them develop their own sense of participation in important work.

A freshman reflecting on one of her "best classes" said of a mentoring professor: "It is actually a lecture course, but somehow he keeps it a dialogue. He's always asking questions. He's more interested in an opinion than an answer. He is willing to talk about himself and doesn't distance himself from the subject. He is willing to say 'from my experience' or 'from my perspective.' He's not saying that his is the 'right one,' but he is willing to share it with us. Once when we happened to bring up a particular film in class discussion, he responded by showing it in class the next day."

A woman well into her professional life in public health remembered:

I had a philosophy teacher whose whole approach was not to teach about philosophers but to teach different ways of thinking. She would teach about Plato, but then in the test not ask you anything at all about Plato. She'd ask you to talk about your own life experience from a Platonic perspective. And then there was my biology teacher, otherwise known as The Ace. She was young—maybe only ten years older than I—and dynamic. It was her enthusiasm that drew me. She was clearly brilliant and very dedicated to her own field of research. . . . I've always been attracted to people who are up on what they do. I didn't have that many classes with her, but what she did for me was serve as a sounding board.

Worthy Dreams

Reflecting on a dinner conversation she and her husband shared with six twenty-somethings (all undergrad university students, most in their last term before graduation), a colleague writes, "We asked some 'big questions' and four hours later pushed away from the table. We had talked about the environment, war, illiteracy, systemic racism, kids in foster care, gender inequality as well as their feelings about what can and can't be done about these issues. The link between these well-articulated concerns and what these students plan to do after graduation was very fragile. They agreed that they had not had any opportunity to reflect on their own or together on this link in the years they had been at the university." This conversation surely reflects that the work of emerging adulthood is not typically accomplished in the early twenties. But I believe it reflects also that it is easier within the life of the academy to serve as a context for asking big questions than it yet is to encourage the worthy dreams that big-enough questions may spawn.

Particularly through the agency of a bold philanthropic initiative, a significant number of colleges across the United States have been encouraged to take up the question of how a worthy sense of purpose and vocation may be fostered within emerging adult lives as an integral part of academic and campus life. The institutions that have responded to this challenge have made considerable progress in exploring this dimension of the potential of higher education and its role as a mentoring environment.[23] The hunger for such efforts can be heard also in the voices of some students at Stanford University, where a course pioneered in the School of Design, titled "Designing Your Life," has attracted significant interest. Applying for the course (which has limited enrollment) three students wrote:

> I've gone through all the motions of an undergraduate career, declared a major, laid out a four-year plan . . . but still feel unfulfilled. It's not that I'm not motivated. I just don't know what direction I want to take in that big scary picture called "life." . . . Through this course I hope to grow the guts to explore what's out there and challenge myself in pushing my potential.
>
> I'm chronically challenged by my tendency to "go with the flow" of things. As much as I enjoy being laid back and accepting, I'd also like to learn how to play a more active role in thinking up and executing a plan or vision for myself. I'd like to challenge the flow. . . .
>
> I hope this course will help me think about my future from different perspectives. . . . I also think it will be interesting to work with other students . . . since my friends and I don't talk much about future plans (probably because it stresses us out too much).

At the close of the course a student reflects:

> Talking with mentors whose opinion you value really helped. The main thing I'm gratified by is the ability understand what I want, and know what I truly value, and design my career around work I really find fulfilling, versus just going somewhere with a brand name or where my friends went. I'm thousands of miles from where I thought I would end up, in a totally different industry, living a totally different life. It [the course] helped me to find a set of problems that I would like to tackle . . . and kind of [gave me] have the courage not only to seek out what I want . . . but my ability to be OK with that.[24]

These are not hungers and conversations that can be addressed by the career counselors in student services alone.

They are the deep question at the core of the big questions—
Where do I put my stake in the ground and invest my life? Every
discipline and program of study has light to cast on this question,
and every member of the faculty and administration—indeed all
who serve the life of the academy—have distinctive opportunities to meet emerging adults as they seek place and purpose in a
world that needs them.

Reflecting on a lifetime of deeply committed scholarship,
teaching, and administration, the dean of a professional school
observed:

> There isn't any question that one of the greatest things that we
> do for anyone else is to show enough confidence to ask them to
> do something which is important—important to them,
> important to you. . . . I've had people around me . . . teachers,
> advisors . . . all of whom have done that. They came and asked
> me to do things that both of us agreed were important, and I
> was willing. I found out the joy of that as well as the duty of it.
> These people saw their role, rightly I think, as cultivators of
> talents and opportunities for young people.

The Courage and Costs of the Intellectual Life

Many thoughtful professors are soberly aware that teaching and
the life of the academy has consequences that touch the whole
life of a student. Here Patricia O'Connell Killen catches the
balance of promise and peril:

> Developing more complex ways of thinking and knowing, of
> perceiving and constructing experience and its meanings,
> changes our students irrevocably. This is the kind of knowing
> that cannot be un-known. For our students this is a process of
> reconstituting themselves as human beings . . . for some
> welcome, for others not. For all, however, it . . . usually
> involves . . . a sense of tension and even betrayal of family, peer
> group, social class, ethnic community, religious denomination,

or political ideology. . . . Anyone who has had occasion to
listen to freshmen students talk in an unguarded manner during
January term about being at home over Christmas break after
their first semester . . . gets a glimmer of the human costs of
education. To have an idea and to know one has an idea can be
a fearsome thing. . . . To formulate a question and to know that
one's question is good is at once exhilarating and terrifying. To
be able to articulate why one's question is good is to have
passed a point of no return. In all of these acts a new and more
complex consciousness emerges in a person, a consciousness
that offers both promise and peril. The promise includes richer,
more nuanced relationships to whomever and whatever is,
including oneself. . . . The peril includes loss of the comfort of
a host of absolute certitudes; the burden of self-
responsibility; . . . and the realization that one's actions,
motivated by the best of intentions, cause harm. The wager of
the humanities has been and still is that the promise outweighs
the peril.[25]

As this quality of reflection conveys, when educators fulfill
their deepest vocation, leading out the next generation by
addressing these larger dimensions of knowing, they do not have
to be on an ego trip. One can teach simply out of a humble
recognition that "one generation owes the next the strength by
which it can come to face ultimate concerns in its own way."[26]

In manifold ways, higher education serves—consciously or
unconsciously—as a mentoring environment for the re-formation
of meaning, purpose, and faith. As higher education reconsiders
its own vocation in the life of today's global commons, the invitation to step up to the adaptive challenges of our time by serving
both what can be known and the one who knows is profound. It
invites all of us to ask bigger questions and to claim worthy
dreams.

Chapter Ten

Culture as Mentor

When the passionate, boundless energy of our youth is wasted
through the failure of our culture to give meaningful direction
and care, we all court disaster. Without elders, who grasp and
protect the mysterious core of culture, inner purpose and spirit
do not get valued and acknowledged by an appropriate
community and people feel like victims and act like outcasts.

—Michael Meade

Every culture is invested in the central task of the twenty-
something era: to discover and compose a critically aware adult
faith—a way of making meaning in its most comprehensive
dimensions—that can orient the self to a worthy adulthood.
Accomplishing this task depends in great measure on the quality
of mentoring environments available to emerging adults. It is not
enough, therefore, to reconsider only the relationship between
emerging adults and particular contexts such as higher education, the workplace, religion, and the family (see the Coda). We
must enlarge our gaze and consider also the whole cultural milieu
in which twenty-somethings move into adulthood.

Every culture serves as a mentoring environment, mediating
expectations of adulthood and the terms of faith. *Culture* as a
word is closely linked with "cultivation." A culture is composed
of the forms of life by which a people cultivate and maintain a
sense of meaning, thus giving shape and significance to their
experience. Culture unfolds in its politics—that is, in the whole

complex of relationships among people in their society—and in myriad forms, both mundane and sublime (symbols, language, institutions, art, practices, customs, and habits), by which people express their convictions of ultimate reality and thereby order their everyday lives.[1] Culture mediates a people's faith as it creates and teaches "how things are" or "how life is." A culture coheres across time through the protection, maintenance, and evolution of what Michael Meade describes as its "mysterious core"—values and practices that nourish essential hungers and animate the imagination of life. A culture dies when the correspondence is lost between its forms and values and the felt conditions of ongoing human experience.

Because the developmental perspective we have described requires us to ask, "What do we now mean to each other?" as a culture we must ask, "What do emerging adults and the present adult culture now mean to each other? Does contemporary culture serve today's emerging adults as a worthy mentoring environment?" Is our present culture accountable to emerging adults—providing recognition, support, challenge, and inspiration in ways that honor both their potential and vulnerability?

Recognition

As conveyed in Chapter One, today's culture is beginning to recognize emerging adulthood as a new era in the human life span—a consequence of a changing cultural milieu. A cultural milieu functions on multiple scales, including local, regional, national, and global. It has many dimensions; thus, we speak, for example, of ethnic, political, religious, business, and popular cultures. Most of today's twenty-somethings dwell in a mix of cultures that sometimes complement each other but just as often collide in their efforts to capture the imagination and allegiance of the next generation. To some degree, this has been true throughout time.

Globalization—a Single Place

But certainly the development of globalization is a primary fact of today's commons that creates a significant change in the cultural milieu defining the imagination of emerging adults. "Globalization" refers both to the compression of the world and to intensifying consciousness of the world as a whole—"turning the world into a single place."[2] The effect of globalization is subjective and objective, and it entails psychological and educational consequences. We are all swept up into an interdependent world, which requires new meaning-making at all levels. Increasingly, hopes and anxieties are fueled by events taking place half a world away.

Two primary features of globalization are its amplification of consciousness-shaping influences through travel and new media technologies and their effect on youth culture. "In a world that is highly interconnected, such influences do not stay in one place. The research on the change of values in the Western world, for example, has made this quite clear. Changing value orientations in youth are not limited to any one country anymore. . . . Such changes spread out like a 'silent revolution.' . . ."[3] Emerging adults in diverse geographical locations long for the same athletic shoes, drink the same beverages, and harbor similar personal and political ambitions. The voices that influence them and their networks of belonging may include others a continent or more away.

It follows that another consequence of globalization is that all cultural traditions are relativized. As the world becomes a single place, simultaneously there is growing awareness of the radical diversity of people and lifestyles and manifold ways of understanding self, other, world, and "God." Especially because emerging adults are often among the first to experience the dissonance between established cultural norms and emerging global realities, and because they are facile in their ability to experiment with new forms, they play a significant role in the globalization of culture.

These dynamics can foster a kind of precocious but conventional relativism. Within this relativism, faith tends to be regarded as a highly subjective and individual matter, leaving the individual to merely "fit in" with little expectation of finding a shared integrity and depth of meaningful community in the vast global sea.[4]

Some cope by making a reflexive grab for security in either an exotic faith identity that "will do for me" or a fundamentalism that offers community and certainty but at the cost of excluding big questions that may give rise to doubt. These dynamics spawn subcultures of all sorts and a renewed tribalism that poses a major threat to the commons and to emerging adults seeking meaningful place and purpose in a globalized world. Yet there is also a quite conscious spirit of exploration and dialogue across differences, motivated by curiosity, compassion, and a clear-eyed view of the reality and implications of the interdependent relatedness of all things.

What globalization does and will mean cannot yet be very richly perceived and understood by any of us. If global consciousness means only the relativization of every culture, and if emerging adults are simply set adrift in a crisis of knowledge and value, so that they must make do in a state of "indecision, confusion and fuzziness"—persuaded that "real knowledge is impossible and genuine values are illusion," then, contemporary culture is not meeting emerging adults in ways that serve the promise of their lives.[5] But to the degree that the globalization of culture reveals and redefines the context of moral action in more adequate terms and spurs the recomposing of yet more inclusive meaning and purpose, globalization can awaken and stir new generations of meaningful discovery and commitment, grounded in more vital forms of inner- and interdependent faith.

Consumers Versus Citizens

Within this changing and globalized culture, a question that must be asked is, Are emerging adults being recognized primarily as citizens or consumers? Are we preparing the next generations to become consumers of stuff (including knowledge, credentials, success, opportunities, and experiences) rather than inviting them first to become stewards and creators of culture—that is, citizen-leaders committed to the creation of the common good? In the absence of a more profound and compelling master narrative, the dominant economic faith of our time has an inside track on claiming the imagination and loyalties of emerging adults. Rooted in the belief that consumption based on individual choice creates a global marketplace that provides what we collectively need, billions of advertising dollars are wagered on the premise that the most meaningful purpose to which one can aspire is to become a successful individual consumer (which in turn shapes a cascade of other life choices). To this end, emerging adults are a favored, "targeted market" because they remain vulnerable to peer expectations and brand loyalty is still being formed.[6]

As most would agree, however, this "Dream" of endless consumption is anchored in poignantly narrow understandings of self, purpose, productivity, wealth, achievement, and success. As Lendol Calder elegantly described in *Financing the American Dream: A Cultural History of Consumer Credit*, from the beginning the American Dream has had a double nature. It is "both a set of 'free' ideals whose worth cannot be measured in market terms, and a wish list of goods with expensive price tags." In this two-sided Dream there lies "a paradox inscribed so deeply in the everydayness of contemporary life it easily goes unremarked." By means of consumer credit, the American Dream has appeared "both fabulously expensive and generally affordable. . . ." Calder is keenly interested in the "core ministry of cultural traditions, the way they address the existential questions that confront all of us as we navigate our way through life: Who am I? What is worth doing? How am I to live, and what is the best way to cope with the hardships I must suffer? Cultures," he writes, "including consumer culture, exist to answer such questions."[7]

Coupling the assumptions of consumer culture with technologies that speed up the pace of expectation and artfully authorize "choice" has left all of us—old and young alike—vulnerable to responding to these big questions in consumerist terms. A culture "always on the run" has limited time to critically examine the nature and effects of our new cultural milieu in the midst of the ever-present and "more alluring universe of distractions. . . ."[8] Consumer-oriented Dreams provide a powerful array of images that weave a narrative of presumed adulthood and, at least implicitly, define a corresponding faith.

This economic orientation has a high level of need for the best and the brightest of the next generation. It needs them to consume and to be consumed, that is, to capture their imaginations and harness and exhaust their talents and passions. To consume means to destroy utterly. Many bright and gifted emerging adults have been heard to say, "Well, I'll aim for working eighty-plus-hour weeks for five to ten years and then I'll be free to live the way I want"—inadequately aware of how formative those years are for setting the trajectory and the habits of their entire adulthood and the costs of the anxiety and stress that such choices demand.

Meanwhile, growing numbers of emerging adults are essentially "unseen"—not simply because culture is still catching on to the fact of this new era in the life span, but also because they are no longer as welcome as they once were. For although there is a need for some highly educated workers, within our current economic arrangements there is a limited need for well-paid workers. Thus the mainstream culture becomes less insistent that everyone become an adult member.[9] To the degree that these conditions gain momentum, the potential and vulnerability of emerging adult lives remain under-recognized, and they become increasingly problematized rather than seen as worthy of being mentored and welcomed into adulthood.[10]

Citizens

If, in contrast, twenty-somethings are recognized as emerging adult *citizens*, they are seen in another light. Although the word *consumer* is individually oriented and depends on a degree of passive compliance, the word *citizen* is relationally cast, suggesting rights, protection, and participation. Citizen is related to *civis*: city. A citizen is a person in responsible relationship to an identifiable sociality.

The rights and responsibilities of citizenship vary from one locale and culture to another, but wherever one is located, being a citizen in today's complex global world requires critical-connective thought, an empathic imagination, and committed engagement—a citizenry well practiced in relentless discernment, complex moral dialogue, skillful knowledge, and the arts of innovation. It is in these terms that a *mentoring culture* recognizes and responds to emerging adults who ask (directly and indirectly), Who am I? What is worth doing? How am I to live, and what is the best way to cope with the hardships I must suffer?

Support

Within a healthy cultural milieu, mentoring presences take many forms, but they are in essence people, communities, places, and institutions that support emerging adults in their distinctive expressions of potential and vulnerability. The question here is, Does today's culture provide broad access to positive, supportive mentoring environments?

On this point, Robert Wuthnow's observations are particularly forceful. He observes that our culture provides institutional (caretaker and developmental) support for children and adolescents and, in some measure, for younger emerging adults in the forms of colleges and universities. But "the amazing thing," he writes, "about this pattern of support and socialization is that it all comes to a halt about the time a young person reaches the age of twenty-one or twenty-two. After providing significant institutional support for the developmental tasks that occurred before then, we provide *almost nothing* for the developmental tasks that are accomplished when people are in their twenties and thirties. And, since more of those tasks are happening later, this is a huge problem. It means that younger adults are having to invent their own ways of making decisions and seeking support. . . ."[11] For large numbers of emerging adults, decision making now occurs through the Internet or at bars, at parties, in cityscapes where emerging adults congregate in typically homogenous, age-determined subcultures. Emerging adults are making major decisions in individual and improvisational ways without the resources of support and stability that a mature and healthy culture could be expected to provide.

For those who go to college after graduating from secondary school, there may be access to a mentoring community, particularly in those colleges where there is a clear commitment to undergraduate teaching and community. Nevertheless, graduation day appears, and as James Keen has observed, despite the virtues of the Internet, we dramatically underestimate the significance of the loss of community that emerging adults experience the day they graduate, whether it be from secondary school or from college.[12] If twenty-somethings who are still making their way into full adulthood do not move directly into graduate school or a stable work position, they face a significant unknown. Often for the first time, their future is their own to design.

Facing the Void

Near the end of her senior year of college, Kate Daloz became aware that she was not the only person undergoing this kind of transition and facing a kind of void. She began to ask her friends for metaphors that captured their experience. One person, recently graduated from college but without much sense of purpose or direction, decided, "It's like a trapeze artist, when it comes to that moment where you're at the end of one swing and you gotta let go and grab onto the other trapeze, but you really just don't want to let go and you're not sure if there's a safety net or not, and you know you can't just swing backward either or you'll hit the wall (and the whole time there are thousands of people watching you)."

A recent university graduate who was about to look for a job in his home city said, "I feel like I got a new set of beautiful angel wings and I'm admiring them and preening them and everyone's giving me compliments, but then I try to fly and jump off a cliff and realize I don't know how to use them. I'm scared to death and flapping and falling, and even though I know I'll never hit the bottom because every once in a while I hit the wind right and bounce up a little, I have that constant tension in my stomach."

Another graduate, sorting through possible career and location options, yearned for access to a broader perspective: "I feel like I'm a pioneer, trying to make my way west on no trail. I'm kind of lost in the bushes and tumbleweeds and don't know which way to go, and what I really want is some sort of guide to stand up on a cliff above me, where they can see the place I'm trying to get to, and call down directions to me about which way to head."

This absence of accompaniment was evident also in the experience of a notably fine twenty-six-year-old attorney just out of law school. Choosing to work in the office of an admired state attorney general, he expected that in the course of his work he would be learning aspects of the law and the legislative process from association with her. Their paths rarely crossed, however, and though the young attorney carried significant responsibilities, there was very limited opportunity to work at the issues aligned with his central aspirations.

Still seeking a place where he could work on key issues having long-term importance for the region, he moved into a large private law firm, assured that he would work with someone who shared his interests. The promise of shared work proved illusory, and when he looked elsewhere in the firm for mentors, they did not seem to exist. He asked others in the firm just slightly older, "Where did you get feedback when you were first working here?" The response was, "We didn't get it either."

There was a time when informal mentoring did occur within the professions and notably within law, but now we are at least two generations deep in the erosion of that kind of natural mentoring. As one attorney put it, "It isn't profitable for two lawyers to talk with each other; when they do, they aren't billable hours."

Each of these emerging adults reflects a mix of strength and vulnerability and the legitimate need for the support of mentoring in the transitions now at hand. Though it has been said that the world is always ready to receive talent with open arms, this is not the experience of many emerging adults. To be sure, there are some enterprises that actively seek the best talent. But this is not the same as providing time, presence, meaningful respect, and other forms of support for emerging adults in "the in-between" when they must discern and test the pathways available to them. How cultural norms and structures for this quality of intergenerational conversation might evolve remains to be seen. In the meantime, however, a culture might usefully ask how the firm, business, department, work crew, or research lab can call forth the best potential of emerging adults—and how policies affecting the health, education, and employment of emerging adults are being adjudicated.

Vulnerability

Meanwhile many emerging adults are paying a high price for a changing culture in which there is inadequate access to even minimal emotional and practical support. Among those on the privileged side of the economic divide, there are emerging adults who appear to harbor an inappropriate sense of entitlement, but this often obscures growing levels of stress, loneliness, and depression. These also share with those on the other side of the divide evidence of record levels of alcoholism and other substance abuse along with early death from various forms of accidents and suicide.[13] Those at the furthest margins of culture are vulnerable to the exploitative, numbing, and even deadly effects of prostitution, prisons, and warfare. Cleary, too many emerging adults on both sides of the economic divide are under-recognized and bereft of the support that is their birthright.

A dominant example is observed in the life-world of a growing number of young men as today's culture is recomposing the meaning of traditional male roles and the expectations to procreate, provide, and protect. Rendered distracted, numb, and passive by the pervasive realities of violent video gaming, casual and predatory sex, binge drinking, and barbaric hazing, they are vulnerable to becoming "man-boys," arrested in conventional thought. Lacking the engaged presence of mature male models, they are reduced to initiating one another into a pseudo-manhood.[14] These vulnerabilities (directly and indirectly affecting young women as well as young men) are compounded within institutions of higher education that tolerate the demeaning and dangerous features of "collegiate culture," authorized, in effect, by the wider culture.

Emerging adults who have suffered significant wounds in childhood and adolescence bear additional vulnerabilities, as many in a changing culture with strained and weakened social bonds have experienced. Yet as the young adult self begins to individuate from powerful and painful relationships, reflect critically on the world of others who have inflicted pain, he or she can reassess the implications for the self. For these as for all emerging adults, with appropriate support from a mentoring culture, meaning, purpose, and faith can be recomposed.

Indeed, emerging adulthood can be a time of healing—and significant redirection. The twenty-something years have been likened to a "stem-cell" moment in human development, when possibilities are uniquely open. Such encouragement requires a culture that not only recognizes and systemically supports a longer transition into adulthood but also provides access to rightly timed and worthy challenges.[15]

Challenge

At this time in history and in the lives of emerging adults, the challenges and opportunities of citizenship are heightened by unprecedented conditions that present a significant array of adaptive challenges. For example, it is increasingly evident to growing numbers that a central challenge of our time is posed by threats to the integrity of our planet. No longer can ecological concerns merely be taken as a favorite issue in a long list of possible choices or be perceived as comparable trade-offs vis-à-vis economic concerns. Rather, this set of challenges is so fundamental to human existence that serious engagement with them touches every domain of our common life: health, education, economics, politics, religion, energy, and commerce.

At the core of this challenge is a cluster of big questions: How wili we all dwell together on the small planet home we share? How will we reimagine what we mean by quality of life? Will we have the psychic energy, the soul energy, the spiritual energy for the discernment and innovation that is now required? What do we now need to learn, through science, the arts, the humanities, and through relationships with the vast numbers of others (human and the more-than-human) who constitute our world?

These are some of the great questions of our time, arising from our present cultural circumstances. Our response to them is further challenged by the intensification of social and cultural diversity within which our collective discernment and meaning-making must take place. Some describe (and dismiss) emerging adulthood as a time of self-absorption and preoccupation with personal questions such as building a résumé, choosing a mate, and landing a career. But it must be asked, Aren't emerging adults in a real sense being cheated if they are not initiated into the great questions of their time and encouraged to make their life choices in relationship to the larger world of which they are a part—invited, that is, to a more meaningful fulfillment of the promise of their lives?

There is evidence on every hand that emerging adults can hear and respond to such questions. But as we have seen, they are appropriately dependent on a mentoring milieu that presents challenges they can rise to and wrestle with—a mentoring culture that supports and enlivens rather than discourages and defeats their best aspirations.

Mentoring Institutions

A mentoring culture mediates meaningful challenges by offering opportunities to work alongside mentoring presences, stimulating critical-connected thought and inner-dependent faith. Here is where mentoring institutions that might especially support emerging adults in their postundergrad years (ages twenty-two to thirty-two) are notably lacking. To be sure, initiatives such as Peace Corps, VISTA, City Year, Teach for America, some travel programs, fellowships, and internships (and some would add the military) provide templates. Such templates can inform a broader cultural imagination of how emerging adults could be met—not only through governmental initiatives or the nonprofit sector but also through any enterprise that is willing to contribute to a new social architecture that will recognize, welcome, challenge, and significantly give form to the energies of emerging adulthood.

Adaptive Leadership

The adaptive challenges our times present, the big questions to which they give rise, and the deep purposes they inspire are the birthright challenges of emerging adults, calling for adaptive leadership. As we saw in Chapter Seven, in a radically interdependent world, leadership can be practiced "from wherever you sit." This means that a mentoring culture that serves today's world does not merely single out "leader types" in which to invest time and treasure. Rather, every emerging adult is recognized as a person who is capable of contributing to the larger commons and deserving of being challenged and of being schooled in the arts of citizen-leadership and the practical politics of our common life.[16]

Inspiration

A primary task of emerging adulthood is the formation of a worthy Dream that coalesces a relationship between the self and the suffering and wonder of the world that is authentic, practical, and honors the potential and highest aspirations of the emerging adult. But, again, emerging adults are vulnerable to the Dreams—worthy or not—to which they have access. As social beings, emerging adults are dependent on the inspiration that an adept mentoring culture can be.

In today's culture, what Dreams are made accessible to in-spirit emerging adults? What do they "breathe in"? What images, narratives, and ideologies are offered for the formation of the emerging adult soul? What passions are they encouraged to imbibe?

In the life of our new global commons, it is plain that emerging adults can be distinctively recruited on the one hand to terrorism and on the other hand to peaceful protest. Both groups are responding to a call for cultural transformation. Both responses are conditioned by the ambitions of the mentoring cultures that inspire them.

In the United States, as the post–9/11 generations come into adulthood, equally affected by global economics and heightened uncertainty, two notable patterns may be observed, among others. Some emerging adults, responding to a culture grown more fearful and seeking personal security, believe that they can make little or no difference in their world and must simply "get theirs" as best and while they can. Others are making their mark by learning second languages and reaching out with curiosity and imagination, willing to take risks on their own behalf and on behalf of the common good—local, regional, and beyond. They are seeking to work as journalists, in the state department, as entrepreneurs, educators, ecologists, or in other roles in our new commons—nonprofit, governmental, and commercial. They are keenly attuned to what the world will ask and allow—and they believe that they can make a positive difference. The subtext in both of these patterns is located in their networks of belonging and what they "breathe in" as they are making meaning and composing a faith to live by.

As we have seen, because emerging adult faith is yet fragile in its capacity for inner-dependent meaning-making, yet is distinctively poised to grasp the ideal it is inevitably ideological, and ways of seeing that appear both worthy and potent may be fiercely grasped and incorporated into the emerging adult Dream. Thus the ideologies—systems of images and their effects—that a culture makes available are a central ingredient in the formation of emerging adult faith. The ideology may be conventional, radical, conservative, progressive, political, economic, religious, or of some other type. It may be held cynically or reverently, but it is what the emerging adult breathes in and becomes.

Transforming the Dream

The formation of a worthy Dream during the emerging adult years matters not only because it completes the work of emerging adulthood, but also because the Dream plays a central role in further development throughout adulthood, an ongoing recentering process that can yield yet more mature strength over time. Particularly times of transition—those developmental openings termed midlife crisis or other life transitions—can become occasions when adults may reclaim, renew, or otherwise come to terms with their own young-emerging adult Dream. Though the Dream may in some measure move underground in the more tested adult years, the Dream resurfaces in later adulthood, at forty, fifty-five, sixty, or beyond. If the Dream is to serve the full potential of self and world, it needs to be critically reexamined across time. Whenever the Dream resurfaces, however, depending on the person's willingness to wrestle yet again with what it asks, it can be welcomed or muzzled. And either one may exact a cost. If the Dream is welcomed, it must be re-known, and the formative power it has held—for better or worse—must be re-engaged.

The emerging adult Dream that dwells in the older adult was initially formed in an historical era that is no more and in a place and circumstance that have now passed. If the adult is to continue to become at home in the world, big questions—old and new—must be entertained to realign the Dream with the evolving motion of life both personal and public. What was worthy and full of promise may now re-inspirit, re-inspire, and recenter a yet deeper sense of purpose, and what was limited and limiting—even destructive to the self and others—may be grieved and relinquished. Wounds in which the Dream was embedded, and any wounds the Dream created, may now be laid open for healing.

This is not easy work.[17] A man in his fifties realized that his young adult Dream had been simply to stay out of the Vietnam War. He accomplished that through educational deferments, which landed him in an admired profession, in which he did achieve a measure of meaning and success. But his own deep spirit had never been invited into the kind of exploration and imagination that he could claim as his own. Recognizing that the formation of his Dream had been constrained by historical circumstance and family expectations, he began to interrogate it and recompose a yet more faithful adulthood for all the good years still ahead—returning to formal studies and entering another profession in his sixties. This kind of recentering process, although not always this dramatic, can take place in dialogue with the emerging adult's Dream across all the years of a long adulthood.

Similarly, if a culture is willing to undergo critical reexamination of its Dream, a renewed, deepened, more mature, and wise passion may become available over time, as each generation receives, re-creates, nurtures, and passes on "that mysterious core of culture." It is difficult, however, for adults in any society to serve as citizens of a mentoring culture if they themselves are cynical, burned out, sold out, or otherwise bereft of worthy meaning, purpose, and faith. Thus it is of enormous importance that a culture supports the ongoing development of meaning and faith throughout adulthood—and a matter of urgency as we live on a new threshold in history. We especially need adults who are willing to reconnect with their own essential, vitalizing spirit so as to mentor the future. How is this to be done?

The American Dream

Few cultures are as explicit about their Dream as the United States, where we regularly appeal to the power of the "American Dream." A primary feature of this Dream is the individual's right to "life, liberty, and the pursuit of happiness" and the imagination of a society in which that right can be claimed. In *The Real American Dream: A Meditation on Hope*, Andrew Delbanco contends, however, that as genuine individual power has shrunk, we have replaced it with a heightened but superficial individualism so that "today hope has narrowed to the vanishing point of the self alone." And although "the most striking feature of contemporary culture is the unslaked craving for transcendence," he goes on, "the symbols that might link us with this transcendence—[with a sense of larger belonging and purpose]—have been terribly weakened. Surely something new will emerge," but, he adds, "The question is, what will it be?"[18]

At this transitional time in history, the American Dream is being interrogated as we reexplore and renew Meade's "mysterious core of culture." A touchstone question in this process is, How does the American Dream serve today's emerging adults and those who will come after them? In a global commons, how does the American Dream contribute to the imagination of a positive and worthy future for emerging adults in an interdependent world?

Worthy Dreams

If a culture's Dream has exhausted its initial energy or has become too limiting, there arises a hunger for an imagination that can re-enliven the faith at the core of culture. This requires a recovery of spirit, a reconnection with the master currents of the soul—the mysterious core that is worthy of being protected, sustained, and renewed across the generations. It requires reassembling the community—networks of belonging, trust, and commitment—in which ongoing discernment is practiced and positive images can thrive.

In uncertain times, the interdependencies of cultural values are subject to polarization. Within the American Dream, for example, it is all too easy to split the value of *liberty* from *justice for all*. Yet as an increasingly global society creates a new mentoring culture for an emergent world, Americans are called to reimagine the interdependent reality in which we dwell and to nourish a new faith, a transcendent imagination within which the indivisible linkage of "liberty and justice for all" reanimates the deep current of democracy. In this imagination of culture, an ethic of rights, competition, and detached justice is rejoined with an ethic of responsibility, connection, and love. The motion is toward wisdom, toward maturity as a culture, and toward a faith that knows that the one who is "other" is the one to whom, inextricably, the self is related in the mutual interdependence that reconstitutes the Dream of "We the people."

If we are to transcend the poverty of "the self alone," then images of interdependence and renewed practices of the commons are among the most significant strengths that a mature culture has to offer to a emerging adult world. Consciousness of the wholeness—the holiness—of life confirms the lives of emerging adults while inviting their participation in commitments beyond mere self-interest, narrowly defined.

This kind of faithful alignment with the motion of life invites emerging adults to imagine not only a job, a career, or a lifestyle. It also invites them to claim Dreams that are the fruit of a deep sense of purpose and vocation. It welcomes their participation in what some have spoken of as the Great Work of our time.[19]

To this end, it is said that the test of a culture is its capacity to nurture and to receive its idealistic youth.[20] In the interdependent cogwheeling of the generations, the mentor needs the protégé as much as the protégé needs the mentor, and the renewal of a mentoring culture takes place in the dialectic with the promise of the emerging adult—the promise of the future. To accompany the emerging adult in faith can mean a reawakening of a culture's potential for compassion, excellence, and vocation, for within the promise of the emerging adult lies the power to beckon the spirit of weary, routinized, or cynical adults who may respond to serve as mentors, joining shoulder to shoulder with emerging adults to build a worthy dream—a beacon for the future. History shows that emerging adults have a particular capacity to see that beacon—a potential dependent on the faithful imagination of older adults who embody a generous, mature, and mentoring adulthood.

Coda: Mentoring Communities

Professional Education and the Professions ▪ The Workplace ▪ Travel ▪ Families ▪ Religious Faith Communities ▪ Media ▪ Social Movements

The institutions and practices that are needed to support the twenty-something era may take many forms within a wide range of contexts, each having particular opportunities to honor and participate in the emerging adult's search for meaning, purpose, and faith. These seven environments, in addition to higher education as addressed in Chapter Nine, are selected somewhat arbitrarily, but with an eye toward identifying places that—intentionally or by default—typically serve as mentoring contexts for emerging adults.

Professional Education and the Professions

In the experience of emerging adults, the boundary between higher and professional education and the professions themselves is often highly permeable for two reasons: First, emerging adulthood takes time. Not only has every field of endeavor become more complex, but also the transformation from conventional meaning-making, through the formation of inner-dependent adult faith to a tested adult faith, requires living through a series of transformations. Though the development of critical thinking and the unfolding of its substantial implications may begin early on in the twenty-something years, they typically extend through the process of further schooling and into the initial professional position(s).

Second, and consequently, for many the journey into adulthood wends its way through an ecology of institutions. At any juncture, formal study may be suspended for a work opportunity, or work may be laid down to pursue more study. Community learning projects, internships, residencies, and the like blur the boundaries between formal study and the practice of the profession itself.

Thus professional education is well perceived as taking place a complex of institutions constituting a mentoring ecology. A question to be asked is, Does this ecology of institutions as a whole serve as a mentoring environment for forming a worthy sense of meaning and vocation? Are the objectives of these related but differing institutions well aligned for the formation of the young professional? Is there collective commitment to the full potential of emerging adults, or are they vulnerable to being exploited for purposes too small to match the promise of their lives?

Future of Callings

A symposium titled "Future of Callings" addressed the shared concern across a wide range of professions that something has been lost in the education of professionals.[1] What emerged in the dialogue was the recognition that one does not enter a profession simply to have a career and a means of livelihood for oneself, nor does one serve as a professional only on behalf of one's individual clients. A sense of working on behalf of our common life—a sense of calling—has traditionally been a central strength of the professions. The symposium on the future of callings bore witness to "the unanimity of agreement regarding the common vocation of the professions to address the interconnected and multi-layered issues of society within the confines of daily work."[2]

In today's cultural climate, however, no matter which profession a young adult enters, the perception persists among many that all professions are becoming simply commercial enterprises and that the goal of professional practice is to succeed primarily in monetary terms. It has been remarked by some emerging adults themselves, "What they believe in most is money because any-thing else is too risky."[3] Although an element of economic prag-matism is appropriate within any profession, what is at stake here is the emerging adult's capacity for idealism, which orients and fuels both the Dream of the emerging adult and the potential renewal of the profession in every generation. Professional schools are the primary places where the veil is lifted on the profession for the first time and the complex terrain between idealism and cynicism is initially revealed.

Thus there is a renewed call to the ethical questions that are integral to professional life. Some believe that this is prompted only by scandals of various kinds that have tarnished the profes-sions and eroded the public trust. A closer look, however, reveals that this turn to ethics arises also from a deeper cause. That is, everyone now works within a dramatically changing world, standing on new moral and ethical frontiers that pose big questions and present unprecedented, adaptive challenges. Many of the canons of yesterday that provided guidance through established professional custom no longer suffice or even pertain.

Yet no matter what form the ethics curriculum may take, it is not compelling in the young adult imagination unless it cor-responds with the perceived requirements of the profession as emerging adults believe they will be asked to practice it. Moreover, whenever "ethics" (issues of right and wrong, legal compliance, fairness, justice, compassion, meaning, and purpose) is cast in a circumscribed place as a special subject rather than appearing as an integral part of the practice of the profession, ethics becomes marginal in the minds of emerging adults who are so acutely attuned to the real terms of participation in the world of adult work.[4] In other words, when matters of conscience, meaning, and the wider welfare of the commons are defined as "externals," or worse, "soft" in contrast to "hard," the message, intended or not, is clear.

Some question whether there is any purpose in teaching ethics to emerging adults. They assume that the conscience has been formed long ago, "at the mother's knee," but this is decidedly not the case. As the emerging adult is engaged in "the wary probe," seeking a place of viable engagement in a relativized and complex world, the emerging adult conscience is ripe for orientation and ongoing formation.

An Interpersonal Versus a Systemic Ethic

I have observed, for example, that despite other forms of obvious sophistication, many emerging adults enter professional education with only an interpersonal ethical frame.[5] They have not yet been initiated into critical thought and a connective-systemic way of perceiving the world that would yield a more comprehensive understanding of the significance of their chosen profession and the broad, systemic reach of their own actions. When business students were asked to think about who or what they might hurt across the years of their professional life, they typically hoped they "wouldn't hurt anyone." Given further time for reflection, they sometimes recognized that they might have to hurt their families because of the demands on their time or perhaps they might have to "fire someone." They did not yet recognize that they aspired to positions in which they would inevitably have to make complex decisions that would affect, for good and ill, people whom they would never meet.

Part of the work of professional education is to deepen and broaden the scope of meaning-making on the basis of which young professionals will make critical decisions. When the big questions of ethics and meaning are honored within the process of professional education, the learning that ensues can foster real transformation in the life and direction of emerging adults. After being asked to grapple with a number of situations common to business, a young man in an MBA program that taught ethical reflection as an integral feature of business practice pondered the consequences of dealing with big questions as part of being initiated into critical and connected thought: "It has changed the way I was viewing the role of a businessman. It enhanced my sensibility as a business leader—being a part of a much broader system which includes countries, cities, local communities and understanding that whatever decision I make can have an impact which can go much further than just increasing the bottom line."

Mentoring communities within the professions can evoke big questions, crack open unexamined assumptions, awaken the imagination of emerging adults, and birth worthy Dreams. Graduate and professional education at its best lends itself to the practices of contemplation, hearth, table, and commons in ways that can rekindle the calling and art of each profession—the creative imagination on which the evolution of culture and civilization depends.[6]

Many Forms of Mentoring

For the emerging adult in search of a mentor, the discovery of a mentoring community can reveal a yet more significant gift. I spoke with an international student who came to the United States from Latin America for graduate study in business administration. He was twenty-six and prepared to use the program well. He was highly intentional about his search for "the person" to mentor him so that "we can work together on a short-term and medium-term business plan for my company." Yet when I spoke with him two years later, he had found not one mentor but five: "[Professor A] has been involved from the beginning, and he liked the challenge. He visited the company and we've continued it until right now. [Professor B] has been very, very helpful in giving me a broad picture of where the industry's going, whom should I talk to, what kinds of things I should think of. And then [Professor C], he gave me very good advice, more on the personal side. And then [Professor D] was also very helpful." This young man created a modest mentoring community around his Dream.[7]

A woman who is now a research physician remembers a particular professor who created a mentoring community for her students in medical school through the practices of hearth and commons:

> Dr. Sagov would run weekly research seminars where everybody would sit around a room and literally shoot the breeze—every idea you could think of. She could generate enough questions in an hour or two of conversation that the rest of us could go out and research for the next three years. What she taught me to do was ask the question, "Why?" and how to try to get at the answer. She taught me how to form the question in the scientific field, because once you can form the question, you can begin to generate a way to answer it. During the course of my residency she held Friday afternoon sherries in her office and all the residents would show up. She was a real mentor.

Becoming a Mentor

When professional education happens well, young professionals become mentors themselves early on and create mentoring communities even in the course of their early work. Susan Bratton remembers how when she was still doing her doctoral work in biology, she went to Costa Rica for more training. She took an undergrad student with her, although she had only seven hundred dollars for both of them. "Mentoring," she says, "isn't something you do 'later.'" Across the years she has developed the fine art of conducting her field research in the company of her students.[8]

Apprenticeship

The Future of Callings symposium described previously noted that a significant shift in the development of the professions is the loss of the "apprenticeship." As professional education has moved into the academy and has been affected by the rupture between knowledge and faith, theory and practice, the relationship between "master and apprentice" along with a shared sense of the common good have been eroded. Brian Johnson clarifies the point:

> [This is] not to suggest that the professions were taught better in another day—though they might have been—or that apprenticeships were without fault—which they were not. What is being proposed, however, is that as a change in pattern occurred that favored an emphasis on learning and acquiring knowledge as a . . . scientific endeavor, the other . . . contributions cultivated in the relationship between master and apprentice were lost. Once this trajectory began, the professions lost their sense of themselves as an art. It was then simply a matter of time before individual students filled this vacuum with an emphasis on success and achievement, while the relationship with the public good [and a sense of vocation] became overlooked or was at least attended to after "work was done."[9]

What might it mean to learn to practice a profession as an art? For example, in the fine arts as well as in some other contexts, the time-honored practice of the master-apprentice relationship can still be found. The apprentice chooses a master in the presence of whom he believes there is an opportunity to become not only skilled but "master-full"—meaning that more is learned than the skill narrowly defined. The work of the head, the heart, and the hand is transformed into a larger consciousness, into new ways of seeing, being, knowing, and acting in the world.

This happens most profoundly if the "master" is committed to the flourishing of the "apprentice"—that is, if the master is a mentor, and better yet, if the master creates a mentoring community. This quality of engagement and investment is conveyed in an account of an apprentice working with a master fiber artist:

> Nell . . . would go home and ponder her pupils, she would meditate on them. Then she would come in and say something right into what you were agonizing over in a piece and didn't want to face. She would say, "Here it is—do it." There were about eight of us working with her that summer in a huge barnlike studio. I had a deadline on my first appliqué piece. I had been working on it for at least three weeks and I was stuck. It wouldn't go. It wasn't resolved. She came up to me and said, "Where are your scissors?" I gave them to her and she said, "Let's see, suppose you just sort of cut into this," and she cut it and handed me a piece, "and then, you see, there's an opening here—oh, and let's cut over there. . . ." This went on for about fifteen minutes. I was standing there in absolute shock. She cut my piece to ribbons. The room got very quiet. Everybody stopped and watched. She turned to me and said, "Well now, see what you can do with that." I turned around with this stuff in my hands, and everybody was looking at me. I wanted to cry. . . . [Then] John smiled at me and said, "Don't feel too bad. The first time she did that to me she didn't hand the pieces to me. She dropped them on the floor."
>
> That was a whole new way for me to live. Nell taught me that if I'm not ready to cut my piece to smithereens I can quit. If I'm stuck on a piece, or if I'm stuck in my life, I can look at something I'm protecting, something I feel I must have, something that is my favorite, a fabric I've fallen in love with. If I can identify what it is that I'm protecting and take it out, then it just goes, everything opens up.[10]

Here, in the vortex of the master-apprentice relationship, set within a small mentoring community, we can see a complex mix of recognition, challenge, support, and inspiration, opening into a whole new way of life and vocation. Every profession is an *art* and a practice. Becoming a professional requires knowledge of the field and the development of compassion and competence, grounded in a sense of deep purpose that can orient adaptive learning and adaptive leadership. It requires an initiation into practice, practice, practice (including always working on the edge of one's own knowing and learning from failure), which the art and practice of any true profession demands.[11] If the promise of emerging adult lives is not met by this quality of commitment to excellence, professional education may be reduced to the acquisition of mere training and credentials.

Emerging adults in every generation represent a readiness—either conscious or inchoate—for the formation of a worthy dream and commitment to a true profession. Roberto Unger addressed the betrayal of this trust in the contemporary academy at a critical legal studies conference attended by law faculty from throughout the United States. After he had brilliantly described the post-Enlightenment divorce of legal method from a transcendent ethical vision and called for a reformulation of that linkage, he closed, as I recall, by simply saying to his colleagues: the task is large and there are so few of us. But we know that we came to the study of law committed to the linkage between the practice of law and moral values. We found institutions prepared to flatter our vanity at the price of our self-respect. It is as though we found a priesthood that had lost its faith, tediously worshipping at cold altars. We find our intellectual work in the heart's revenge.[12]

The Workplace

One of the primary questions of young adulthood is, "How do I find my place in the world of adult work?" The workplace, in whatever sector of the commons, is a primary testing ground, not only for achieving adulthood in conventional terms but also for exploring and claiming a worthy dream of the future for both self and society. As emerging adults begin to take up adult responsibilities, they ask, "Who am I as a worker? What is the work reality within which I must find my place? What and who is trustworthy? What is going to really matter? Can I make a difference?" In workplaces, fundamental patterns of life and images of adulthood, citizenship, and leadership are being laid down in a primary way.

Trying to be cool on his first day as a construction worker, wearing a brand-new leather tool belt overstocked with gear, Eric Wallen, a computer engineer, confidently swings twenty-five feet up the scaffolding, watches his tape measure plummet to the ground, promptly drops his hammer, and nearly kills a fellow carpenter.

> My boss had patience with my seemingly non-existent common sense during my first two months working in construction, while I tried to learn the arts of carpentry and good old-fashioned thorough thinking. I've been chewed out on more than one occasion for having my head in the clouds when it should have been on the ground. . . .
>
> "Mindful" is my boss's favorite word out on the site. He continually urges us to pay attention . . . , to think things through while keeping the big picture in mind. The shocking and revealing thing about it is that I thought I was already "mindful." . . . I was wrong.
>
> The wonderful—and sometimes frightening—thing about this type of work is that the results of my thought processes and actions have immediate physical manifestations. . . .
>
> I want to be a person who does things well, but I am only that person sometimes, in some situations, and not in others. Unlike construction work, mistakes or shoddy performances in some white-collar jobs can sometimes be temporarily ignored or hidden. The in-your-face confrontation of construction has made me realize that I have spent far too much time and energy trying to rationalize away the inconsistencies in my life, rather than simply doing things right the first time. . . .
>
> And gradually, I am at last curing my own disease of self-deception, and becoming the kind of person who genuinely cares about his work.[13]

Mentors

Supervisors, coworkers, and colleagues can individually and together serve as mentors. A young and effective captain in the

Coast Guard attributed his success to his first captain, who was a powerful mentoring figure. He watched as this captain, unlike many others, spent time up on the deck talking with his crew. The patterns of presence and communication that he observed became a powerful and orienting image, which he has subsequently carried into other contexts, seeing every organization as in some measure a boat with a crew. Since then, working in educational and then corporate settings, he has demonstrated a distinctive though quiet commitment to succeed in "the mission" in ways that include the survival and achievement of all. His account serves as a reminder that senior colleagues are always being watched—sometimes unawares.

An executive remembers that in her first position in an international corporation she served as an administrative assistant. One day her boss suggested that she apply for a higher-level position elsewhere in the company. She was taken aback and hesitantly responded, "I thought you were pleased with my work." He said, "Yes, and I would hate to lose you. But if you remain in this position it won't be good for you, and it won't be good for our company." These gifts of mentoring—recognition, challenge, and support—demonstrate the generosity of soul (and a part of the art of good management) that marks the practice of great mentoring.

Deep Purpose

It is essential to remember, however, that one can be mentored into the Mafia as well as into work that is morally responsible. The content or deep purpose of the work environment has significant influence in shaping the ethical imagination of the emerging adult. Many emerging adults struggle with an apparent trade-off between "doing work I value" and "doing work where I will make money—a lot of money." Where does support for the former come from? The stakes seem high in an economy with a yawning gap between the wealthy and the poor, and mentoring presences are loath to counsel what they themselves cannot model or what they fear may quite literally cost the emerging adult too much. This feature of economic life, coupled with the fact that there is ever less expectation that one will remain with a given firm (a form of community), can mean that neither potential mentors nor protégés can see much point in making an investment in the relationship. Individual tracks to success become the norm, utilitarian relationships abound, and the kind of support that makes it possible to flourish in place or to entertain an alternative and more meaningful pathway shrivels.

In both not-for-profit and for-profit enterprises, however, this period of initiation into the world of adult work can set in place a positive image of what work means. How the enterprise is undertaken; how its purposes are named; who matters; how moral choices are or are not recognized, engaged, and decided—all affect the emerging adult's sense of self and world and shape major features of the emerging adult's meaning-making and faith.[14]

Recognition as an Adult Worker

The importance of giving emerging adults opportunity for genuine adult work and a felt sense that they are recognized as having the capacity to share shoulder-to-shoulder work with other adults cannot be overestimated. A young woman, twenty-four, teaching general education and adult literacy in a community college serving students from very diverse backgrounds and often considerably older than herself, described what mentoring recognition and support feels like from the inside:

> In general I get excellent support from all the other teachers in that they listen to my theories and ideas as much as to each other's, even though I have ten or more years less experience than they do. My boss comes to me for ideas, shares his ideas with me, and has on occasion used my worksheets with his class. He has really made me feel like a peer, even though I am

closer to his children's age than his. He and I are teaching the same level class right now, in the same time slot, so we entered this semester trying to figure out some curriculum we could work on jointly. It sort of fell through because the students' reading level was so low, but we both ended up teaching a book I remembered from when I was in about fifth grade. He hasn't even read the whole thing yet, but he agreed to teach it based on my advice. His support is really, really encouraging and has made me feel very welcome at the school. He has prepared me to lead my classes, backed me up when I'm frustrated— basically, it's like being a real part of the team. I guess the very nature of that interaction makes me feel like an adult.

I had a recent situation with my class in which a few of the younger students were giving me a hard time, and when I complained in frustration, I was given only support and the benefit of the doubt. . . . That kind of belief in me as a teacher and leader in a classroom, from someone whom I really respect, makes me feel like a capable teacher and an adult.

This engagement in adult work that matters can serve the kind of faith development that is so critical in the emerging adult years because it builds a sense of trustworthy belonging in the larger adult world and a sense of one's own power and agency. Reflecting how engagement in real work in a mentoring community helped to teach both a sense of power and a systemic perspective, an African American religious leader who was very active in community development recalled:

If the black teachers and professionals in my community saw a young person who had talent and ability, they wouldn't let you stop. From them I learned the role of black professionals and intellectuals in the struggle. I saw the importance of having people who could strategize, who could see the larger picture, the institutional relationships. . . . I actually got to sit in on some of the strategy sessions where they were analyzing the political situation, seeing whose interests were at stake, and looking at the black community to see where we could engender support. I asked to be allowed to do it, and I was encouraged. It was just so important to be there because I had to know that somewhere people weren't just being beaten down and just taking it on the chin. There was a thinking group that looked ahead and said, "This is what we've got to do next." I had to be part of that for my own sanity. One began to see that there was a cadre of leaders and thinkers who saw far beyond Dallas and connected us with what was going on around the world and around the United States, so one didn't feel so powerless.

Emerging adults seek places, albeit on their terms, where they can roll up their sleeves and pitch in, ready for adult work in a challenging world. When they are perpetually offered only unpaid internships, temp jobs, and little challenge; when their hours are kept low so benefits don't have to be paid and the justification is that "they can still live at home"; or when they are asked to carry significant responsibility but are under-recognized, "kept in their place," or dismissed as "too different, too young, too idealistic"; or when they are overworked in "high-powered" eighty-hour a week burnout jobs, too often their true potential is squandered, and we are all the poorer for it.

In a conference setting, a group of emerging adults working in a wide range of organizations were asked what they desired in a workplace. They responded:

Being on this end of power relationships makes us vulnerable.

Believe in my potential, so I can be vulnerable.

Understand my uniqueness: you may have seen twenty-five idealists before but this is my first time doing it.

Don't make me just sink or swim.

Give me room to fail and walk me through it; make it safe for me to fail.

Ask me tough questions.

Tell me about your life—not just your job; tell me your failure and not just the good stuff.

I may look like I'm after your job when I'm just caring as much as you are.

Recognize that my sense of "responsibility" is huge because we know so much about the world—bear it with us.

I still need access to you after you have given the responsibility to me.

Don't believe everything the media says about my generation—it's not all true.[15]

The constant throughout these comments is a request for the practices of a mentoring environment—recognition, support, challenge, inspiration, and accountability.[16]

Institutions That Work

Experience early on in "institutions that work" may anchor hope in the possibility of good work and good workplaces. In today's complex societies, big questions are likely to spawn worthy Dreams that cannot be achieved alone and require working closely and cooperatively with many others. We are learning that the world's deep hungers can only be adequately met with the collective wisdom and passion of a host of inspired hearts and competent minds. Thus, the realization of the potential of emerging adults depends, in part, on the availability of meaningful opportunities within organizations and institutions, places where they can contribute their part as an element of a larger and more effective effort than the self can achieve alone.

In our study of the formation of people who can sustain commitment to the common good, we have come to believe that most had the opportunity during their formative years to be part of a workable, effective institution. Participating in an organization that successfully enacts a worthy purpose gives flesh to the intuition that one's own power is amplified when joined with others who seek a common goal. This sensibility is at risk if cynicism regarding virtually every form of institutional life abounds.

Almost every organization has the opportunity, as a mentoring environment, to gift the emerging adult imagination with an experience of an organization that works. Though the emerging adult may not find the same again, the conviction takes root that collectively we can take on ambitious dreams in a complex world.

Travel

As emerging adults begin to develop a sense of inner-dependence and a yearning to know for themselves, there is a distinctive readiness for exploration and adventure that may take the form of travel. Whether through a formal program, a job, or as a vagabond pilgrimage, travel can become a mentoring environment. It is difficult to overestimate the potential significance of travel in the formation of faith during the emerging adult years. Transformative travel experiences do not necessarily require emerging adults to cross oceans and continents. Across town or down the hall is sometimes enough to prompt a reimagination of self and world and a stretch of faith. Whatever the distance, travel can be a powerful means of becoming more at home in the universe.

Critical and Connected Thought

Many people, however, travel and remain inside their cocoons, insulated with a tribe of their own kind, armored with unexamined assumptions. They never truly engage with the local culture and return home essentially unchanged. Travel is often informative but too seldom transformative. Transformative travel does not happen simply by means of a shift in geographical location. But as one steps out of one's own tribe and encounters the other, travel can encourage the emergence of critical thought. One's familiar experience is cast in a new light, and new, often big, questions emerge.

Providing provocative pathways and hospitality that are both welcoming and challenging for young explorers can be a critical mentoring function. This may involve creating learning opportunities, internships, short-term employment, and other ways of getting off the beaten track of one's own assumptions into places that awaken curiosity, evoke awe, deepen compassion, inform the mind, and open possibilities. Or it may take the very practical forms of offering a place at the table, a bed to sleep in, or a hearth conversation that lingers into the night.

A significant part of the power of programs such as the Peace Corps and City Year is the combination of travel combined with good adult work. This kind of opportunity fosters encounters with otherness and a mentoring community of peers and advisors who encourage critical-connective thought and the prospect of changing one's mind. Such mentoring environments often feature powerful life-shaping images for the emerging adult imagination to work with over time, grist for the ongoing formation of citizenship and leadership.

Todd Daloz harbors this set of images from a two-week stay in a Nicaraguan village to assist in building a health clinic when he was a freshman in college:

> We arrived in a town made up of a few brick buildings and a lot of cardboard/plywood/pressboard shacks with tin roofs that were tied on with wire or held down with stones. The night we arrived, we stepped off the buses into teeming masses of children—most of whom had no fathers because of the war. We hurried into the cinderblock church where we were to stay. Most of us were blown away by the poverty, the dirt, the children, and the place in which we found ourselves. We all slept on the floor, gringos complaining about how cold it was, not realizing that the forty of us had brought more stuff with us for three weeks than the people in the village had, period.

But the children were mischievous, teasing the young volunteers for attention, pelting them with cicada bugs, and pestering them for gifts. When it came time to leave, some of the volunteers were more than ready to go.

In the last few days before we left, all the kids wanted *memorias*, gifts of remembrance; otherwise, they threatened, they would not remember us. There was one kid I had hung out with quite a bit, his name was Lenin. As we were leaving, he wouldn't stop bugging me about giving him a "memory." I knew he had more money than other kids and didn't "need" anything, and initially I refused. Finally, I gave him my hat and he ran off with it—I thought I would never see him again. "Greedy little kid," I thought, "our communication didn't mean anything. He gained nothing from meeting me, and all he wanted was that hat."

But he did come back, and he was crying as we said goodbye. Perhaps it was as touching as I remember it to be. What I came to realize was that I was being overly materialistic and morally way too heavy-handed in my thinking. He was a kid, just eleven or so, and he just wanted a hat with a Nike symbol on it. It didn't hurt me at all to give it to him. If anything, my refusal to give it to him had hurt our friendship more.

As we left, a lot of us felt relief, but also a sadness. I still remember the faces, always dirty, hanging at the windows, yelling to us to come outside to play with them. So many times we refused because we were scared or tired. I have a sense of a lost opportunity, of a duty that I skipped out on or didn't try hard enough to achieve. What I gained from it the most, something that Mom told me, was that the real connection that you make with people of such different cultural and economic backgrounds is that no matter how different someone seems or in fact is, there is a certain bond of shared human experience.

Travel can be a means of becoming a part of a larger commons, and it can serve the formation of a more spacious faith. A critical element, however, is located in what occurs after returning home. Travel becomes a pilgrimage when mentoring communities on the road and back at home create contexts in which emerging adults can debrief—tell their stories, surface their questions, and thus repattern their meaning-making on behalf of a more adequate knowing of self and world. If this happens well, emerging adults become more adequately prepared for leadership in an increasingly diverse and complex world.[17]

Families

Rabbi Zalman Schacter-Shalomi has observed that although mentoring is an activity that is usually placed outside the family, "the model for mentoring clearly comes from the multi-generational family."[18] Families play a significant, inextricable, and under-recognized role in the recomposing of self and world and the development of purpose and faith in the emerging adult years.[19]

As emerging adults seek to become at home in an enlarging world, there is an appropriate hunger to travel beyond the boundaries of family—and the family system can be shaken up by the emerging adult's new interests and behaviors, leading to new ways of relating to parents, siblings, and relatives. But we never outgrow our need for connection and confirmation within that primary network of belonging. Indeed, if development is perceived less as a journey (leaving previously valued people and earlier ways of making meaning wholly behind) and more as a process of learning how to take more into account (a process of expansion and recentering), families can meaningfully provide some of the gifts of a mentoring community.

I discovered this once in a fresh way at a family reunion. We are a close but scattered family, presently living in three countries and ten cities. At the time of the reunion there were fifteen of us, including seven emerging adults. Honoring an occasion in my mother's life, we managed to get all of us together for twenty-four hours and have one meal around the same table. I found myself wishing that we might have some way of sharing what was happening in our varied lives.

After we concluded dinner with a yummy cake to celebrate also both a twenty-first and a fiftieth birthday, I suggested with some trepidation (knowing the resistance of emerging adults to anything that seems contrived and inauthentic) that around the table we each take a turn, sharing something that had been particularly satisfying in the previous year and something that we expected would be particularly challenging in the year to come. As each one did just that, we were able to catch a glimpse of each other's lives in new and deeper ways. And then as mother/grandmother/step-grandmother affirmed the love and aspirations of the family circle, the kind of anchoring power that a family can provide was recentered for all of us.

In these and other ways, families can serve to confirm a worthy identity and continuity of self and integrity as young adults change across time. In many families this requires healing—recomposing the family story in more adequate terms to ground a more trustworthy faith. In a good-enough family, however, the family primarily needs to practice the art of recognizing the emerging adult in new terms rather than simply drifting with the currents of prevailing patterns. Then visits home or other ways of touching base may add new layers of meaning to family belonging and play an important function as the emerging adult recomposes self, other, world, and "God."

This is easier said than done. Many emerging adults feel keenly the expectations held within their familial network of belonging. A thoughtful professor reflected on how many times students had thanked him "for permission" to choose a direction other than the pathway laid down by family expectations—evidence that the emerging adult is still, though in a new way, dependent on Authority "outside the self." In some families, by contrast, there is permission and support for dreaming good—though perhaps unexpected—Dreams. Nevertheless, this is often hard work for parents who have made deep investments in their own Dreams for their emerging adult children. In A *Gravestone Made of Wheat*, by Will Weaver, we learn that Walter Hansen, well loved by both of his parents, grew up on a farm learning everything fathers can teach their sons about the land: the crops, how to work the machinery, the cycle of the seasons, and all the rest. Walt goes away to the university and at age twenty is the only undeclared major on campus. Returning home for his birthday he dreads the looming conversation with his father. As he arrives, his father is in the field beginning to plant the corn for the coming season. They greet each other, make small talk about a dragging disk on the tractor, and then his father asks:

"So how's the rat race, son?"

"Not so bad," Walter said.

His father paused a moment. "Any . . . decisions yet?" His father said.

Walter swallowed. He looked off toward town. "About . . . a major, you mean?" Walter said.

His father waited.

"Well," Walter said. His mouth went dry. He swallowed twice.

"Well," he said, "I think I'm going to major in English."

His father pursed his lips. He pulled off his work gloves one finger at a time. "English," he said.

"English," Walter nodded.

His father squinted. "Son, we already know English."

Walter stared. "Well, yessir, that's true. I mean, I'm going to study literature. Books. See how they're written. Maybe write one of my own some day."

His father rubbed his brown neck and stared downfield.

Two white sea gulls floated low over the fresh planting.

"So what do you think?" Walter said.

His father's forehead wrinkled and he turned back to Walter. "What could a person be, I mean with that kind of major? An English major," his father said, testing the phrase on his tongue and his lips.

"Be," Walter said. He fell silent. "Well, I don't know, I could be a . . . writer. A teacher maybe, though I don't think I want to teach. At least not for a while. I could be . . ." Then Walter's mind went blank. As blank and empty as the fields around him.

His father was silent. The meadowlark called again.

"I would just be myself, I guess," Walter said.

His father stared a moment at Walter. "Yourself, only smarter," he added.

"Yessir," Walter said quickly, "that's it."

His father squinted downfield at the gulls, then back at Walter. "Nobody talked you into this?"

Walter shook his head no.

"You like it when you're doing it?" his father asked. He glanced across his own field at what he had planted.

Walter nodded.

His father looked back to Walter and thought another moment. "You think you can make a living at it?"

"Somehow," Walter said.

His father shrugged. "Then I can't see any trouble with it myself," he said. He glanced away, across the fields to the next closest set of barns and silos. "Your uncles, your grampa, they're another story, I suppose."

"They wouldn't have to know," Walter said quickly.

His father looked back to Walter and narrowed his eyes. "They ask me, I'll tell them," he said.[20]

In this conversation we can hear a relationship between a father and a son being recomposed. We can imagine the cost to the father. We also see that he does not simply respond with resignation. He asks four significant, mentoring questions: "What could a person be with that kind of major? Nobody talked you into this? You like it when you're doing it? You think you can make a living at it?"

Walter's responses are "I would just be myself I guess." "No." "Yes." "Somehow." On the strength of the first three responses and despite the vagueness of the fourth response, this father has the grace to affirm his son's bid for integrity and a worthy Dream. He also has the wisdom to insist that there will be no dissembling within the wider family circle.

When families serve well as part of an emerging adult's mentoring environment, their members become gracious and skilled in recognizing that we all change over time. Their support, challenge, and inspiration carry great weight, if offered in ways that make sense in terms of the emerging adult's own experience. Indeed, as the emerging adult self is still appropriately fragile, families err if it is assumed that the emerging adult is now simply on her or his own. The phenomenon of "helicopter-hovering" parents, however, may provide an important anchor or may seriously undercut the development of the emerging adult in the task of moving toward more inner-dependent ways of composing self and world.

The primary work within families is to find a new quality of conversation and relationship with emerging adult children who still return (often unexpectedly) and in some cases actively resist moving out. Discovering that right mix of challenge and support (both emotionally and financially) is the mentoring two-step that is particularly complicated for parents. Sometimes an aunt, uncle, grandparent, or other family member or family friend may offer a "less weighted" but valued mentoring voice within the family circle.

Families as Healers

Some families serve as a mentoring community for other people's emerging adult children who are assessing possible templates of their future adulthood and recomposing their own family stories. In *Resilient Adults: Overcoming a Cruel Past*, Gina Higgins recounts the experience of "Grady," who came from a family where his father was "severely alcoholic" and his mother was repeatedly hospitalized for depression. "It was really bad stuff, toxic stuff." His girlfriend's family became a surrogate family and she later became his wife. Yet later in his thirties, he reflected, "She was a normal kid [from a] normal family. . . . I threw the anchor out, and it hooked onto that island. . . . What I really liked was that the parents respected each other, and they were nice to each other. . . . There was love; there was warmth. . . . I'd never seen that sort of respect that they had for each other. . . . I wanted something stable."[21]

Diana, an emerging adult with a very painful family background, had the opportunity during her university years to spend time in the home of her aunt and uncle. "I used to go out to their house and then all their friends would come over, and they'd sit around usually and have dinner, and their kids, who were slightly younger than I was, would come and go . . . and their kids would tell a joke and everybody would laugh. . . . I thought this was unbelievable. I'd never been listened to long enough to have a joke. . . . So I really got a lot from that family."[22]

Higgins observed that for many of the adults she studied (all of whom had suffered profoundly in childhood but were able to love well in adulthood), the capacity for critical reflection and experiences in surrogate families during their emerging adult years meant that they "gradually cast their previous family experience in high relief and then relativized them." In this process they were "aggrieved but relieved." She concludes, "For those who are adept at sowing their seeds outside the gardens into which they were born, recruited love certainly seems to have the capacity to flourish and thereby restore."[23]

Parent as a Keeper of the Promise

If emerging adults suffer from false mentoring, the absence of mentoring communities, and a variety of temptations to a lesser life, families may often be the primary safety net—stewards of the promise of the emerging adult life. Some parents experience considerable anguish as they sift and sort, trying to discern what powers they do and do not have if their emerging adult children flounder and sometimes head down ill-advised and dangerous paths. In Chapter Two, we spoke of parents and other caregivers in the life of the infant as "keepers of the promise." Parents and families can be keepers of the promise for emerging adult lives as well.

One divorced mother shared with me this account of her relationship with her son when he was a twenty-five-year-old. Each parent thought the son was spending the holidays with the other. When he did turn up, he had just returned from Europe with entirely too much unaccounted-for money. He would not tell his parents where he lived, though he gave them a number for his cell phone. Later, he arranged to visit his mom for a couple of days.

"I struggled," she said, "with the question of how I would be with him. And after a long time, I had an image that helped me. I imagined that I had already totally lost him; he had died or simply disappeared forever. But he was going to be coming back for just two days. How would I want to be with him?" She continued, "Then I was able to be with him from a loving, not bitter, less fearful, un-accusing place. We had a remarkable visit. We could begin to at least walk around the things that matter. I could ask him, 'Can I rule out terrorism?' He said, 'Yes.' 'Can I rule out child prostitution?' Again, 'Yes.'"

Tempted to just cut him off because the pain was so great, this mother found the strength of soul and imagination to remain connected, knowing her voice did matter, letting go to the degree she must, yet still conveying to her son that his life and his choices matter. On his behalf, she holds the hope of a worthy Dream.

Religious Faith Communities

Following a long telephone conversation, a young woman—twenty-seven years old and wrestling with questions of career choices along with her growing recognition of suffering and death—sent a message of appreciation. She wrote, "I got a tremendous amount out of that conversation, especially your reminder that there is something bigger than me playing out in my life." When we wrestle with hope and fear, power and powerlessness, the known and the unknown, we gain consciousness of the Mystery we all share—something bigger, perhaps, than our finite agendas (significant though they be). When a friend is dying too young, when the plan that everything hinges on is in disarray and then comes together in ways we could not have anticipated, when we are stressed out and someone surprises us with a bit of gentleness, we are awakened to wonder—discovering ourselves again on the edge of our knowing about how life really works. Our imagination is activated and our soul leans into another turn in the motion of our becoming. As the questions brew, at least at times, we may seek a language and a home in which to work them. We long for a religious faith.

If "spirituality" is understood as one's lived relationship with Mystery, a religion is a *shared* way of making meaning of that relationship. At its best, religion is a distillation of shared and worthy images powerful enough to shape into one the chaos of our existence. Neither mere dogma nor simply an optional thread in the composing of a lifestyle, religion functions religiously when it serves as a shared means of interpreting the whole of life—continually tested and revised in the ongoing lived experience of individuals and their communities.

In a time of profound cultural change, as science makes demands on religion, as the boundary between religious and political commitments blurs (in both positive and dangerous forms), and as all religious traditions now share a single global commons, every religious tradition is necessarily under review. In the words of physicist Arthur Zajonc, "The venerable and beautiful traditions in which we were educated are losing their hold on human belief, day by day; a restlessness and dissatisfaction in the religious world marks that we are in a moment of transition. . . . The old forms rattle, and the new delay to appear. We are born too late for the old and too early for the new faith."[24] This complex reality is the milieu in which emerging adults are making meaning of self, world, and "God" and seeking viable networks of belonging. Within this dynamic reality, religious faith communities can play a vital, mentoring role in the development of emerging adult, inner-dependent faith.

Some religious communities, however, primarily appeal to the undertow longing for security and certainty, simply offering refuge in a conventional, unexamined faith. Well-intentioned religious communities of this sort often convey zealous care for the integrity of conventional faith mediated by Authority; they reach out to those of emerging adult age in these terms, frequently with obvious success.

Other religious communities assume that, indeed, emerging adults are questioning Authority in the process of seeking adequate and owned faith, and that young adults naturally may be expected to push away from the dock and explore a "far country." These religious faith communities assume, therefore, that during the process of coming to critical thought and mature faith, emerging adults want to distance themselves from their inherited religious communities. It is also assumed that later, when they are older, they will come back. Neither is necessarily the case— and these assumptions become moot in the reality that there are growing numbers of emerging adults who have grown up without a religious community.

Emerging adults are naturally renegotiating questions of their personal future, the meaning of happiness, suffering, and death, their sense of "God," and the ethical dimensions of their choices. Both personally and communally, these are big questions that condition the prospect of worthy Dreams. These are religious questions because they touch the whole of life. If they become mute because there is no place for them, no language to give them public voice, the development of meaning and faith becomes disjointed.

A group of emerging adults, recently out of college, were speculating over coffee in Manhattan. They had attended colleges and universities where there was no particular encouragement to explore questions of spirituality and religious faith. They wondered together how it was that their consciousness of faith had been alive before they entered college but then seemingly had gone underground. Now, in the harsh light of big-time needs for a faith that made sense, they were clearly in a new place and scrambling for a faith to live by. Collectively they came up with this analogy to describe their experience:

> It's like high school was the period when you're trying to think up the paper topic, and you get a rough thesis, an idea of what you want to find out or prove, and the questions you need to ask in your research. Then you spend four years in the library researching, and you find out more than you ever knew you would, and maybe you lose sight of what you were supposed to be researching in the first place, and maybe think of a couple of new ideas while you're at it, or discover something that changes the entire idea you had coming in. And after four years, you step out of the library (where it's been very dark and quiet and safe) and it's noisy and you're blinking in the sun and you have a messy stack of note cards that you're supposed to organize into something cohesive to write the paper, and your original idea sort of comes back to you. But you know way too much to do that thesis, and you're disoriented and have no idea where to start, and the last thing you want to do, having been in the library for so long, is write the damn paper.

Even so, their shared intuition is that life is not likely to unfold well if that "damn paper" is never written.

Religious faith development happens best in tandem with the intellectual and emotional flow of one's life. This means that emerging adults need felt access to religious faith communities while they are "in the library." Such communities need to provide meaningful networks of belonging; extend hospitality to big questions; recognize the claims of a plurality of religious traditions; give access to viable stories and myths, symbols, and songs; inspire meaningful purpose and vocation; recognize the promise and contributions of emerging adult lives; and hold mentors and emerging adults alike in a viable hope.[25]

Communities of Belonging—Comfort and Challenge

Emerging adults are attracted to places where they can be truly at home. They are attracted to places of belonging that can embrace the whole self as it is emerging in its new integrity. In the ongoing search for meaningful belonging, emerging adults, like the rest of us, value places and people where the spiritual dimensions of life are acknowledged and where it is possible to work that delicate mix of sustaining comfort and solace, along with a healthy dollop of stimulation and challenge. A young woman completing her senior year at a major university reflected, "One of my current unresolved questions is that I don't know where to tie my spirit into—there are the confines and dangers of different religions, yet religion provides a place of community and hope like no other." In her question we hear the potentially fruitful tension between her capacity for critical thought, consequent skepticism, and her recognition of the vital role of community as a place to "tie her spirit into."

Hospitality to Big Questions

In conversation with a seasoned pastor, I asked, "Why do you think that so many emerging adults are present in your congregation?" Rather than referencing the size of the congregation, the kind of music, use of media, or charismatic leadership, he thoughtfully responded, "I think it is because we are willing to welcome a lot of questions."[26] This means, of course, not simply responding with traditional or easy answers or mere tolerance, but rather engaging in serious and sustained dialogue. It means a willingness to recognize the Mystery we all share.

The changing milieu of today's world asks religious faith communities to create natural opportunities to gather with emerging young adults in ways that may be a depart from earlier forms. Rabbi Dan Smokler has argued for creating the option of the "Third Space"—neither formal religious nor school settings but rather kitchen tables, coffee shops, and other settings where emerging adults may find—to their surprise—that they are engaged in conversations of significant inquiry and meaning.[27] Traditional religious rituals may also serve mentoring purposes, especially on those occasions that inevitably appear in the lives of emerging adults and their friends—for example, funerals and marriages, experiences that open into faith-sized territory.

A Plurality of Religious Traditions

Contending with another kind of faith-sized challenge, emerging adults now wander and wonder in a dramatically pluralistic landscape, exploring and sometimes discovering deep meaning in religious traditions other than those presumed to be their own. For some, this landscape is both "out there" and within. Reflecting the experience of growing numbers of emerging adults who live a multiethnic, multicultural identity, Eboo Patel has written the following:

> I am an American Muslim from India. My adolescence was a series of rejections, one after another, of the various dimensions of my heritage, in the belief that America, India, and Islam could not co-exist within the same being. If I wanted to be one, I could not be the other. My struggle to understand the traditions I belong to as mutually enriching rather than mutually exclusive is the story of a generation of young people standing at the crossroads of inheritance and discovery, trying to look both ways at once. There is a strong connection between finding a sense of inner coherence and developing a commitment to pluralism. And that has everything to do with who meets you at the crossroads.
>
> When I was in college, I had the sudden realization that all of my heroes were people of deep faith: Dorothy Day, the Dalai Lama, Martin Luther King Jr., Mahatma Gandhi, Malcolm X, the Aga Khan. Moreover, they were all of different faiths. A little more research revealed two additional insights. First, religious cooperation had been central to the work of most of these faith heroes. The Reverend Martin Luther King Jr.

partnered with Rabbi Abraham Joshua Heschel in the struggle
for civil rights. Mahatma Gandhi stated that Hindu-Muslim
unity was just as important to him as a free India. Second, each
of my faith heroes assumed an important leadership role at a
young age. King was only twenty-six years old when he led the
Montgomery bus boycott. Gandhi was even younger when he
started his movement against unjust laws in early-twentieth-
century South Africa.[28]

In his own journey from rage to the possibility of a meaningful pluralism, Patel was met at the crossroads by embodied images
and narratives of possibility offering an alternative imagination.
He realized, however, that the faces of religious fanatics were
young and the faces of interfaith cooperation were old. Believing
that in a world of global, religious conflict, "something had to
change," he has become a public voice on behalf of a religious
pluralism that is neither mere coexistence nor forced
consensus.

Religious faith communities that serve as mentoring communities have a distinctive opportunity and an increasing responsibility to provide religious leadership in a world where growing
numbers of emerging adults must find their own integrity and
faith within an inheritance of multiple identities. In a world
often divided by religious passions, there is a call for leadership
that recognizes that religious truth does not lie in religious
systems but in persons. We are asked to enter and engage imagi-
natively with what it means to be a particular Buddhist, Hindu,
Muslim, Jew, or Christian. From this perspective, a society in
which religious pluralism is possible depends on a robust capacity
for an empathic imagination and respectful dialogue.

It may be said that religious leadership in the contemporary
world is at once more adept than leadership in other sectors in
understanding the nature of religion, yet unpracticed in interreligious dialogue. The quality of empathic dialogue now needed
may include but moves beyond the teaching of the "isms" or the
"ologies."[29] If Harvey Cox has it right in *The Future of Faith*, the

deep currents beneath the religious divides worldwide are transforming religious cultures and we are moving from an Age of Belief and institutionalized dogma to an Age of Spirit and revitalized imaginations of faith.[30] Emerging adults are playing a role in this transformation. There is a hunger for religious leadership that can meet them there.

Emerging adults, meanwhile, are on the one hand vulnerable to easy assumptions about truth in all religions based on a shallow understanding of cultural relativism; on the other hand, they are the souls within which "the new faith" will be imagined. As critical thought develops and a stronger inner authority emerges, a new readiness forms to transcend tribal norms and revise one's boundaries outward. A campus minister who worked to create a climate in which people could express their religious identities while honoring the experience and commitments of others described a poignant moment in her day. Celebrating the High Holy Days, the Jewish students had built the traditional Sukkos. After the services were over, a young Israeli woman was putting the Sukkos away when a Palestinian student happened by. He spontaneously offered to help carry one of the long beams. Then each of them paused a moment, recognizing that if they had been "at home," this simple gracious gesture would not have been possible. Even such momentary encounters can awaken the potential of a larger religious imagination. If emerging adults have access to mentoring communities that will meet them at the crossroads of suffering and wonder in today's world, their faith can be recomposed profoundly and durably.

Often, it is feared, this means that students will no longer hold the faith of their inherited traditions. Sometimes this is the case. Very often it is not. When we encounter the other, there often arises not just greater appreciation for the integrity of the other but new appreciation as well for one's own heritage and its gifts. Through our encounter with the faith of others, we may come to a deepened experience of our own.

One young Jewish woman grew up in a very Protestant city with a small but strong Jewish community. In her college years, she participated in the E Pluribus Unum (EPU) program, which brought Catholic, Jewish, and Protestant students together for three weeks to practice and learn from interfaith dialogue and interreligious collaboration on issues of social justice. Later, she reflected:

> After I went back home, I became friends with a Catholic. We had a big conversation one time after lunch about two big things, abortion and the death penalty. Before EPU, I was always afraid to bring up things like that. But now, as in EPU, we were able to talk with each other and to share with each other without being mad and without getting defensive. At the end, we agreed to disagree, but it was so good that I could come back home and still be able to talk in that way.
>
> The first time I went to services after I returned home was for Rosh Hashanah and Yom Kippur, which of course are the big, huge services every year where everyone comes. It was so good to be able to stand there and to not really feel the need to exactly follow along in the prayer book because I knew from the EPU experience that I could find a prayer inside of me. I had my own spirituality, and it didn't need to be fed to me before like it was, from the prayer book and from the rabbi standing up there talking at me. And so as I stood near the back of the synagogue, I just looked at all the people and was totally in a world of complete prayer just standing there. On those holidays we're continually asking for forgiveness, and it was an amazing experience to stand there and genuinely be able to ask for forgiveness instead of just rambling off all the prayers as I had done in the years past. . . . I'm getting older and my thoughts are becoming more my own, just as my faith is.[31]

This young woman is discovering a deeper experience of her own religious meaning-making. What is also clear when we listen to those who have been engaged in genuine dialogue is that irrespective of what particular religious community one may claim as one's own, one does not remain untouched by the genuine faithfulness of others and the forms in which it is manifest. Increasingly, we all have opportunities to observe and in some measure participate in the practices and beliefs of others. Religion is slowly but surely being reshaped in our time by this fact. As in every generation, emerging adults are leading the way.

Stories and Myths, Symbols, Songs, and Practices

Religion can offer a community "like no other" in part because of its capacity to give language to spirituality and faith. Even in a time between stories, if the great traditions offer their images— stories, symbols, and songs—less as dogma and more as gifts to the work of a faithful imagination—then with critical awareness they can be received as finite vessels to be treasured, reshaped, or cast aside according to their relative usefulness. This is not well done if it is merely a matter of individuals making their private selections from a religious smorgasbord. It is best done in the context of a discerning community—and for emerging adults, a mentoring community. We all need stories to live by, symbols to anchor our meanings by, and songs and dances that confirm that we belong with each other within a yet larger reality. More, we need practices that discipline us into trustworthy ways of discerning worthy forms of meaning and purpose. Religious communities at their best provide access to languages of meaning-making and faith in profound measure. If its offering is resonant with the emerging adult soul, then the spiritual quest may lead to a worthy religious home.

Some religious faith communities within urban, campus, and military environments that harbor large populations of emerging adults are tentatively but necessarily and increasingly serving as sites for creative abrasion and often remarkably meaningful experimentation among differing religious traditions. There is a great deal at stake for all of us within these mentoring communities, and they may appropriately be recognized (not uncritically but respectfully) as zones of sacred possibility in the human community.

Recognition of Emerging Adult Gifts

The religious community does not fulfill its role in the formation of emerging adult faith unless it can welcome and confirm the emerging competence of twenty-somethings. A minister reflecting on his own formation wrote the following:

> Attending a youth conference as a young minister to youth, I was in awe of some of the other ministers present. Men and women whom I respected, they were . . . inspirations to me. . . .
>
> One morning one of these men came up to me and said, "I would love the privilege of getting together with you. How about over a Coke this afternoon?"
>
> I couldn't believe what I had heard. This successful, highly regarded man wanted to sit down with me? . . . Why? I felt both honored and scared. . . .
>
> That afternoon we did get together . . . and had a great time getting to know each other. I can't recall all that this man shared with me, but I do remember one statement he made that has stayed with me as a real source of encouragement.
>
> As our conversation came to a close he said, "Michael, I want to tell you something. This afternoon I'm buying stock in you as a person and as a minister. Right now, as you begin your ministry, the stock is not 'at a high.' But one day stock in you is going to pay big dividends, and I'm buying into it right now, because I believe in you. . . ."
>
> . . . Now, years later, this incident, along with many others, brings to my mind the realization that God placed certain people in my life to be a source of encouragement and support both to my ministry and to me personally.[32]

Very frequently when people in later life reflect on how religious faith communities have been part of their formation, they identify someone, lay or ordained, who singled them out in their emerging adult years and conferred a deepened sense of trust in their own potential. Yet in a recent conversation with a small group of remarkable senior clergy, I learned that during their formative years, each of them had been gifted by significant mentors. They realized that now, however, they were not doing the same for the next generation.

Tasks to Do

Recognition of emerging adults and their gifts also takes the form of giving them meaningful tasks to do—especially providing pathways, forms of institutional support, that lead to engagement in situations that call for compassion and justice and seed worthy dreams. In this kind of real work in the world, emerging adults may discover a sense of purpose that deepens into vocation. Adulthood takes form as one is called to a problem, a meaningful challenge, and tasks, around which the adult self becomes. This is a primary domain in which religious faith communities may significantly meet the hungers of emerging adults for meaning, purpose, and a grounded hope.

A Viable Hope

When I asked a group of civic leaders what they thought religion contributed to the new commons, the first reply was, "Hope." Hope is nourished in a host of ways, but one of the forms that is now needed is experiences of the commons—places where we can come together across differences, recognize our interdependence, and gain access to symbols that open us to the Mystery that transcends us all, while at the same time we are invited to moral responsibility. At their best, religious faith communities can offer emerging adults a micro experience of the new commons, mediating hope—not in terms of guaranteed outcomes—but as a posture in the world informed by a critically aware and worthy faith.

But it is a two-way street. In *Virtual Faith*, Tom Beaudoin observes that many emerging adults tend to exhibit on the one hand an experimental and skeptical attitude toward orthodoxy and a heightened ambiguity in their experience of faith. On the other hand, they are creating new forms of searching for and articulating their faith, new images to convey their experience of Spirit, unprecedented modes of music—in short, new and often seemingly "irreverent" forms of credo. Great liturgy—the work of the people—is always an artful juxtaposition of the novel and the familiar. Communities of religious faith that respond to the hunger for mentoring environments are being stretched, sometimes almost to the breaking point, to maintain their embrace of these two poles. Embedded, however, in the irreverence, new sounds, and syncopations are gifts to the religious imagination of both younger and older generations.[33]

Religious faith communities grounded in vibrant practices of ongoing discernment can serve as communities of shoulder-to-shoulder mentor-protégé relationships, inspiring purpose and faith across the generations in traditional, hybrid, and other creative, emergent forms.

Media

Although today's emerging adults may live in different media cultures shaped in part by gender, ethnicity, and social class, "the media" have become so pervasive, so integral to the surround of emerging adult lives, that our media technologies have become more than mere tools. They constitute a powerful environment—inevitably playing a mentoring role.

The jury is surely still out on what this perpetually "new" surround means for any of us—how media will recompose the experience, knowledge, meanings, and ultimately the faith of the human community. What we do know is that these technologies evoke big questions. Sherry Turkle, founder and director of MIT's Initiative on Technology and the Self, has been studying the evolving relationships among self, society, and technology for thirty years. She captures the heart of the matter when she reflects, "Thinking about robots . . . is a way of thinking about the essence of personhood. Thinking about connectivity is a way to think about what we mean to each other."[34]

These questions—What does it mean to be a human being? What do we mean to each other?—are the overarching questions within which we consider the media as a worthy mentoring environment. Surely such questions are not easily answered, but we can suggest criteria with which such questions may be engaged. To that end and in keeping with our purposes here, I suggest that we might assess the media by posing the questions we would ask of any mentoring environment: How does the media environment recognize, support, challenge, and inspire emerging adults? Do the current practices of media use among emerging adults (which according to some evidence can be distinguished from the media use of teen-agers[35]) assist us in being accountable to the potential and vulnerability of emerging adult lives in their formation of meaning, purpose, and faith? These questions carry us into complex, swampy, yeasty terrain. Here we can only begin to trace some of the broad contours of that terrain.

Recognition

Emerging adults need to be recognized—to be seen—as they are and as they could become. How are emerging adults "seen" through the eyes of the media? First, what are the prevailing images of emerging adults in advertising, film and other media that serve as "mirrors" shaping the identities and aspirations of emerging adults? Second, it is surely arguable that social networks provide a forum in which an emerging adult may be "seen" on an unprecedented scale. Especially as text gives way to more visual modalities, the opportunities to be "seen" will continue to proliferate. Although the range of connectivity is dramatically extended, the depth of communication is, however, highly variable, and sorting out the appropriate depth at which one is "seen" in these ways is a critical task. It is also argued that those who are socially shy are empowered by digital communication, and when people are developmentally trying on various identities, social media provide a space in which to do so with less risk. Yet the latitude for posturing and dissembling is also broad—that is, people can simply lie. Who is it that is "seen"?

As a thoughtful parent and provost put it, "Where are the edges, the boundaries?" Over time, in relationship to other powerful aspects of human life—food and eating, for example—we develop practices, norms, and laws that distill experience into wisdom and orient a civilization. Our media technologies are relatively very new and evolving at such a rapid pace that we have not yet had the time to distill shared patterns of "right use." We are all in an experimental mode with human subjects.

Support

In this experimental mode, how does the media provide for or erode the mentoring support and the positive networks of belonging that emerging adults require? Emerging adults are typically connected to families and friends in ways that provide for some forms of emotional and practical support far exceeding the experience of earlier generations. The Web supports vast realms of inquiry and exploration. Media—newscasts, magazines, film, music, games, and all the rest—may inform, entertain, and significantly enrich a sense of a world full of possibility, supporting the ambitions and aspirations of emerging adult lives.

We can also read media use as a reach for support. Claire Gordon, a Yale graduate student, posted the following on *The Huffington Post* in defense of her generation:

> Young people today aren't so much narcissistic as needy. If anything, we are obsessed with relationships. We don't hurl our bursting egos into the Internet, but build our self-esteem through likes, re-tweets, views, and comments.

Young people don't blog out of self-love, but in pursuit of affirmation. We didn't grow up "amid a chorus of applause," but with intense parental pressure, as competition for college spots soared. We got the message not that we surpassed all expectations, but that expectations surpassed our human limits.[36]

In what ways does media use reflect the hungers of emerging adults for appropriate support?

And in what ways does the media feed on the appetites of all of us, including emerging adults, addressing all as passive consumers to be exploited for the purposes of markets—distracting and arresting, if not derailing, the development of a more inner-dependent imagination? How does the media assist the emerging adult who is vulnerable to merely floundering in a sea of "targeted" images? What mentoring supports are in place for the development of media consciousness and information literacy—means by which the flow of images may be assessed and integrated?[37]

Challenge

That is, as emerging adults are ripe for meaningful challenges, are they challenged to think critically, especially in regard to media messages and other dimensions of media use so as to become media savvy in ways that serve the process of learning to "superintend" the imagination? And does the media catalyze other key challenges that are germane to young adult development—encounters with otherness, big-enough questions, and engagement in adaptive learning that fosters development from conventional assumptions to more adequate adult meaning-making, a more adequate faith?[38]

Reflecting on "challenges" from another perspective, it must be observed that many nondigital natives are challenged by how tremendously capable some emerging adults are in using the media as a means of self-expression, collaboration, and as a medium of enormous creativity in art, communication, and politics—sometimes in notably courageous ways. Encouraging the talent and imagination of emerging adults in the media environment is a role that some mentors have taken on, building significant partnerships across generational lines, working in highly adaptive territory.

Media can also bridge the "digital divide"—an issue of class and race—challenging the imagination of some who are otherwise denied access to civic life. Joseph Kahne has found evidence that working-class and less fortunate young people who play games with civic content—"including games that raise ethical questions, those that offer leadership roles, and those that offer gamers the opportunity to help novices—can encourage youths to get involved off-line in civic efforts. . . . These games are not the 'chocolate-covered broccoli' learning games of the past . . . that espouse poorly concealed civic lessons. These are games . . . which allow people to form and run their own societies, or to tackle issues such as pollution and poverty by organizing and cajoling thousands of other real-life players to cooperate for the greater good." Kahne has also found that other forms of digital media, including social networks and blogs, expose people to both those who agree and those who disagree with them, leading to greater civic engagement. Many of those who don't go to college do use digital media, and it can and could be a way of challenging their imaginations and smoothing their transition to adulthood.[39]

Inspiration

The media can inspire—inspirit and enliven—and it can also narrow and numb the life of the emerging adult's imagination. As we assess the potential and perils of the media environment, a central fact is that the media has enormous power to create and amplify images and to pour them into the heart and hearts of our new global commons. The media determine in significant measure what emerging adults are breathing in and breathing out. One of the great powers of the new media is its capacity to serve as a conduit of narratives inspiring the imagination of emerging adults in positive ways as they seek to compose a coherent adult narrative worthy of the promise of their lives, as exemplified in the film *Invictus,* the magazine *Yes!* and the Web site *Why do you do what you do?* (www.wdydwyd.com).

But the media environment is also replete with missed opportunities and luminous distractions. Out for dinner, my husband and I are waited on by an obviously highly capable, personable young man. We ask him what he does when he isn't waiting tables. We learn that he is thirty years old, and he tells us that he "has graduated from high school but has yet to go to college" and knows it's high time to get on with it, but isn't sure what he wants to study, and he is thinking about it because his girlfriend—a junior in molecular biology—wants him to and "then I could have a career—instead of 'this,' which is just a job." Then, returning to our initial question, he tells us that in his free time, he is home watching (ironically, we think) the last three seasons of the "reality" TV show *Lost.*

David Whyte has observed how helpless any of us may be before our highly portable access to digital media and every flickering screen. Most significantly he also observes that "the need for a larger, mythological context has an enormous percentage of young men sinking their ambitions and hopes into virtual games which feed them endless false triumphs and a sense of almost other-worldly accomplishment that bears no relation to the world they actually inhabit. Without discipline and artfulness, it is hard to break out of the increasingly narrow contexts that these technologies so conveniently provide."[40]

Accountability

The media conversation is being taken up in most quarters not only to keep pace with technological innovation but also because we are beginning to deepen the questions of media accountability. In the early stages of this adaptive challenge, the work of paying attention in the midst of running experiments is paramount—especially as our media-saturated environment lures all of us into a state of continuous partial attention.

Two key elements that most obviously might command our attention as we consider issues of accountability are (1) *What is the content of the images that dominate the emerging adult media culture?* The media can serve as sources of identities and enterprises that are worthy of emulation and others that limit or denigrate the more positive aspects of human potential.[41] What does it mean, for example, that gaming is dominated by an imagination of violent conquest? Do some forms of celebrity glamour instill mere consumerist and cynical worldviews? (2) *How does today's media interact with the processes of human becoming?* For instance, what does it mean that many emerging adults, whose bodies are rarely where their minds are, live in what one young adult has described as a "chronic state of dislocation"? What does it mean to have the expectation that life can be negotiated "fast and free"? Does the media environment foster both a greater connectivity and a greater loneliness? How do we adjudicate the differing merits of screen-to-screen and face-to-face communication? Is the media an "indoor" environment in relationship to an "outside" world? If our most meaningful experiences occur through what media artist Ken Burns describes as duration and sustained attention,[42] how does the media environment serve or fail the formation of worthy Dreams? In short, how does our understanding of the potential and vulnerability of the twenty-something years and the gifts of a mentoring imagination inform our aspirations and practices in a media environment?

In his thoughtful essay, "Hacker Ethics and Higher Learning: The Moral Clash Determining the Future of Education," Gerardo Marti recognizes the idealism and virtues embedded in the moral code of the "Hacker Culture."[43] This moral orientation celebrates the values of openness, freedom, connectivity, new spaces, access, intelligence, creativity, experimentation, passion, playfulness, problem solving, speed, efficiency, self-confidence, volunteerism, personal and social transformation—and a new release of the human spirit (along with suspicion of Authority). These are qualities that also mark some of the most positive features of the twenty-something era.

Marti then directs our attention to the tension between Hacker values and the moral code of educational contexts as we have known them, a code anchored in commitments to human formation and virtues, including responsibility, discernment, the pursuit of wisdom, and the values of place and face. Interestingly, he suggests that this tension turns on the question of who qualifies as an adult. I do not believe these two codes define an unbridgeable gap, rather they invite us into big questions: That is, if twenty-somethings are "emerging adults" and formation toward adulthood is still under way, how then do the virtues of positive mentoring environments both affirm and challenge the virtues of the Hacker ethic? Or to return to Turkle's pivotal inquiry: Where, with whom, and by what discipline and artfulness do today's generations creatively, critically, and contemplatively negotiate the terms by which we evolve our understanding of the formation of personhood and what we mean to each other?

Social Movements

Social movements serve inevitably as powerful mentoring environments in the lives of those emerging adults who find within them a sense of transcendent meaning and purpose. The reach for the ideal and a place of meaningful contribution in the adult world uniquely positions the energies of emerging adults to serve as vital fuel for positive transforming social movements (though "movements" can surely also exploit the emerging adult vulnerability to false mentors, who lead to death rather than to life). Not every generation has an opportunity to be part of a great social turning. But those who do tend to feel in later life a kind of privilege in having had one's adulthood forged in the fire of social conflict, in the service of high purpose.

If there is a groundswell of resistance to injustice and oppression and a stirring of the collective conscience that makes a claim for more life-bearing patterns of institutional and communal practice, we can count on emerging adults to show up, especially when their own futures are at stake in the outcome.[44] In the light of today's media technologies, the power of emerging adults to participate in creating and shaping narratives of possibility and strategies for action has been dramatically amplified.

On whatever scale, a movement can become a mentoring community, as critical dialogue, conscious conflict, powerful images, a host of mentors, a call to action, and a public stage on which to test one's powers create a confluence of recognition, support, challenge, and inspiration—a crucible for the formation of emerging adult meaning-making and faith. It might be said that until we achieve a just and sustainable Earth community, every generation of emerging adults deserves access to a worthy social movement. Movements are inevitably messy as well as meaningful, and they have their own kind of casualties. But it must be acknowledged that in the context of a great movement, many emerging adults discover purposeful participation in something larger than the self and gain access to worthy Dreams.

Notes

Chapter One: Emerging Adulthood in a Changing World

1. Kristen Scharold, guest blogger. http://blog.christianitytoday.com/women/2010/09/an_argument_against_settling_down, September 14, 2010.
2. See Jeffrey Jensen Arnett. *Emerging Adulthood: The Winding Road from the Late Teens Through the Twenties.* New York: Oxford University Press, 2004. Kenneth Keniston. *Youth and Dissent: The Rise of a New Opposition.* Orlando: Harcourt Brace, 1960. Sharon Parks. *The Critical Years: Young Adults and Their Search for Meaning, Faith, and Commitment.* San Francisco: Harper San Francisco, 1986. See also Daniel Levinson. *Seasons of a Man's Life.* New York: Knopf, 1978; Daniel J. Levinson with Judy D. Levinson. *Seasons of a Woman's Life.* New York: Knopf, 1996; and John Kotre and Elizabeth Hall. *Seasons of Life: The Dramatic Journey from Birth to Death.* Ann Arbor: University of Michigan Press, 1990, Chapters Ten through Twelve.
3. Keniston (1960), pp. 17–18.
4. See for example Richard Settersten and Barbara E. Ray. *Not Quite Adults: Why 20-Somethings Are Choosing a Slower Path to Adulthood, and Why It's Good for Everyone.* New York: Random House, 2010; Robin Marantz Henig. "What Is It About 20-Somethings?" *New York Times Magazine,* August 22, 2010, pp. 28–37, 46–47, 49; Anastasia Snyder, Diane McLaughlin, and Alisha Coleman-Jensen. *The New, Longer Road to Adulthood: Schooling, Work, and Idleness Among Rural Youth.* Dartmouth: Carsey Institute, University of New Hampshire, 2009; William A. Galston. "The Changing

Twenties," monograph presented at a meeting hosted by the National Campaign to Prevent Teen and Unplanned Pregnancy, October 2007; and Christian Smith. "Getting a Life: The Challenge of Emerging Adulthood," *Books & Culture*, November/December 2007, pp. 10–12.

5. See Laurent A. Parks Daloz. *Sons, Fathers, and Mentors: Manhood for the Twenty-first Century*, forthcoming.

6. Meaning is, broadly speaking, the awareness of connectedness, importance, and felt significance among perceived objects both external and internal; narrowly speaking, it is the attribution of positive value to a particular configuration of attitudes, ideals, and connections that stand close to the center of one's identity and are the key to judging importance in relation to time, person, events, and the natural world. Adapted from William R. Rogers. "Defense and Loss of Meaning." Paper delivered to the Society for Scientific Study of Religion, Philadelphia, 1976, p. 8. See also Michael Lerner. *The Politics of Meaning: Restoring Hope and Possibility in an Age of Cynicism*. Reading, MA: Perseus, 1996, p. 21.

7. Levinson (1978), p. 73.

8. Zalman Schachter-Shalomi. *From Age-ing to Sage-ing*. New York: Time-Warner, 1995, p. 192.

9. See Laurent A. Parks Daloz, Cheryl H. Keen, James P. Keen, and Sharon Daloz Parks. *Common Fire: Leading Lives of Commitment in a Complex World*. Boston: Beacon Press, 1996, pp. 2–4.

10. Daloz, Keen, Keen, and Parks (1996), Chapter Four.

11. See Douglas Jacobsen and Rhonda Hustedt Jacobsen (eds.). *The American University in a Postsecular Age*. Oxford, UK: Oxford University Press, 2008; Robert Kiely. "Notes on Religion at Harvard: Out of the Closet & into the Classroom, the Yard, & the Dining Halls," *Liberal Education*, Fall 2001, 24–30; Parker J. Palmer and Arthur Zajonc with Megan Scribner. *The Heart of Higher Education: A Call to Renewal*. San Francisco: Jossey-Bass, 2010; Alexander W. Astin, Helen S. Astin, and Jennifer S. Lindholm. *Cultivating the Spirit: How College Can Enhance Students' Inner Lives*. San Francisco: Jossey-Bass, 2010.

12. "New England's First Fruits," quoted in S. E. Morrison. *The Founding of Harvard College*. Cambridge, MA: Harvard University Press, 1935, p. 168. See also Perry Miller. *The New England Mind: The Seventeenth Century*. Cambridge, MA: Harvard University Press, 1939, pp. 75–76.

13. Kotre and Hall (1990), p. 221.

Chapter Two: The Deep Motion of Life

1. Stephen Sundborg, S. J. Presentation. Executive Leadership Program. Seattle University, October 22, 2010; and Harvey Cox. *The Future of Faith*. New York: HarperOne, 2009, Chapter Two.

2. Parker Palmer. *The Courage to Teach: Exploring the Inner Landscape of a Teacher's Life*. San Francisco: Jossey-Bass, 1998.

3. Wilfred Cantwell Smith. *Belief and History*. Charlottesville: University Press of Virginia, 1977, pp. 41–45.

4. Smith (1977), pp. 13–61.

5. Smith (1977), p. 78.

6. William F. Lynch, S. J. *Images of Faith: An Exploration of the Ironic Imagination*. Notre Dame, IN: University of Notre Dame Press, 1973, p. 9.

7. Lynch (1973), p. 125.

8. Charles Spezzano. "Prenatal Psychology: Pregnant with Questions," *Psychology Today*, May 1981, pp. 49–57.

9. Erik Erikson. *Childhood and Society*. (2nd ed.) New York: Norton, 1963, pp. 247–251.

10. James W. Fowler. *Stages of Faith: The Psychology of Human Development and the Quest for Meaning*. San Francisco: Harper San Francisco, 1981, pp. 16–23; and *Faithful Change: The Personal and Public Challenges of Postmodern Life*. Nashville: Abingdon Press, 1996, pp. 20–22.

11. H. Richard Niebuhr. *Radical Monotheism*. London: Faber and Faber, 1943, p. 25. In this sense, virtually all human beings may be understood as "theists." From this perspective, a "true atheist" would be one "who loves no one and whom no one loves; who

does not care for truth, sees no beauty, strives for no justice; who knows no courage and no joys, finds no meaning, and has lost all hope." Wilfred Cantwell Smith. *Faith and Belief*. Princeton, NJ: Princeton University Press, 1979, p. 20.

12. Sharon Lea Parks. "Faith Development and Imagination in the Context of Higher Education." ThD dissertation, Harvard University, Cambridge, MA, 1980, p. 42.

13. Smith (1979), p. 13.

14. Niebuhr (1943), pp. 24–39.

15. John Tarrant. *The Light Inside the Dark: Zen, Soul, and the Spiritual Life*. New York: HarperCollins, 1998, p. 114.

16. Anthony Lawlor. *A Home for the Soul: A Guide for Dwelling with Spirit and Imagination*. New York: Clarkson Potter, 1997, p. 26.

17. Smith (1979), pp. 61–62.

18. Smith (1979), pp. 65–66.

19. William Damon. *The Path to Purpose: Helping Our Children Find Their Calling in Life*. New York: Free Press, 2008, pp. 33–34. See also Robert J. Nash and Michelle C. Murray. *Helping College Students Find Purpose: The Campus Guide to Meaning-Making*. San Francisco: Jossey-Bass, p. xx; and Lara Galinsky with Kelly Nuxoll. *Work on Purpose*. New York: Echoing Green, 2011.

20. Damon (2008), p. 39.

21. Lynch (1973), pp. 39–40.

22. Richard R. Niebuhr. *Experiential Religion*. New York: HarperCollins, 1972, pp. 42–43. See also Tom Beaudoin. *Virtual Faith: The Irreverent Spiritual Quest of Generation X*. San Francisco: Jossey-Bass, 1998, especially Chapter Six.

23. Niebuhr (1972), pp. 91–104.

24. Karen Thorkilsen helpfully recognized that though the structure of an earlier faith may undergo collapse, often it is some element of the wreckage that saves our lives until the new shore appears.

25. Viktor Frankl. *Man's Search for Meaning: An Introduction to Logotherapy*. New York: Washington Square Press, 1963, p. 106.

26. Niebuhr (1972), p. 97.

27. James Carroll. *A Terrible Beauty*. New York: Newman Press, 1973, p. 102.
28. Lynch (1973), p. 25.
29. Tarrant (1998), p. 106.
30. James Fowler and Sam Keen. *Life Maps: Conversations on the Journey of Faith*. (J. Berryman, ed.) Waco, TX: Word Books, 1978, p. 37.

Chapter Three: Becoming at Home in the Universe

1. Jedediah Purdy. *For Common Things: Irony, Trust, and Commitment in America Today*. New York: Knopf, 1999, p. 25.
2. Parker Palmer. *Let Your Life Speak: Listening for the Voice of Vocation*. San Francisco: Jossey-Bass, 2000, p. 70.
3. Smith (1979), p. 12. For a history of the idea of a hospitable universe in American religion, see William A. Clebsch. *American Religious Thought: A History*. Chicago: University of Chicago Press, 1973.
4. See Vasti Torres, "Mi Casa Is Not Exactly Like Your Casa: A Window onto the Experience of Latino Students," *About Campus*, May–June 2003, 2–7; Jean S. Phinney, "Ethnic Identity Exploration in Emerging Adulthood." In Jeffrey Jensen Arnett and Jennifer Lynn Tanner (eds.). *Emerging Adults in America: Coming of Age in the 21st Century*. Washington, DC: American Psychological Association, 2006, pp. 117–134.
5. Erik Erikson. *Childhood and Society*. (2nd ed.) New York: Norton, 1963, Chapter Seven.
6. See Daloz, Keen, Keen, and Parks (1996), Chapter Two.
7. Robert Fulghum. *All I Really Need to Know I Learned in Kindergarten: Uncommon Thought on Common Things*. New York: Villard Books, 1988, pp. 6–7.
8. Emily Souvaine, Lisa Laslow Lahey, and Robert Kegan. "Life After Formal Operations: Implications for a Psychology of the Self." In E. Langer and C. Alexander (eds.). *Beyond Formal Operations*. New York: Oxford University Press, 1990, p. 8.

9. See "Reconstructing Larry: Assessing the Legacy of Lawrence Kohlberg." *Harvard Education Bulletin*, 1999, 43(1), 6–13.

10. Robert Kegan. "There the Dance Is: Religious Dimensions of a Developmental Framework." *Toward Moral and Religious Maturity*. Morristown, NJ: Silver Burdett, 1980, p. 407. Robert Kegan. *The Evolving Self: Problem and Process in Human Development*. Cambridge, MA: Harvard University Press, 1982; Robert Kegan. *In over Our Heads: The Mental Demands of Modern Life*. Cambridge, MA: Harvard University Press, 1994; Robert Kegan and Lisa Laskow Lahey. *Immunity to Change: How to Overcome It and Unlock the Potential in Yourself and Your Organization*. Boston: Harvard Business Press, 2009.

11. Kegan (1994).

12. Carol Gilligan. *In a Different Voice: Psychological Theory and Women's Development*. Cambridge, MA: Harvard University Press, 1982.

13. Carol Gilligan. "Remapping the Moral Domain: New Images of Self in Relationship." Paper presented at Reconstruction Individualism, Stanford University Humanities Center, February 1984.

14. Kegan (1980), p. 409.

15. Kegan (1980), p. 410.

16. Fowler (1981).

17. See James W. Fowler. *Faithful Change: The Personal and Public Challenges of Postmodern Life*. Nashville: Abingdon Press, 1996.

18. See William G. Perry Jr. *Forms of Ethical and Intellectual Development in the College Years: A Scheme*. San Francisco: Jossey-Bass, 1998.

19. Keniston (1960), p. 7.

20. Keniston (1960), p. 5.

21. Keniston (1960), p. 6.

22. Arnett (2004), p. 8. The identification of this era as "self-focused" may be less descriptive of emerging adults in other cultures or subcultures. See for example, Michelle Sarna, "An Emerging Approach to Emerging Adulthood and Modern Orthodoxy." Presentation at the conference, "Toward a Third Space—New

Dimensions of Jewish Education for Emerging Adults." New York City, June 21, 2010.

23. See Parks (1986).

24. See John Broughton. "The Political Psychology of Faith Development Theory." In Craig Dykstra and Sharon Parks (eds.). *Faith Development and Fowler*. Birmingham, AL: Religious Education Press, 1986.

25. See Laurent A. Daloz. *Mentor: Guiding the Journey of Adult Learners*. San Francisco: Jossey-Bass, 1999. (First edition published 1986)

26. For a compelling use of the journey metaphor as "the journey to self authorship" built on a study of eighteen- to twenty-year-olds, see Marcia B. Baxter Magolda. *Authoring Your Life: Developing an Internal Voice to Navigate Life's Challenges*. Sterling, VA: Stylus, 2009.

27. Joseph Campbell. *The Hero with a Thousand Faces*. Princeton, NJ: Princeton University Press, 1949, p. 30.

28. Nancy Chodorow. *The Reproduction of Mothering: Psychoanalysis and the Sociology of Gender*. Berkeley: University of California Press, 1978.

29. Kegan (1982), pp. 107–108.

30. Mary Belenky, Blythe Clinchy, Nancy Goldberger, and Jill Tarule. *Women's Ways of Knowing: The Development of Self, Voice, and Mind*. New York: Basic Books, 1986.

31. Sharon Daloz Parks. "Home and Pilgrimage: Companion Metaphors for Personal and Social Transformation." *Soundings*, 1989, 52(2–3), 297–315; and Sharon Daloz Parks. "To Venture and to Abide: The Tidal Rhythm of Our Becoming." In Richard R. Osmer and Fredrich L. Schweitzer (eds.). *Developing a Public Faith: New Directions in Practical Theology*. St. Louis: Chalice Press, 2003, Chapter Three.

32. Richard R. Niebuhr. "Pilgrims and Pioneers." *Parabola*, 1984, 9(3), 6–13.

33. Martin Heidegger. *Poetry, Language, Thought*. New York: Harper-Collins, 1975, p. 147.

34. Tarrant (1998), pp. 37–38.
35. See Daloz, Keen, Keen, and Parks (1996), Chapter Three.

Chapter Four: It Matters How We Think

1. Perry used initial capitals for the terms *Authority* and *Truth* to indicate the particular way these are constructed in early developmental positions. The same pattern is followed here.
2. Perry (1998), p. 33.
3. Belenky, Clinchy, Goldberger, and Tarule (1986), Chapter Two.
4. Perry (1998), pp. 121–148.
5. For the term *unqualified relativism*, I am indebted to George Rupp's work *Beyond Existentialism and Zen*. New York: Oxford University Press, 1979, Chapter One.
6. Perry (1998), pp. 36–37.
7. "Although the road of reflection . . . increases the adaptive repertoire of individuals, it does not guarantee good adaptation. . . . That is, high levels of conceptual complexity can also serve maladaptive functions. . . . For this reason, in my own work I have emphasized that successful adaptation requires individuals to coordinate a concern with complexity . . . with the ability to maintain sufficiently positive levels of positive affect and to ward off extreme levels of negative affect. In recent work, I referred to these different strategies as differentiation and optimization." Gisela Labouvie-Vief, "Emerging Structures of Adult Thought." Arnett and Tanner (2006), p. 75.
8. Quoted in Robert Rankin. "Beginning." In Robert Rankin (ed.). *The Recovery of Spirit in Higher Education: Christian and Jewish Ministries in Campus Life*. New York: Seabury Press, 1980, p. 10.
9. Kegan and Lahey (2009), p. 52.
10. Erik H. Erikson. *Identity: Youth and Crisis*. New York: Norton, 1963, pp. 261–263.
11. Erikson (1963), p. 211.
12. Fowler and Keen (1978), p. 70.

13. Keniston (1960), p. 8. (The language in the citation has been modified to be inclusive in terms of gender.) This is resonant with "subjective knowing" as described by Belenky, Clinchy, Goldberger, and Tarule (1986) and discussed in Chapter Five of this book.
14. Keniston (1960), p. 6.
15. Ernest L. Boyer Jr. A Sailor's Journal. Volant, PA: Napier Press, 1974, pp. 19–20.
16. Keniston (1960), p. 8.
17. This "ambivalence" is akin to Arnett's "instability" spawned by exploration but does not carry the same pejorative connotation.
18. Perry (1998), pp. 149ff.
19. Boyer (1974), pp. 27–28.
20. Keniston (1960), pp. 8–9.
21. For further description of cognitive development in emerging adulthood, see Labouvie-Vief (2006), Chapter Three.
22. Howard Brinton. Quaker Journals. Wallingford, PA: Pendle Hill, 1972, pp. 6–68. In the study described in Common Fire (Daloz, Keen, Keen, and Parks, 1996), it was similarly observed that a coalescence of identity and vocation typically occurred by the ages of twenty-six to twenty-eight.
23. Ann S. Masten, Jelena Obradovic, and Keith B. Burt. "Resilience in Emerging Adulthood: Developmental Perspectives on Continuity and Transformation." Arnett and Tanner (2006), p. 177.

Chapter Five: It All Depends . . .

1. Kegan (1980), p. 408. See also "Emerging cognitive capacities transform the very functioning of emotions, even causing at times the emergence of new emotions that appear to be linked to higher levels of complexity." Labouvie-Vief (2006), p. 75.
2. Note that this volume addresses the mind-heart dualism but often assumes, and only modestly addresses, the body-embodied dimension of human personality. This undoubtedly reflects in part the body-spirit dualism that prevails in much of Western culture.

Beverly Harrison traced the fallacies and dangers of the traditional body-spirit or heart-mind dualisms that fail to recognize persons as fully embodied, psychosexual, spiritual unities: "We are not split, 'compounds' of mind and emotion or body and spirit. Our emotions mediate our basic interactions with the world. Our minds are an integrated aspect of our body-systems, shaped by the matrix of our sensuous being in the world" (p. 147). "With bodily repression comes a loss of a sense of our connectedness to the rest of nature, the cosmos, and to each other" (p. 148). Beverly Wildung Harrison. "Human Sexuality and Mutuality." In Judith L. Weidman (ed.). *Christian Feminism*. San Francisco: Harper San Francisco, 1984. See also Tu Wei-Ming. "The Confucian Perception of Adulthood," *Daedalus*, Spring 1976, p. 115.

3.   My awareness of dependence as a key dimension of development was initially informed by the work of William Weyerhaeuser; see "One Person's View of Conscience with Special Reference to His Therapy." PhD dissertation, Fuller Graduate School of Psychology, Pasadena, CA, 1975.

4.   Patricia O'Connell Killen and John de Beer. *The Art of Theological Reflection*. New York: Crossroad, 1994, pp. 27–28. See also David Brooks. *The Social Animal: The Hidden Sources of Love, Character, and Achievement*. New York: Random House, 2011.

5.   Mirra Komarovsky. *Women in College: Shaping New Feminine Identities*. New York: Basic Books, 1985, p. 10.

6.   See George C. Lodge. *The American Disease*. New York: Knopf, 1984.

7.   "While there is solid conviction as well as psychological wisdom in both religious and general cultural manifestations of independence, the excess of such claims easily leads us to the suspicion that they may betray more underlying anxiety about forms of dependence." W. R. Rogers. "Dependence and Counterdependency in Psychoanalysis and Religious Faith." *Zygon*, September 1974, 9, 191.

8.   See maps of individual phases on the journey. Marcia B. Baxter Magolda (2009).

9. This shift in the construal of authority is interestingly linked with a gentler sense of self. Indeed, Gilligan's studies suggest a corresponding motion in the dimension of care. People (especially women) who have tended to extend care to others while neglecting themselves (because only others had the authority to claim care) can now as a consequence of the capacity to include the self in the arena of authority extend care also to the self. Gilligan (1982).
10. Kegan and Lahey (2009), p. 52.
11. Belenky, Clinchy, Goldberger, and Tarule (1986), pp. 52–62.
12. Robert E. Quinn. *Deep Change: Discovering the Leader Within*. San Francisco: Jossey-Bass, 1996, pp. 73–78.
13. Fowler (1981), pp. 197–198.

Chapter Six: . . . On Belonging

1. James W. Fowler. "Stages in Faith." In T. Hennessey, S.J. (ed.). *Values and Moral Development*. New York: Paulist Press, 1976, p. 184.
2. Sharon Daloz Parks. "Theme Dorms: Mixing Academic and College Life." Palmer and Zajonc (2010), pp. 175–178.
3. See Daloz, Keen, Keen, and Parks (1996), Chapter Three.
4. Kegan (1982), p. 90.
5. For an elegant reflection on the influence and interaction of multiple social environments in relationship to emerging adults, see Brian J. Mahan. *Forgetting Ourselves on Purpose: Vocation and the Ethics of Ambition*. San Francisco: Jossey-Bass, 2002, pp. 156–157.
6. Seminar conversation with Dwayne Huebner, Auburn Theological Seminary, March 1982.
7. See Kegan (1980), pp. 411–413.
8. John Henry Newman. *The Idea of a University*. Notre Dame, IN: University of Notre Dame Press, 1982, p. 110.
9. Damon (2008), p. 38.

10. Keniston (1960), pp. 18–21.

11. Early on, Fowler observed that individuating faith sometimes has to collapse the dichotomies one way or another; elsewhere he suggested that the tensions could be tolerated. I believe that this contradiction in Fowler's early work is another instance of the discrepant data that, under reexamination, distinguish the emerging adult from the tested adult.

12. Ronald Marstin. *Beyond Our Tribal Gods: The Maturing of Faith.* Maryknoll, NY: Orbis, 1979.

13. Marstin (1979), p. 34.

14. Marstin (1979), p. 34.

15. Marstin (1979), p. 44.

16. Marstin (1979), p. 37.

Chapter Seven: Imagination

1. Scott R. Sanders. *Hunting for Hope: A Father's Journeys.* Boston: Beacon Press, 1998, pp. 8–9.

2. Phillip Wheelwright. *The Burning Fountain.* Bloomington: Indiana University Press, 1954, p. 82.

3. See Richard R. Niebuhr. "Symbols in Reflection on God and Ourselves." *Princeton Seminary Bulletin,* new series 1999, 20(2), 131–137.

4. Samuel Taylor Coleridge. *Biographia Literaria,* Vol. 1. (Two volumes; J. Shawcross, ed.) Oxford, UK: Oxford University Press, 1907, p. 202. (Originally published 1817)

5. Coleridge (1907), Vol. 1, p. 202.

6. In the Enlightenment (1675–1830), it was as though Western philosophical-theological thought came to the same point in the epistemological pilgrimage as does the emerging adult, recognizing the powers and limits of the human mind. Kant made distinctions among forms of knowing (theoretical, speculative, practical), particularly distinguishing knowing of the sensible world from that of the supersensible. In his view, only what could be apprehended through the five senses could be "known." Apprehension of moral

and religious claims was perceived as inaccessible to knowing but he affirmed the postulation of religious categories as essential to practical or moral life, where human actions have consequences. Philosophical and theological reflection became more fully aware of and responsible for its own composing activity, particularly in relationship to spiritual, theological, and moral questions. (Similarly, in the postmodern period, there is a recognition of the relative character of all perception, that is, the culturally conditioned nature of every claim to truth and the exercise of power justified by such claims.)

As part of his critique of the powers of the human mind, Kant identified imagination as the active, creative, constructive power of the knowing mind, essential to all perception and to the power of the mind to hypothesize. Thus, though giving imagination this critical role in knowing the sensible world, he did not allow it a central role in practical reason and therefore no role in faith and moral choice. Lindsay suggests that Kant never saw that freedom and necessity had to be reconciled within reason itself. See his *Critique of Practical Reason*. (L. Beck, trans.) Indianapolis: Bobbs-Merrill, 1956 (Originally published 1788), especially pages 3–19 and 92–93. See also A. D. Lindsay. *Kant*. London: Ernest Benn, 1934, in particular pages 95 and 275.

7.   See Suzanne Langer. *Philosophy in a New Key: A Study of Symbolism of Reason, Rite, and Art*. Cambridge, MA: Harvard University Press, 1942, p. 42.

8.   Coleridge remarked in a notebook entry: "How excellently the German *Einbildungskraft* expresses this prime and loftiest faculty, the power of coadunation, the faculty that forms the many into one—in-eins-bildung!" Quoted in Ray L. Hart. *Unfinished Man and the Imagination: Toward an Ontology of Rules and Rhetoric*. New York: Herder and Herder, 1968, p. 338.

9.   Lynch (1973), p. 119. See also Charlene Spretnak. "Don't Call It Romanticism!" In *The Resurgence of the Real: Body, Nature, and Place in a Hypermodern World*. Reading, MA: Addison-Wesley, 1997, Chapter Four.

10. Coleridge was a powerful thinker, but not a systematic one. His thoughts on imagination are tucked into notebooks, elaborated on in poetry and woven into other writings as fleeting flashes of insight. His most focused statement is a brief, packed definition in his *Biographia Literaria*: "The IMAGINATION then, I consider either as primary, or secondary. The primary IMAGINATION I hold to be the living Power and prime Agent of all human Perception, and as a repetition in the finite mind of the eternal act of creation in the infinite I AM. The secondary Imagination I consider as an echo of the former, coexisting with the conscious will, yet still as identical with the primary in the kind of its agency, and differing only in degree, and in the mode of its operation. It dissolves, diffuses, dissipates, in order to re-create; or where this process is rendered impossible, yet still at all events it struggles to idealize and to unify. It is essentially *vital* . . ." Coleridge (1907), Vol. 1, p. 202.

11. D. W. Winnicott addressed this paradox by observing that the child composes that which the child finds. *The Maturational Processes and the Facilitating Environment*. New York: International University Press, 1965. See also Ana-Maria Rizzuto. *The Birth of the Living God: A Psychoanalytic Study*. Chicago: University of Chicago Press, 1979.

12. Samuel Taylor Coleridge. "The Statesman's Manual." In R. White (ed.). *Lay Sermons*. Vol. 6 of K. Coburn (gen. ed.). *The Collected Works of Samuel Taylor Coleridge*. Princeton, NJ: Princeton University Press, 1972, pp. 59–61.

13. Ronald A. Heifetz, *Leadership Without Easy Answers*. Cambridge, MA: Harvard University Press, 1994. See also Ronald Heifetz and Marty Linsky. *Leadership on the Line: Staying Alive Through the Dangers of Leading*. Boston: Harvard Business School Press, 2002.

14. Heifetz and Linsky (2002), pp. 14–15.

15. Sharon Daloz Parks. *Leadership Can Be Taught: A Bold Approach for a Complex World*. Boston: Harvard Business School Press, 2005, pp. 8–10.

16. See Thomas Berry. *Dream of the Earth*. San Francisco: Sierra Club Books, 1988, Chapter Eight.

17. James W. Botkin, Mahdi Elmandjra, and Mircea Malitza. *No Limits to Learning: Bridging the Human Gap*. Oxford, UK: Pergamon Press, 1979, pp. 17–44.

18. See James E. Loder. *The Logic of the Spirit: Human Development in Theological Perspective*. San Francisco: Jossey-Bass, 1998; and John Paul Lederach. *The Moral Imagination: The Art and Soul of Building Peace*. Oxford, UK: Oxford University Press, 2005.

19. For example, see C. Otto Scharmer. *Theory U: Leading from the Future as It Emerges*. Cambridge, MA: SoL, 2007.

20. Loder (2005), p. 113. Note that this sequence as it appears here for heuristic purposes does not presume that the process always has the same entry point and proceeds in a linear manner.

21. William Sloan Coffin. *Letters to a Young Doubter*. Louisville, KY: John Knox Press, 2005.

22. Wheelwright (1954), p. 79.

23. Barbara E. Rooke (ed.). *The Collected Works of Samuel Taylor Coleridge*. (K. Coburn, gen. ed.) Vol. 4: The Friend (Vol. 1 of Vol. 4), p. cii.

24. Lederach (2005), p. 35.

25. Lederach (2005), pp. 35–36.

26. James E. Loder. *The Transforming Moment: Understanding Convictional Experiences*. San Francisco: Harper San Francisco, 1981, p. 53.

27. Loder (1981), p. 32. Loder draws on Harold Rugg, who described this moment as allowing the "transliminal mind to be at work. The true locus of the creative imagination is the border state that marks off the conscious from the nonconscious. This is the stage between conscious alert awareness, . . . and the deep nonconscious in which Freud was intensely absorbed. James was aware of it, calling it 'the fringe,' 'the waking trance.' . . . This is the Taoists' state of 'letting things happen,' where day dreaming and reveries go on, where Whitehead's prehension and Wild's intuition as primal awareness function; where we know before we know we

know . . . the true creative center. . . . I think of it as 'off-conscious,' not unconscious, for the organism is awake, alert, and in control." Harold Rugg. *Imagination*. Orlando: Harcourt Brace, 1963, pp. 39–40.

28. Gaston Bachelard. *The Poetics of Space*. (M. Jolas, trans.) Boston: Beacon Press, 1969, p. xviii.
29. Coleridge (1907), Vol. 1, pp. 85–86.
30. Coleridge (1907), Vol. 1, p. 167.
31. Parks (2005), pp. 130–131, 161–162.
32. Lao Tsu. *Tao Te Ching*. (Stephen Mitchell, trans.) New York: Harper and Row, 1988, Chapter Fifteen.
33. Evelyn Fox Keller. *A Feeling for the Organism: The Life and Work of Barbara McClintock*. New York: Freeman, 1983, pp. 115, 117.
34. Loder (1981), p. 36.
35. H. R. Niebuhr. *The Meaning of Revelation*. New York: Macmillan, 1952, p. 93.
36. Niebuhr (1952), p. 109.
37. Niebuhr (1952), p. 93.
38. Niebuhr (1952), p. 154.
39. Horace Bushnell. "Dissertation on Language." A chapter in *God in Christ*. Hartford, CT: Brown and Parsons, 1886, pp. 20–21.
40. Bushnell (1886), p. 52.
41. Bushnell (1886), pp. 24–25.
42. Parks (2005), p. 192.
43. Langer (1942), pp. 40–41.
44. Niebuhr (1999), p. 130.
45. Sara Eileen Kelly, college application essay, 1998.
46. This is what Whitehead understood when he wrote that the essence of all true education is religious. Alfred North Whitehead. *The Aims of Education and Other Essays*. New York: Free Press, 1929, p. 25.
47. Beaudoin (1998), pp. 74–77.
48. Loder (1981), p. 55.
49. Lynch (1973), p. 63.

50. Lederach (2005), p. 18.
51. Northrop Frye. "The Expanding World of Metaphor." *Journal of the American Academy of Religion*, 1985, *53*(4), 591.
52. Loder, unpublished paper.
53. Niebuhr (1952), p. 73.
54. Patricia M. Sparks. *The Female Imagination*. New York: Avon, 1976, p. 4.
55. Owen Barfield. *What Coleridge Thought*. Middletown, CT: Wesleyan University Press, 1971, p. 155.
56. Niebuhr (1952), p. 96.
57. Niebuhr (1952), p. 80.
58. Niebuhr (1952), pp. 96 and 108.
59. Arthur Zajonc. "Molding the Self and the Common Cognitive Sources of Science and Religion." In Victor H. Kazanjian Jr. and Peter L. Laurence (eds.). *Education as Transformation: Religious Pluralism, Spirituality, and a New Vision for Higher Education in America*. New York: Peter Lang 2000, pp. 61–63.
60. See Sharon Parks. "Reimagining the Role of the Human in the Earth Community." In Fritz Hull (ed.). *Earth and Spirit*. New York: Continuum, 1993.
61. Lederach (2005), p. 34.
62. Daloz, Keen, Keen, and Parks (1996), Chapter Three.
63. Lederach (2005), p. 39.
64. Parks (2005), pp. 40, 125.
65. Mary Moschella, baccalaureate address, Harvard Divinity School, June 8, 1983.

Chapter Eight: The Gifts of Mentorship and a Mentoring Environment

1. For an excellent portrayal of the mentor in relationship to older adults, see Laurent A. Daloz. *Mentor: Guiding the Journey of Adult Learners*. (2nd ed.) San Francisco: Jossey-Bass, 1999.

2. Agnes K. Missirian. *The Corporate Connection: Why Executive Women Need Mentors to Reach the Top.* Upper Saddle River, NJ: Prentice-Hall, 1982, p. 47.

3. Christian Smith with Patricia Snell describes key conditions that have fostered the relativism that directly and indirectly creates "indecision, confusion, and fuzziness." See *Souls in Transition: The Religious & Spiritual Lives of Emerging Adults.* New York: Oxford University Press, 2009, pp. 292–294.

4. Gary Whited. Essay in Edward F. Mooney (ed.). *Wilderness and the Heart: Henry Bugbee's Philosophy of Place, Presence, and Memory.* Athens: University of Georgia Press, 1999. See also Daloz, Keen, Keen, and Parks (1996), pp. 80–101.

5. See the twenty-two-minute video with teaching guide for Daloz, Keen, Keen, and Parks's *Common Fire: Leading Lives of Commitment in a Complex World.* (Terry Strauss, producer, 1997). www .newcommons.org.

6. Coleridge (1907), Vol. 1, p. 98.

7. A. Storr. *Feet of Clay. Saints, Sinners & Madmen: A Study of Gurus.* New York: Free Press, 1996.

8. Richard J. Light. *Making the Most of College: Students Speak Their Minds.* Cambridge, MA: Harvard University Press, 2001, pp. 45–50. Richard J. Light. "The Harvard Assessment Seminars: Explorations with Students and Faculty About Teaching, Learning, and Student Life." Harvard University Graduate School of Education and Kennedy School of Government, 1992.

9. David Evans. See course description "Designing Your Life" at Stanford University. Steve Garber has observed that people who have formed a viable adult faith have in their young adult years "(1) formed a worldview that could account for truth amidst the challenge of relativism, (2) found a mentor whose life 'pictured' that possibility of living with and in that worldview, and (3) forged friendships with folk whose common life offered a context for those convictions to be embodied." *The Fabric of Faithfulness: Weaving Together Belief & Behavior.* Downers Grove, IL: Inter-Varsity Press, IVP Books, 2007, p. 174.

10. Heifetz and Linsky (2002), pp. 102–107; and Parks (2005), pp. 220–221.

11. Mary Jo Bona, Jane Rinehart, and Rose Mary Volbrecht. "Show Me How to Do Like You: Co-Mentoring as Feminist Pedagogy." *Feminist Teacher*, 1995, 9(3), 116–124.

12. Daloz, Keen, Keen, and Parks (1996), pp. 45–46, 206–207.

13. J. P. Keen. "Appreciative Engagement of Diversity: E Pluribus Unum and the Education as Transformation Project." In Kazanjian and Laurence (2000).

14. See Sharon Daloz Parks. "Is It Too Late?" In T. Piper, M. Gentile, and S. D. Parks. *Can Ethics Be Taught? Approaches, Perspectives, and Challenges at Harvard Business School*. Boston: Harvard Business School, 1993.

15. Michael Jones. *Artful Leadership: Awakening the Commons of the Imagination*. Toronto: Pianoscapes, 2006, p. 43. See the Web site created by Rabbi Josh Feigelson, www.askbigquestions.com.

16. See Daloz, Keen, Keen, and Parks (1996), Chapter Three.

17. Douglas Steere. *Dimensions of Prayer*. New York: General Board of Global Ministries, United Methodist Church, 1982.

18. See Jon C. Dalton and Anne Marie Petrie. "The Power of Peer Culture." *Educational Record: The Magazine of Higher Education*, Summer/Fall 1997, pp. 19–24.

19. Pamela Paul, "From Students, Less Kindness for Strangers?" *New York Times*, June 27, 2010, reporting on paper presented to the Association for Psychological Science: "Changes in Dispositional Empathy in American College Students over Time: A Meta-Analysis" by Sara Konrath, a researcher at the University of Michigan. See *Personality and Social Psychology Review* at http://psr.sagepub.com. See also Jeremy Rifkin. *The Empathic Civilization: The Race to Global Consciousness in a World in Crisis*. New York: Tarcher, 2009.

20. Carol Trosset, "Obstacles to Open Discussion and Critical Thinking: The Grinnell College Study." *Change*, September/October 1998, pp. 44–49.

21. See Daloz, Keen, Keen, and Parks (1996), Chapter Four.

22. Diana Eck. *Encountering God: A Spiritual Journey from Bozeman to Banaras*. Boston: Beacon Press, 1993, p. 37.

23. Renee Lertzman. "Living on the Rim: Notes from the Ontologically Insecure." *The Symposium*, 1999, *1*(6), 1–2, 5.

24. See www.contemplativemind.org.

25. Levinson (1978), pp. 91–93; and Levinson with Levinson (1996), pp. 238–239.

26. Carol Gilligan. "Moral Development." In Arthur W. Chickering and Associates (eds.). *The Modern American College*. San Francisco: Jossey-Bass, 1981, pp. 139–157. Note that for Kohlberg, "principled moral judgment solved the problem of moral relativism; for Perry, relativism found the problem in principled moral judgment" (p. 153).

27. See Frederick Bueckner. *Wishful Thinking: A Theological ABC*. New York: HarperCollins, 1973. See also Daloz, Keen, Keen, and Parks (1996), Chapters Five and Seven; Tarrant (1998); Gregg Levoy. *Callings: Finding and Following an Authentic Life*. New York: Harmony Books, 1997; Palmer (2000); and John Neafsey. *A Sacred Voice Is Calling: Personal Vocation and Social Conscience*. Maryknoll, NY: Orbis Books, 2006.

28. See Daloz, Keen, Keen, and Parks (1996), p. 148.

29. See Sharon Daloz Parks. "How Then Must We Live: Suffering and Wonder in the New Commons." In Sam M. Intrator (ed.). *Living the Questions: Essays Inspired by the Work and Life of Parker J. Palmer*. San Francisco: Jossey-Bass, 2005, pp. 298–307.

30. Julie E. Neraas. *Apprenticed to Hope: A Sourcebook for Difficult Times*. Minneapolis: Augsburg Books, 2009.

31. Rosemary Radford Ruether. "Beginnings: An Intellectual Autobiography." In Gregory Baum (ed.). *Journeys*. New York: Paulist Press, 1975, pp. 40–41.

32. See Dorothy Bass (ed.). *Practicing Our Faith: A Way of Life for a Searching People*. San Francisco: Jossey-Bass, 1996; and C. Dykstra. *Growing in the Life of Faith: Education and Christian Practices*. San Francisco: Jossey-Bass, 1999.

33. Aaron Ausland reflects on the mutuality of the communion table, the influence of the negotiation table, the competence of the

study table, the humility of the operating table, and the celebration of the hearthing table in "Come to the Table: Five Values for the Global Citizen." *The Global Citizen: A Journal for Young Adults Engaging the World Through Service*, 2006, 3, 6–18. (from the Krista Foundation)

34. Daloz, Keen, Keen, and Parks (1996), Chapter One.
35. Bachelard (1969), p. 6.

Chapter Nine: Higher Education as Mentor

1. Jennifer Lynn Tanner, "Recentering in Emerging Adulthood: A Critical Turning Point in Life Span Human Development." Arnett and Tanner (2006), pp. 48–49.
2. Confirming the work of Burton Clark and Martin Trow in the 1960s, Arnett describes four student subcultures: "The collegiate subculture centers around fraternities, sororities, dating, drinking, big sports events, and campus fun. Professors, courses, and grades are a secondary priority. . . . Students in the vocational subculture have a practical view of their college education. . . . The purpose of college is to gain skills and a degree that will enable them to get a better job. . . . Typically they work 20–40 hours a week to support themselves and help pay for tuition. . . . The academic subculture is the one that identifies most strongly with the educational mission of college. . . . Drawn to the world of ideas . . . they study hard, do their assignments. . . . These are the students whom professors like best. . . . Students in the rebel subculture are also deeply engaged with ideas. . . . Unlike academics, rebels are aggressively nonconformist . . . tend to be critically detached . . . skeptical. . . . Rebels enjoy learning when they feel the material is interesting and relevant to their lives, but they are selectively studious. . . ." Arnett (2004), pp. 135–136.
3. See Smith's review of "The University: The Anatomy of Academe" by Murray G. Ross. *Dalhousie Review*, 1977, 57, 546.
4. Smith (1977).
5. Arthur Zajonc, "Beyond the Divided Academic Life." In Parker J. Palmer and Arthur Zajonc with Megan Scribner. *The Heart of*

Higher Education: A Call to Renewal. San Francisco: Jossey-Bass, 2010, pp. 70–71.

6. Zajonc (2010), p. 93.
7. See Michael D. Waggoner (ed.). *Sacred and Secular Tensions in Higher Education: Connecting Parallel Universities.* New York: Routledge, 2011.
8. See Alexander W. Astin, Helen S. Astin, and Jennifer A. Lindholm. *Cultivating the Spirit: How College Can Enhance Students' Inner Lives.* San Francisco: Jossey-Bass, 2010; Arthur Schwartz. "Spirituality During the College Years." *Liberal Education,* Fall 2001, 31–35. Sharon Daloz Parks. "Leadership, Spirituality, and the College as a Mentoring Environment." *Journal of College and Character.* October 2008, 10(2).
9. See Derek Bok. *Universities in the Marketplace: The Commercialization of Higher Education.* Princeton, NJ: Princeton University Press, 2003.
10. Harvey Cox. *Seduction of the Spirit.* New York: Simon & Schuster, 1973, pp. 100–101, 103–104.
11. Nancy Malone. "On Being Passionate: Reflections on Roman Catholic Approaches to Spirituality." In R. Rankin (ed.). *The Recovery of Spirit in Higher Education.* New York: Seabury, 1980, pp. 58–67.
12. Dennis C. Roberts. *Deeper Learning in Leadership: Helping College Students Find the Potential Within.* San Francisco: Jossey-Bass, 2007, p. 17.
13. See Thomas Berry. *The Great Work: Our Way into the Future.* New York: Bell Tower, 1999, Chapter Seven; David Orr. *Earth in Mind: On Education, Environment, and the Human Prospect.* Washington, DC: Island Press, 1994; and the TED Talk, "Liz Coleman's call to reinvent liberal arts education" by Elizabeth Coleman, 2009.
14. R. Eugene Rice. "Faculty Priorities: Where Does Faith Fit?" In Douglas Jacobsen and Rhonda Hustedt Jacobsen (eds.). *The American University in a Post Secular Age.* Oxford, UK: Oxford University Press, 2008, p. 110.
15. Cheryl H. Keen. "Spiritual Assumptions Undergird Educational Priorities: A Personal Narrative." Kazanjian and Laurence (2000).

16. Andrew Delbanco, "A Forum on Helping Students Engage the 'Big Questions.'" *Liberal Education*, Spring 2007, 93(2), 32.

17. See, for example, bell hooks. *Teaching to Transgress: Education as the Practice of Freedom*. New York: Routledge, 1994; Stephen Brookfield. *The Skillful Teacher*. San Francisco: Jossey-Bass, 1990; Palmer (1998); and Daloz (1999).

18. Kenneth Keniston. *The Uncommitted: Alienated Youth in American Society*. New York: Dell, 1960, pp. 338–339.

19. See Light (2001), pp. 93–98.

20. Coleridge (1907), Vol. 2, pp. 5, 16. "The imagination of the poet remains under . . . control of will and understanding, but its vocation above all is to make manifest . . . the depth and height of the ideal world around forms, incidents, and situations, of which for the common view, custom had bedimmed the luster, had dried up all the sparkle and the dew drops." Vol. 2, p. 11, and Vol. 1, p. 59.

21. Coleridge (1907), Vol. 1, p. 59.

22. Jacques Barzun. *Teacher in America*. Indianapolis: Liberty Press, 1981, pp. 42–43. (Originally published 1945)

23. See Timothy Clydesdale. *When Students and Professors Find Their Callings*. Chicago: University of Chicago Press, forthcoming; and http://www.cic.edu/netvue/netvue_website/index.html Supported by the Lilly Endowment.

24. See www.designingyourlife.org.

25. Patricia Killen. "Gaps and Gifts." *Prism*, Spring 1999, *12*, 8.

26. Erik Erikson. *Insight and Responsibility*. New York: Norton, 1964, p. 133.

Chapter Ten: Culture as Mentor

1. See Andy Crouch. *Culture Making: Recovering Our Creative Calling*. Downers Grove, IL: IVP Books, 2008, especially Chapter Four.

2. Friedrich Schweitzer. "Global Issues Facing Youth in the Postmodern Church." *1998 Princeton Lectures on Youth, Church, and Culture*. Princeton, NJ: Princeton Theological Seminary, 1999, p. 73.

3. Ronal Inglehart quoted in Schweitzer (1999), p. 74.

4. Smith (2007), p. 293.
5. Smith (2007), pp. 292–293.
6. Sharon Daloz Parks. *The University as a Mentoring Environment.* Indianapolis: Indiana Office of Campus Ministry, 1992.
7. Lendol Calder. *Financing the American Dream: A Cultural History of Consumer Credit.* Princeton, NJ: Princeton University Press, 1999, pp. 4–6.
8. Andrew L. Shapiro. "The Net That Binds: Using Cyberspace to Create Real Communities." *The Nation*, June 21, 1999, p. 14.
9. James E. Cote. "Emerging Adulthood as an Institutionalized Moratorium: Risks and Benefits to Identity Formation." Arnett and Tanner (2006), pp. 91ff.
10. See Henry A. Giroux, "Left Behind? American Youth and the Global Fight for Democracy." *truthout*, February 28, 2011.
11. Robert Wuthnow. *After the Baby Boomers: How Twenty- and Thirty-Somethings Are Shaping the Future of American Religion.* Princeton, NJ: Princeton University Press, 2007, pp. 12–13.
12. James P. Keen, personal conversation.
13. See "Depression, Lack of Social Support Trigger Suicidal Thoughts in College Students." Johns Hopkins Children's Center, 2010, www.hopkinschildrens.org/Depression-Lack-of-Social-Support-Trigger-Suicidal-Thoughts-in-College-Students.aspx#. "A Snapshot of Annual High-Risk College Drinking Consequences," July 2010. www.colegedrinkingprevention.gov/StatsSummaries/snapshot.aspx.
14. See Michael Kimmel. *Guyland: The Perilous World Where Boys Become Men.* New York: Harper, 2008; and Laurent A. Parks Daloz, *Sons, Fathers, and Mentors: Manhood for the 21st Century* (forthcoming).
15. Labouvie-Vief (2006), p. 80.
16. Anne Colby and others have argued persuasively that though many students in higher education are given opportunities to be engaged in service and community learning, most often they are working in nonprofit and other community organizations where they gain only a limited understanding of the work of public gov-

ernance and political processes. See Anne Colby, Thomas Ehrlich, Elizabeth Beaumont, and Jason Stephens. *Educating Citizens: Preparing America's Undergraduates for Lives of Moral and Civic Responsibility*. San Francisco: Jossey-Bass, 2003; and Anne Colby, "Intersections of Political and Moral Development." *Journal of College and Character*, September 2008, *10*(1).

17. See Palmer (2000), especially Chapter Four.
18. Andrew Delbanco. *The Real American Dream: A Meditation on Hope*. Cambridge, MA: Harvard University Press, 1999, pp. 103, 113, 114.
19. Berry (1999).
20. Erikson (1964), p. 127.

Coda: Mentoring Communities

1. "The Future of Callings—an Interdisciplinary Summit on the Public Obligations of Professionals into the Next Millennium." *William Mitchell Law Review*, 1999, *25*(1), 43–192.
2. "The Future of Callings" (1999), p. 186.
3. Purdy (1999).
4. See T. Piper, M. Gentile, and S. D. Parks (1993).
5. Parks (1993).
6. For a widely used course addressing medical education as a profession see *The Healer's Art* copyright 1991 by Rachel Naomi Remen, MD, at the Institute for the Study of Health and Illness at Commonweal. www.ishiprograms.org.
7. See Herminia Barra. "Provisional Selves: Experimenting with Image and Identity in Professional Adaptation." *Administrative Science Quarterly*, December 1999, 764–791; and "Making Partner: A Mentor's Guide to the Psychological Journey," *Harvard Business Review*, March–April 2000, 146–147.
8. Susan Bratton is a professor of biology at Whitworth University. See also Light (2001), pp. 94–96.
9. Brian T. Johnson. "An Essay on Lost Arts and Common Callings," *Mitchell Law Review*, 1999, *25*(1), 184.

10. Adelaide Winstead with Catherine Kapikian. *In the Awful Rowing Toward God*. Washington, DC: Potter's House Press, 1988, pp. 16–18.
11. See Sharon Daloz Parks (2005), Chapter Nine.
12. See also Roberto Mangaberira Unger. "The Critical Legal Studies Movement." *Harvard Law Review*, January 1983.
13. Eric Wallen. "The Mindless Carpenter." *The Symposium*, 1999, *1*(6), 1, 4–5.
14. See Douglas A. Hicks. *Money Enough: Everyday Practices for Living Faithfully in the Global Economy*. San Francisco: Jossey-Bass, 2010.
15. Leadership Conference, The J. M. Murdock Trust, Vancouver, WA, December 2009, facilitated by Robert McKenna and Ron Carrucci.
16. See Lois J. Zachary. *The Mentor's Guide: Facilitating Effective Learning Relationships*. San Francisco: Jossey-Bass, 2000.
17. See Daniel Wejremfemmog (ed.). "Olive Tree Initiative." *Expressions/Impressions*. University of California-Irvine, Spring 2009, 6; the travel component in a three-course sequence in the Hart Leadership Program at Duke University taught by Alma Blount in the Institute of Public Policy in Parks, 2005, pp. 188–195; and Ronald Frase. *Discovering the Stranger Next Door* (unpublished manuscript).
18. Schachter-Shalomi (1995), pp. 204, 203–207.
19. See William S. Aquilino. "Family Relationships and Support Systems in Emerging Adulthood." In Arnett and Tanner (2006), pp. 193–218.
20. Will Weaver. "The Undeclared Major." *A Gravestone Made of Wheat*. New York: Simon & Schuster, 1989, excerpt quoted in *Leading Lives That Matter: What We Should Do and Who We Should Be*. Mark R. Schwehn and Dorothy C. Bass (eds.). Grand Rapids, MI: William B. Eerdmans, 2006, pp. 365–367.
21. Gina O'Connell Higgins. *Resilient Adults: Overcoming a Cruel Past*. San Francisco: Jossey-Bass, 1994, pp. 166–167.
22. Higgins (1994), pp. 156–158.
23. Higgins (1994), pp. 158, 169.

24. Zajonc (2000), p. 68.

25. See Wuthnow (2007), Chapter Eleven; Keith R. Anderson and Randy D. Reese. *Spiritual Mentoring: A Guide for Seeking and Giving Direction*. Downers Grove, IL: Inter-Varsity Press, 1999; and Rev. Scotty McLennan. *Finding Your Religion: When the Faith You Grew Up with Has Lost Its Meaning*. San Francisco: Harper San Francisco, 1999.

26. See the Web site created by Rabbi Josh Feigelson, www.askbigquestions.com, and www.wondercafe.ca, an initiative of the United Church of Canada led by Rev. Keith Howard; and Wuthnow (2007), Chapter Ten.

27. See Rabbi Daniel Smokler. "Toward a Third Space—New Dimensions of Jewish Education for Emerging Adults." Keynote address, Third Place Conference, New York, June 21, 2010.

28. Eboo Patel. *Acts of Faith: The Story of an American Muslim, the Struggle for the Soul of a Generation*. Boston: Beacon Press, 2007, pp. xxvii–xxviii. See also Susan Saulny. "Black? White? Asian? More Young Americans Choose All of the Above." *New York Times*, January 30, 2011, pp. 1, 20–21.

29. "Smith . . . thought the many professionals in the field treated religion as a system, an 'ism,' a simplistic and sterile, overly conceptualized static entity that had little to do with the personal and historical reality that we label 'religion.' . . . Pursuits that are far removed from the mystery and manure of real-life persons trying to make sense of a world that is often boring and meaningless, and at the same time seemingly in danger of falling apart at the seams. . . . Christianity neither eats nor sleeps. Christians do. . . . Islam does not recite the Qur'an. Muslims do. . . . [Smith] upheld the view that religious truth does not lie in religious systems but in persons. . . ." Donald K. Swearer. "The Moral Imagination of Wilfred Cantwell Smith." *Harvard Divinity Bulletin*, Winter/Spring 2011, 22–23.

30. Cox (2009).

31. Interview by James Keen in the E Pluribus Unum program. See also Keen (2000).

32. Michael Slater. *Stretcher Bearers: Giving and Receiving the Gift of Encouragement and Support.* Ventura, CA: Regal Books, 1985, pp. 16–18. The mentoring pastor is my father, Emmett F. Parks. Though it is characteristic of his life, I did not know about his encounter with Slater until I received the book after my father's death.

33. Beaudoin (1998), Chapter Seven and pp. 56–57.

34. Sherry Turkle. *Alone Together: Why We Expect More from Technology and Less from Each Other.* New York: Basic Books, 2011, p. xvii.

35. S. Craig Watkins. *The Young and the Digital: What the Migration to Social-Network Sites, Games, and Anytime, Anywhere Media Means for Our Future.* Boston: Beacon Press, 2009, pp. 63–64.

36. Claire Gordon. "The Narcissism Myth." *Utne Reader*, May–June 2011, 43, excerpted from *The Huffington Post* (February 3, 2011).

37. See Jane D. Brown. "Emerging Adults in a Media-Saturated World." Arnett and Tanner (2006), pp. 279–295.

38. Recall the makeup of the human brain in two primary respects relative to the media. First, the limbic brain plays a vital though primitive function, alerting us to danger. Anything that may be dangerous can command our attention. But as soon as we discover that there is no immediate danger, the limbic mind is bored. Market-driven media succeeds if it can appeal to anxiety or terror, and to sustain our attention, the message must change and the charge must escalate. A subtlety here is that what appears only beautiful, glamorous, or entertaining can be designed to raise the fear that without it we are not attractive and do not belong (another means of evoking anxiety). The second aspect of mind is that what we "breathe in" remains imprinted within. It may fade from the conscious mind but takes up residence within us. We become what we "breathe in."

39. Settersten and Ray (2010), pp. 115 and 166–167.

40. David Whyte. "Letter from the House." Fall 2007. www.davidwhyte/house/letter.

41. Brown (2006), pp. 290–291.

42. See Timothy Mitt Robinson. "Things That Require Sustained Attention." http://timothymittrobinson.com/2009/08/31/things-that-require-sustained-attention/.

43. Marti Gerardo. "Hacker Ethics and Higher Learning: The Moral Clash Determining the Future of Education." *The Cresset*, April 2011, 17–27.

44. See Eric Greenberg with Karl Weber. *Generation We: How Millennial Youth Are Taking Over America and Changing Our World Forever*. Emeryville, CA: Pachatusan, 2008.

The Author

Sharon Daloz Parks has taught, studied, and worked with young, emerging adults in higher education and other settings for more than forty years. During her own "twenty-something" years she served as a residence hall director at the University of Redlands and was an associate chaplain at Whitworth University. For more than sixteen years after completing her doctorate at Harvard University, she held faculty and research positions at the School of Divinity, School of Business, and the Kennedy School of Government. She has also served on the faculty at the Weston Jesuit School of Theology. She is now a senior fellow at the Whidbey Institute and teaches at Seattle University, both at the Albers School of Business and the School of Theology and Ministry. Her other publications include *Leadership Can Be Taught: A Bold Approach for a Complex World* (Harvard Business School Press, 2005) and, co-authored, *Common Fire: Leading Lives of Commitment in a Complex World* (Beacon Press, 1996). She speaks and consults nationally and is principal of Leadership for the New Commons www.newcommons.org. She lives with her husband, Larry Parks Daloz, on Whidbey Island and in Vermont.

Name Index

Subject Index

Loss: as adaptive challenge, 142, 161; faith and, 38–43; inner experience of, 94–95, 107–109; of life assumptions, 76–77
Lost, 284
Loyalty, 119, 131

M

Man-boys, 234
Massachusetts Institute of Technology (MIT), Initiative on Technology and the Self, 279–280
Master-apprentice relationship, 249–251
Meaning, defined, 290n. 6
Meaning-constitutive evolutionary activity, 56
Meaning-making: affective dimensions of, 94–97; aspects of, 20–45; being at home and, 46–69; community and, 114–133; culture and, 224–242; dependence continuum and, 96–113; developmental stages of, 12, 49–69, 70–93; faith as form of, 27–29, 156; higher education and, 16–19, 60–61, 203–223; ideology and, 123–128; imagination and, 134–164; mentoring communities and, 177–202; networks of belonging and, 114–133; professional education and, 243–251; in religious communities, 267–279; stages of knowing and, 70–93; steps and activities of, 12, 27–28; as task of emerging adults, 8–11, 132–133; in work world, 253–254. *See also* Faith; Faith development; Knowing
Medea, 37–38
Media: accountability of, 284–286; as authority, 72; big questions and, 279–280; challenge in, 282–283; as distraction, 284; emerging adults and, 5; false images in, 160; images in, 160, 283–284, 285; inspiration from, 283–284; limbic brain and, 316n. 38; as mentoring environment, 279–286; recognition in, 280–281; self-involvement and, 183; and shared suffering, 42; support from, 281–282. *See also* Information technology
Medical school mentoring, 248, 313n. 6
Meditation, 148
Men, changing roles of, 234
Mentor(s): accountability of, 173; in apprenticeships, 248–251; books as, 172; challenge role of, 168–169; complex call to, 19; in dialogue, 170–173; digital technologies as, 172–173; emerging adults as, 196–197, 248; faculty as, 168,

213–222; gifts of, 165–173; inspirational role of, 169–170; mutual respect with protégé and, 170, 173, 217; overuse of term, 166–167; overview of, 13–14; power of, 105–106, 165–166, 170–173; in professional education, 247–251; recognition role of, 167; research on, 174; as self-selected authorities, 105–106, 109; support role of, 167–169; in workplace, 121, 167–168, 252–258
Mentor: Guiding the Journey of Adult Learners (Daloz), 305n. 1
Mentoring communities and environments: big-enough questions and., 177–181, 271–272; as communities of practice, 197–202; critical-connective thought and, 182, 186–192, 246–247, 258–261; culture as, 13–14, 19, 224–242; discernment in, 159; encounters with otherness in, 181–184, 258–261, 272–276; families as, 167, 261–267; features of, 176–202; habits of mind developed in, 185–189; in higher education, 17, 18–19, 203–223; images and, 192–197; the media as, 279–286; as networks of belonging, 120–123, 124, 133, 174, 176–177, 261–267; overview of, 13–14; in professional education, 243–251; religious, 267–279; research on, 174; social movements as, 286–287; systemic thought and, 188–192, 246–247; travel as, 258–261; value of, *versus* one-on-one mentoring, 174–175; workplace as, 251–258; worthy dreams and, 190–192, 220–222, 237–242. *See also* Culture and cultural milieu; Higher education
Mentoring institutions, 236
Mentoring moments, 172
Metaphor(s): of battle, 65; of "getting on the balcony," 151–152; image as, 151–152, 154, 157; of journey, 65–67, 68, 69, 295n. 26; of post-school emerging adults, 231–232
Midlife: community in, 131; developmental stage of, 50, 111–113; Dream realignment in, 238–240; interdependence achieved in, 111–113; meaning-making in, 46
Mind: contemplative, 147–150, 189; development of, 51–55; the media and, 316n. 38; orders of, 12; vital habits of, 185–189
Mirror test, 110
Monotheism, radical, 32